THE WORKING MEN'S
COLLEGE

AUSPICIUM

MELIORIS

ÆVI

MDCCCLIV

Purchased

R.E.T... L.     1913     F.H.F... Sc.

# THE TRANSFORMATION
# OF INTELLECTUAL LIFE
# IN VICTORIAN ENGLAND

CROOM HELM STUDIES IN SOCIETY AND HISTORY
Edited by Richard Price

# The Transformation of Intellectual Life in Victorian England

T.W. Heyck

CROOM HELM
London & Sydney

ST. MARTIN'S PRESS
New York

© 1982 T.W. Heyck
Croom Helm Ltd, Provident House, Burrell Row,
Beckenham, Kent BR3 1AT
Croom Helm Australia Pty Ltd, First Floor,
139 King Street, Sydney, NSW 2001, Australia
Reprinted 1984

British Library Cataloguing in Publication Data

Heyck, T.W.
    The transformation of intellectual life in Victorian England.
    (Studies in society and history)
    1. England — Intellectual life — 19th century
    I. Title  II. Series
    942.081    DA533

    ISBN 0-7099-1206-4



All rights reserved. For information, write:
St. Martin's Press, Inc., 175 Fifth Avenue, New York, NY 10010
First published in the United States of America in 1982

Library of Congress Cataloging in Publication Data

Heyck, Thomas William, 1938-
    The transformation of intellectual life in
Victorian England.

    Bibliography: p. 240.
    Includes index.
    1. England — Intellectual life — 19th century.
I. Title.
DA533.H48    1982    305.5'52'0942    82-840
ISBN 0-312-81427-5                      AACR2



Printed and bound in Great Britain by
Billing and Sons Limited, Worcester

# CONTENTS

# ACKNOWLEDGEMENTS

I am very pleased to have the opportunity to thank a number of people and organizations for their assistance to me while I worked on this book. Since the book offers in part a synthesis, I am very much indebted to many scholars on whose work I have depended. I hope the notes pay adequate thanks to them. In particular I wish to acknowledge my debt to three scholars — none of whom have I had the good fortune yet to meet — whose work has been especially influential: John Gross, whose book on the men of letters first set me to thinking about them as a group; Raymond Williams, whose various works led me to the history of words and concepts; and Sheldon Rothblatt, whose books on Victorian university education provoked many questions about the social function of universities.

To a large number of friends and colleagues I also owe thanks. Jonathan Freedman worked as my research assistant in 1976 and helped me sort out my ideas in the earliest stage of the project. To my good friend James J. Sheehan I owe an enormous debt of gratitude; he talked for hours on end with me about my interpretations, offered me much guidance along the way, and gave the final draft a helpful reading. David Roos and Chris Herbert of the Northwestern English Department assisted immensely by sharing their knowledge of Victorian literary culture. Rosemary Jann taught me a great deal about Victorian historical writing. A number of colleagues in the Northwestern History Department gave the penultimate draft the benefit of their criticisms: Lacey Baldwin Smith, Robert E. Lerner, Jock McLane, David Joravsky, and Robert Wiebe. Sarah Maza contributed an especially thorough and perceptive critique. Standish Meacham (University of Texas) and Martin Wiener (Rice University) gave me the benefit of their expertise in the form of close reading of the final draft. Richard Price, the editor of this series, has offered both encouragement and criticism at various stages of the manuscript's life. But the scholar to whom I owe the most is Denis Lynn Heyck, who was a patient listener, shrewd critic, and supportive friend throughout.

Finally, I want to thank several institutions for their help. The American Council of Learned Societies and the College of Arts and Sciences at Northwestern financed leave time for research and writing. The Northwestern University Library, and especially the Interlibrary

## Acknowledgements

Loan Department, have provided marvellous support as well as a splendid place to work.

Evanston

To my mother and father,
my wife and my children

# PREFACE

The purpose of this book is to illuminate one aspect of Victorian cultural history — the transformation of concepts and institutions governing intellectual life from the 1830s through to the 1890s. The main theme concerns the emergence of 'the intellectuals', the other face of which is the fragmentation of high culture. The argument is that in the early and mid-Victorian periods (1830-70), the English did not think of their society as having a separate, distinct class of people known as 'intellectuals', but that in the late-Victorian years (1870-1900), they generally adopted this concept and its associated terminology. The key idea in the new concept of the intellectuals was that they were a self-conscious, distinct group with common attitudes of superiority, aloofness and detachment. Further, the argument is that while the people who became known as the intellectuals did not show *all* the characteristics of a social class, they did in fact come to share enough views about themselves and their relations with society to warrant designation as a quasi-class. In his recent history of *Modern European Thought,* Franklin L. Baumer says that 'the intellectuals do constitute a distinct class, relatively detached from the everyday struggles of the marketplace or forum . . .'[1] The contention of this book is that for England, even as recently as the early nineteenth century, this was not true, but that by the end of the century it had largely become so.

A major task of the book is to try to explain *how* and *why* the concept of the intellectuals emerged — to account for the changes in the defining ideas and conditions of intellectual life which eventually required new terms like 'the intellectuals' so that people could speak meaningfully about them. The thesis of the book is that three 'forces' were largely responsible for the emergence of the concept of the intellectuals: (1) the rise of natural science; (2) the reform of the universities; and (3) the tradition of culturally-oriented criticism of society. Furthermore, while these three forces are analytically separable, in the actual events of the century, they often overlapped; indeed, by the end of the century they converged in extremely important ways. A number of other themes weave in and out of the story — secularization, specialization, professionalization, and alienation — but each finds its place in the development of the main forces. I try not to treat any of these themes as living things or independent causes. They are labels which can be applied to certain phenomena of serious intellectual work, but — with the possible exception of professionalization — they were not goals consciously pursued or conditions consciously avoided. They were more descriptions than causes of the changing conditions of intellectual life.

I have deliberately avoided presenting a 'Whiggish' interpretation of the rise of the intellectuals. That is, I do not mean to argue that the production and support of serious thought has progressed from the benighted and shallow world of the men of letters and amateur cultivators of science in the first half of the nineteenth century to an enlightened and excellent condition at the turn of the century. As a matter of fact, that was the view held by the late-Victorian 'intellectuals', but it is not one that I share. My view is that early and mid-Victorian England had a system of concepts and support of deep intellectual work with important strengths as well as weaknesses, and that the exchange of this system for what we might call a more modern package has involved losses as well as gains. Indeed, I agree with those who believe that modern English culture, like other modern cultures, has fragmented; and I see the emergence of the intellectuals as both a sign of, and a contribution to, this fragmentation.

**Note**

1. Franklin L. Baumer, *Modern European Thought: Continuity and Change in Ideas, 1600-1950* (New York, 1977), p. 7.

# THE TRANSFORMATION
# OF INTELLECTUAL LIFE
# IN VICTORIAN ENGLAND

# 1 INTRODUCTION

One of the strangest facts about intellectual life in the Victorian years in England is that for most of the period there appears to have been no intellectuals. That is, there was no group of people designated as 'the intellectuals' or even 'the intellectual elite'. Down to the 1870s, no one was called 'an intellectual'. Of course, this would be a trivial point if it had to do simply with usage, for it would matter little that words like 'intellectuals' were not used if the *concept* existed. But the concept of 'the intellectuals' or 'an intellectual' did not exist in the early and mid-Victorian periods (prior to the 1870s) any more than did the terms. The idea of intellectuals as a distinct class of people in any of the various twentieth-century definitions of the term — such as 'a sort of classless class, relatively detached from the everyday struggles of the marketplace', or a class 'for whom thinking fulfills at once the function of work and play', or 'persons possessing knowledge or in a narrower sense those whose judgment, based on reflection and knowledge, derives less directly and exclusively from sensory perception than is the case with non-intellectuals'[1] — was for the most part inconceivable to the early and mid-Victorians. They thought about their society in a different way; and it is in this sense that one can say there were no intellectuals in early and mid-Victorian England.

This proposition — which will be examined in detail further on — seems to fly in the face not only of common sense but of the vast body of sociological literature on intellectuals, which holds that all societies have had their intellectuals. Common sense and sociologists in this case are in one respect right. To adopt a functional definition of intellectuals and then investigate any given society to discover who were the people who performed that function and how, is to engage in a perfectly legitimate enterprise. Seymour Martin Lipset, for instance, defines intellectuals as 'all those who create, distribute, and apply *culture*, that is, the symbolic world of man, including art, science, and religion'.[2] He sees this group as divided into two levels — the creators of culture and the distributors. Equipped with this definition, Lipset proceeds to examine the political attitudes and status of American intellectuals in the recent twentieth century. He concludes, rightly or wrongly, that the left-wing tendency of American intellectuals as compared to those of England and continental Europe is related to the lack in America of a British sense of deference and to the feeling in America among intellectuals that they do not enjoy contacts with the political elite.

Undoubtedly, such sociological procedures are useful. They are basically the method of Edward Shils, who is by a long way the leading theorist of intellectuals. Shils, who has a rather exalted view of intellectuals, says that they are needed in all societies, and the more complex the society, the greater the need.[3] Shils believes that intellectuals arise from those people in any society who have special propensities — from those 'with an unusual sensitivity to the sacred, an uncommon reflectiveness about the nature of the universe, and the rules which govern their society'.[4] This propensity is distributed unequally among the members of a society, but at least intermittently every society as a whole has a need for contact with the essential or 'sacred'. Thus, in Shils's view, the 'intellectuals' activities and their situation in society is [sic] the product of a compromise' between the personal drives of the intellectual and the needs of the society. It follows that the institutional arrangements in which intellectual work goes on have 'varied markedly in history'. The intellectual systems' variations 'have at least in part been affected by the nature of the intellectual tasks, the volume of the intellectual heritage, the material resources necessary and available for intellectual work, the modes of reproduction of intellectual achievements, and the scope of the audience'.[5]

These ideas can be potent analytical tools for the examination of any society; in fact they constitute a programme for comparative cultural analysis, towards the completion of which Shils has himself contributed.[6] This book in part investigates Victorian high culture in terms of Shils's programme. However, this book also concentrates on the *historical* dimension. Many of the sociological theories of 'the intellectuals' are curiously timeless. They lack a sense of the change of cultural formations over time, and they seem to miss the frame of mind — the conceptual categories — of past societies. Sociological definitions of intellectuals are very much products of twentieth-century Western thought: not one major theoretical work on intellectuals as such, was produced before the twentieth century.[7] To use the terms and concepts of the present to discuss a society of the past is to try, in Wittgenstein's phrase, 'to say what cannot be said' about that society. One should, even in the analysis of 'intellectual life' (itself an anachronistic but unavoidable phrase) attempt to recover the 'language game' of a particular moment in the past — in this case to see how the Victorians thought about themselves and their intellectual needs.

By this approach, the change in important sectors of a language from one set of related usages to another becomes an indicator of significant social and cultural developments. Thus the shift from early and mid-Victorian terms like 'men of letters', 'literary men' and 'cultivators of science' to 'the intellectuals' was no trivial alteration in linguistic fashion. Rather, it marked a profound transformation of the economic, social, and conceptual relations in which writers and thinkers stood. The term 'men of letters' and other associated phrases used before the 1870s denoted different groups, with different relations to each other and to the society at large, as compared to terms like 'intellectuals' used from the 1870s onwards. The Victorian years, then, witnessed the origin of the *idea* as well as the *vocabulary* of 'the intellectuals'; and both the idea and the vocabulary have made it possible for modern sociologists to think of all societies — those of ancient Egypt, pre-modern tribal Africa, medieval Europe, as well as twentieth-century Britain — as having intellectuals. The emergence of the idea and the vocabulary of 'the intellectuals' was a historical phenomenon indexing the splintering of earlier Victorian cultural cohesion. As Christopher Lasch has said of American history: 'The intellectual class, then, is a distinctly modern phenomenon, the product of cultural fragmentation that seems to characterize industrial and post-industrial societies.'[8]

To say that the concept and vocabulary of 'intellectuals' emerged in the industrial age, at least in England, is to place this book firmly in the context of work done by Asa Briggs and Raymond Williams. Both of these scholars have noted that alterations in vocabulary point to important social change. Briggs has argued persuasively that the 'language of class' emerged in the last years of the eighteenth century and the first decades of the nineteenth. As the industrial revolution transformed English society, altering a hierarchical social structure into one of antagonistic social classes, so the language referring to social stratification changed from words like 'orders', 'ranks' and 'degrees' to terms like 'aristocracy', 'middle class' and 'working class'. By the mid-nineteenth century, it was difficult for Englishmen to think of their society in any terms other than those of class structure.[9] Raymond Williams some years ago drew attention to many such changes in the language in his book *Culture and Society,* changes which formed a pattern related to the industrial revolution — new words, or new meanings for old words, like 'class', 'art', 'democracy', 'industry', 'society', and above all, 'culture'. These 'keywords', as Williams later called them, 'can be used as a kind of special map . . . to look again at those wider changes in life and thought to which changes in language evidently refer'. The complex of words centring around 'culture' had to do with a reaction to industry and to the 'new kinds of personal and social relationships' that accompanied capitalist industrialism.[10] One of the words that, according to Williams, had acquired a new meaning was the noun 'intellectual'. In *Keywords,* Williams says that 'intellectual' as a noun denoting 'a particular kind of person or a person doing a particular kind of work' dates from the early nineteenth century. He notes that 'intellectualism' dated from earlier centuries 'as a simple alternative to rationalism', with 'implications of coldness, abstraction and, significantly, ineffectiveness'. While 'intelligence' kept a positive connotation in the early nineteenth century, 'intellectual' as a noun took on a negative sense for several reasons: because of widespread orthodox English opposition to rationalist ideologies at the time of the French Revolution; because of a Romantic opposition to separation of the 'head' from the 'heart' (or reason from emotion); and because certain groups doing intellectual work in the eighteenth and nineteenth centuries were gaining independence from established political and religious institutions.[11]

There is brilliant speculation behind Williams' views, and it is true that when 'intellectuals' did come into general use in the nineteenth century, it carried for many (though not all) users a negative connotation, which is probably the main reason why many English intellectuals today are reluctant to apply the term to themselves.[12] However, I believe that Williams dates the arrival into general usage of 'the intellectuals' and the like too early: it happened towards the end and not the beginning of the nineteenth century. The early and mid-Victorians only *very* rarely used 'intellectual' or 'intellectuals' to denote a particular kind of person or persons. It is, of course, impossible to prove a negative, but some evidence can be offered to defend this proposition. The *Oxford English Dictionary* (the appropriate volume published in 1888) has an entry for 'intellectuals' as a noun, but is unable to cite any examples of usage between 1813 and 1884. English dictionaries did not carry 'intellectual' as a noun designating a kind of person until the 1880s.[13] Nor did encyclopaedias — the *Encyclopaedia Metropolitana* (1840s) does not refer to intellectuals, and neither did the *Encyclopaedia Britannica* until 1910-11.[14] I have found three cases of 'intellectual' used as a noun or adjective in a noun phrase between 1820 and the 1870s: (1) De Quincey refers to his mother in *Confessions of An English Opium Eater* (1822) as an 'intellectual woman'; (2) George Eliot in a letter in 1852 said that John Chapman stood out 'even in that assemblage of intellectuals'; and (3) Newman commented in the 'preface' to *On the Scope and Nature of University Education* (1852) that 'An intellectual man, as the world now conceives of him, is one who is full of "views" on all subjects of philosophy, on all matters of the day.'[15] No doubt there are more instances; but such usage clearly was not common in early and mid-Victorian England: it was not remotely like a prevailing way of thinking about cultural activities. In short, I agree with Steven Marcus, who has observed that 'intellectual' in any of the modern senses of the term did not exist as late as the middle of the nineteenth century.[16]

This point suggests that the rise of the terminology of intellectuals was not related to social change in quite the way that Williams thought. He is right to say that industrialization in the broadest sense lay behind the development of the concept of the intellectuals, but he failed to see that a long period of time elapsed between the onset of industrialization and the adoption of the new terminology. In fact, the first, most agonizing period of social and economic change had ended, and the relatively stable and harmonious decades of the 1850s and 1860s, characterized by the moral and material hegemony of the middle class, had passed, before the concept emerged into general usage. It seems likely that the idea of intellectuals as a class was related to particular changes in a comparatively mature industrial society, as well as to the very emergence of the basic class structure. One of the essential tasks of this book is to analyse the precise mental and material mechanisms by which Victorian culture — or at least high culture — was connected to social change.

The proposition that the concept of 'the intellectuals' in England emerged in the late-nineteenth century, and that it evolved in a particular relationship to the class structure, bears on certain questions raised in a current debate within the British left about the 'peculiarities of the English'. This unusually hot dispute began with a series of articles in the mid-1960s by Perry Anderson and Tom Nairn, who wanted to explain the relative moderation and consequent ineffectiveness of British socialism and the Labour Party. Their fundamental point was that any such explanation must be historical; thus they boldly set out in a few pages an interpretation of all of modern British history — with plenty of comparisons to continental developments — an interpretation that ranged over the three centuries since the 1640s and over huge topics like the changes in economic and social structure, the history of culture, and the sociology of knowledge. Along the way, Anderson and Nairn stressed the failure of Victorian intellectuals to be sufficiently rebellious.[17]

Anderson and Nairn contended that the political and social evolution of modern Britain and the orthodoxy of its intellectuals have been intimately related. They asserted that England in the seventeenth century had the first but 'least pure' bourgeois revolution in Europe. Further, the English middle class, having been formed prematurely, losts its 'courage' and merged meekly with the landed aristocracy in the nineteenth century; and this submissive English middle class failed to produce any 'systematic major ideology'. The English working class, which emerged during the period of political reaction against the French Revolution, was itself premature. The working class, existing in a condition of 'apartheid' and misery, and inheriting as an ideology only utilitarianism from the bourgeoisie, failed to produce a comprehensive understanding of their world, or 'universal ideology'.

Here is where the intellectuals failed the working class. Anderson and Nairn assume that intellectuals have always existed in England, but not always separate from the hegemonic class. One reason for the peculiar evolution of English *working-class* consciousness, Anderson wrote, 'was the failure of any significant body of intellectuals to join the proletariat until the very end of the nineteenth century'. The main reason for this failure was the 'peculiar sociological moorings of the intellectuals of the Victorian period'. The aristocracy had deliberately prevented the rise of a secular intelligentsia from the sixteenth century onwards, and as a result the intellectuals were closely related by kinship to the ruling class. Hence in England there has been 'the tradition of a body of intellectuals which was *at once homogeneous and cohesive and yet not a true intelligentsia*'.[18] Nairn described the role of Victorian intellectuals this way:

> The voices of intellectual protest were few, and remote from politics and the working class: distorted by the immense pressures of Victorian conformity, they tended towards an impossible and Utopian rejection of capitalism and industrialism as such (as with Ruskin and William Morris) or retreated into obscurity and eccentricity (like the novelists Meredith and Samuel Butler).[19]

The other side of the dispute was presented (vigorously, to put it mildly) by E.P. Thompson, who agreed with Anderson and Nairn that history should be put to use in understanding the present, but who declared that Anderson and Nairn had got their history all wrong. He contested their views of the seventeenth century, of the nature of eighteenth-century landowners, and of the power of the Victorian middle class. Thompson argued that the Victorian bourgeoisie *was* the dominant class, and that it tolerated aristocratic institutions only because those institutions were useful to middle-class people. Moreover, the Victorian middle class *did* produce impressive intellectual monuments, among them political economy and Darwinian science. As for the intellectuals, Thompson declared that 'it is rubbish to suggest there is some crippling disablement in the failure of British intellectuals to form "an independent intellectual enclave" within the body politic'. He said that there were many such enclaves, which together achieved much in science and in social and political action, but which never were forced into a clear confrontation with the political and social system, and which therefore never formed a French-style intelligentsia.

> The English experience certainly did not encourage sustained efforts of synthesis: since few intellectuals were thrown into prominence in a conflict with authority, few felt the need to develop a systematic critique. They thought of themselves, rather, as exchanging specialized products in a market which was tolerably free, and the sum of whose intellectual commodities made up the sum of 'knowledge.'[20]

The disputants in the 'peculiarities of the English' controversy raise a great many issues beyond the bounds of a study of Victorian intellectual life, and even on that particular subject, the angle from which they view the role of intellectuals is peculiar to their fraternal struggle. Moreover, the heavy-handedness of their generalizations and the casualness of their usage of terms like 'the intellectuals' and 'an intelligentsia' does not inspire confidence. Both interpretations lack a foundation in systematic analysis of the economic and social position of the Victorian thinkers, and of the attitudes and ideas which governed intellectual work. Nevertheless, Anderson, Nairn and Thompson have raised some extremely important questions about the nature of Victorian intellectual life. They disagree on the accomplishments of Victorian thinkers and on the reasons for their particular relationship to the ruling classes; but they agree on the comparative lack of rebelliousness but high cohesiveness among them. The questions brought to mind by these disagreements and agreements alike get to the heart of Victorian intellectual life. How cohesive in reality and in appearance were Victorian thinkers as a group? At what point and for what reasons did these thinkers become 'intellectuals'? What were their relationships to the ruling classes? In what senses, if any, did Victorian thinkers become alienated?

The 'peculiarities of the English' dispute also shows that to avoid confusion in discussing Victorian intellectual life, some assumptions about the development of English economic and social structure must, however briefly, be set out. First, the background to all intellectual activity was the immense expansion of the economy due to the industrial and commercial revolutions. This unprecedented burst of economic growth in the final analysis made possible the support of a widespread and vital high culture. Next, aside from the vast proliferation of wealth itself, the two social developments having the greatest impact on English intellectual activity in the nineteenth century were the growth of the middle class and the expansion of the professions. By 1850, the middle class amounted to more than twenty per cent of the English population. Commercial and industrial men were seen by themselves and others as the men of the future; they were the people who made the great economic machine go. James Mill said that the middle class is 'the class which is universally described as both the most wise and the most virtuous part of the community'.[21] Largely literate, the middle class by the early-nineteenth century comprised the great bulk of the reading public. In fact, public opinion was widely recognized as the opinion of the middle class.[22] The ideals and values of the middle class, often transmitted through Evangelical religion, had a decisive impact on Victorian culture. Indeed, it has been convincingly argued that by the mid-century, the 'entrepreneurial ideal' had triumphed, at least in the sense that middle-class values were accepted by the landed orders and by a significant portion of the labour aristocracy.[23] Inevitably, writers and thinkers had to contend with the ideas, aspirations, needs, and anxieties of the middle class.

The expansion of the professions, however, was scarcely less important. As W.J. Reader has said, the professions in Victorian England both were and were not part of the middle class.[24] In some of their values and styles of behaviour, professionals were much like the hard-working, dutiful commercial and industrial people; but in other ways they sought to rise above the middle class, to become a kind of 'new gentry'. This new gentry proliferated in the nineteenth century. In Georgian England, three occupations were regarded as professions

— the clergy, law, and medicine, or, more accurately, the clergy, the bar, and 'physic'. In the nineteenth century the number of acknowledged professions grew to include architects, engineers, civil servants, and solicitors, among others. As Sir George Kitson Clark has pointed out, in many of these cases the aspiring professionals had 'to organize the profession, in order to make sure that its members maintained standards and that their ranks were not invaded by the unsuitable and the untrained'.[25] In becoming professional, people accepted the social discipline of the group in order to gain the status and autonomy associated with the first three professions.

Professional status was attractive because of the traditional links between the professions and the old ideal of the gentleman; hence professionalization in some ways involved rejection of middle-class ways. In eighteenth-century England, the great dividing line in society was between the landed orders (aristocracy and gentry) on one side and everyone else on the other. By grace of their land, gentlemen lived well, bestowed patronage on their clients, received the deference of people lower in the social hierarchy, and performed important (often unpaid) public services. But they did not work for a living. Their ideal included disinterested public service. Everyone who possibly could aspired to the status of the gentleman and thus to free himself from dependency and servile work. No one within the gentry wanted to lose that standing; consequently, marriages in and out of gentle families were affairs of serious calculation. For eldest sons of a landed family, retention of status was no problem, for they inherited the land and the status that went with it. For younger sons, it was another matter. Some married into bourgeois families or went to work in a firm, with some loss of status but perhaps gain in wealth. Others had to find outdoor relief in one of the three professions — the clergy, bar, or physic. Hence the three professions became the means by which someone in nineteenth-century England could associate himself with high status and authority. By education and training, a man might lift himself above the commercial and industrial middle class, and so achieve the dignity and win the deference owed to the landed class.

The desire to become a professional was not the only factor by any means in the formation of groups which came to be called 'intellectuals', but it was significant. It was one mechanism which connected the functions and roles in intellectual work to the social structure. It affected both the ideas and the institutions which defined intellectual activity. A culture, as Karl Deutsch has pointed out, involves both a content (information, values, customs) and an institutional system through which the content is communicated.[26] These two elements are connected by a relation of mutual cause and effect. The technology and organization of intellectual activities affect what intellectual work is done and for whom; but the ideas themselves help shape the institutions. Moreover, both content and system are connected to the surrounding society as well as to each other. The interplay of these three factors — content, system, and society — at any moment produces a kind of topography of intellectual life. The topography in England changed between 1830 and 1900. The central object of this book is to make maps of the changed topography, and to explain how the Victorians went from one map to the other.

## Notes

1. The definitions come respectively from: Franklin L. Baumer, *Modern European Thought: Continuity and Change in Ideas, 1660-1950* (New York, 1977), p. 7; Christopher Lasch, *The New Radicalism in America: The Intellectual as a Social Type* (New York, 1965), p. ix; and Roberto Michels, 'Intellectuals', *Encyclopaedia of the Social Sciences*, vol. 8 (New York, 1932), p. 118.

2. Seymour Martin Lipset, *Political Man: The Social Bases of Politics* (Garden City, NY, 1963), p. 333.

3. Edward Shils, 'The Intellectuals and the Powers: Some Perspectives for Comparative Analysis' in Edward Shils, *The Intellectual and the Powers* (Chicago, 1972), pp. 3-22. See also Edward Shils, 'Intellectuals', *International Encyclopaedia of the Social Sciences*, vol. 7 (New York, 1968), pp. 399-415; and 'The Intellectuals as Participant in and Critic of Society', *Spectrum* (edited by S. Udin, Jakarta, 1978), pp. 499-531.

4. Shils, 'The Intellectuals and the Powers', p. 3.

5. Ibid., pp. 9-10.

6. Edward Shils, *The Intellectual between Tradition and Modernity: The Indian Situation* (The Hague, 1961).

7. Some of the leading works on intellectuals are: Julian Benda, *The Treason of the Intellectuals* (translated by Richard Adlington; New York, 1928); Florian Znaniecki, *The Social Role of the Man of Knowledge* (New York, 1940); and Lewis Coser, *Men of Ideas: A Sociologists's View* (New York, 1965). A good selection of excerpts of works on intellectuals can be found in George B. de Huszar (ed.), *The Intellectuals: A Controversial Portrait* (Glencoe, Ill., 1960).

8. Lasch, *New Radicalism in America*, p. xi.

9. Asa Briggs, 'The Language of "Class" in Early Nineteenth Century England', in Asa Briggs and John Saville (eds.), *Essays in Labour History* (London, 1960), pp. 43-73.

10. Raymond Williams, *Culture and Society, 1780-1950* (New York, 1966), p. xi.

11. Raymond Williams, *Keywords: A Vocabulary of Culture and Society* (New York, 1970), pp. 140-2.

12. Bertrand Russell is said to have sent this answer to someone asking how he defined 'intellectual':

I have never called myself an intellectual and nobody has ever dared to call me one in my presence. I think an intellectual may be defined as a person who pretends to have more intellect than he has, and I hope this definition does not fit me.

13. Samuel Johnson's *A Dictionary of the English Language* defines the noun 'intellectual' simply as 'intellect; understanding; mental powers or faculties. Little in use.' Charles Richardson's *A New Dictionary of the English Language* (London, 1858) also defines it as mental faculties. He says 'intellectualist' is used in connection with 'sublime philosophies'. John Ogilvie's *The Imperial Dictionary of the English Language* (new edn by Charles Annandale, London, 1885) carries 'intellectual' as an adjective designating a kind of person 'having intellect, or the power of understanding; characterized by intellect, or the capacity for higher forms of knowledge; as an *intellectual* being'.

14. The *Encyclopaedia Britannica,* 11th edn (1910-11) has an article on 'intellect', which says: 'A man is described as "intellectual" generally because he is occupied with theory and principles rather than with practice, often with further implication that his theories are concerned mainly with abstract matters: he is aloof from the world, and especially is a man of training and culture who cares little for the ordinary pleasures of sense.' vol. 14, p. 680.

15. Thomas De Quincey, *Confessions of an English Opium Eater* (New York, 1899; first published in 1822), p. 26; Eliot quoted in Gordon Haight, *George Eliot: A Biography* (Oxford, 1968), p. 110; and John Henry Newman, *On the Scope and Nature of University Education* (London, 1915; first published in 1852), p xxxix.

16. Steven Marcus, *Engels, Manchester, and the Working Class* (New York, 1975), p. vii. See also Christopher Kent, *Brains and Numbers: Elitism, Comtism, and Democracy in Mid-Victorian England* (Toronto, 1978), fn., p. 65.

17. For the Anderson-Nairn position, see: Perry Anderson, 'Origins of the Present Crisis', *New Left Review* (January-February 1964), pp. 26-54; Tom Nairn, 'The English Working Class', *New Left Review* (March-April 1964), pp. 43-57; Tom Nairn, 'The Nature of the Labour Party — I', *New Left Review* (September-October 1964), pp. 38-65; Tom Nairn, 'The Nature of the Labour Party — II', *New Left Review* (November-December, 1964), pp. 32-62; and Perry Anderson, 'Socialism and Pseudo-Empiricism', *New Left Review* (January-February 1966), pp. 2-42.

18. Anderson, 'Origins of the Present Crisis', p. 42.

19. Nairn, 'Nature of the Labour Party — I', p. 41.

20. E.P. Thompson, 'The Peculiarities of the English' *The Socialist Register* (London, 1965), pp. 311-62, espec. p. 333.

21. James Mill, *An Essay on Government* (Bobbs-Merrill, Indianapolis, 1955), p. 89.

22. Briggs, 'Language of Class', pp. 56-7.

23. Harold Perkin, *The Origins of Modern English Society, 1780-1880* (London, 1969), Ch. VIII.

24. W.J. Reader, *Professional Men: The Rise of the Professional Classes in Nineteenth-Century England* (London, 1966), p. 1. My remarks on professionals in the next two paragraphs depend heavily on Reader's lucid account.

25. G. Kitson Clark, *The Making of Victorian England* (New York, 1967), Ch. VIII.

26. Karl Deutsch, *Nationalism and Social Communication,* 2nd edn (Cambridge, Mass., 1966), Ch. 4.

# 2 THE WORLD OF THE MEN OF LETTERS, 1830s-1860s

The topography of early and mid-Victorian intellectual life was marked by a variety of distinct features, and the vocabulary of the day reflected this fact. When Englishmen referred to producers of intellectual objects, they used a number of different terms — men of letters, literary men, poets, novelists, artists, men of science, and scholars, to mention only a few. Generally, they grouped these types of thinkers under three labels — men of letters, men of science and scholars — but they had no term for the members of the three groups lumped together. 'Men of letters' was the broadest, most inclusive term, but through the mid-Victorian years, English men and women did not usually include in its scope either scientists as such or university dons or professors. In the Victorian mind, the sectors of the intellectual terrain occupied by these three kinds of thinkers were as different as mountains are from deserts and rivers.

By 'men of letters' or 'literary men' the Victorians meant more than producers of literature as such. Towards the end of the century, it is true, 'men of letters' was beginning to take on the sense of its most common twentieth-century definition — a quaint, second-rate writer in *belles lettres*. But throughout most of the century, 'men of letters' was a broader and more respectable sobriquet, including a very wide variety of writers — poets, novelists, journalists, biographers, historians, social critics, philosophers and political economists. It was applied to writers of imaginative literature like Dickens, Thackeray and Tennyson; to critics and social thinkers like Carlyle, Ruskin and Arnold; and to political philosophers like Mill, G.H. Lewes, and John Morley.[1] The most eminent and influential among the men of letters sometimes received the label of 'sages' or 'prophets', but these terms signified differences of moral weight rather than of occupation or function. The sage did with greatest power what all the men of letters were supposed to do.

What this wide variety of writers had in common was that they wrote for publication in books or periodicals offered for sale to the public through a market system. Sometimes, the Victorians used 'men of letters' in a narrower sense — to denote 'professional writers', those who actually made their living by writing, especially for periodicals. Trollope, for instance, usually had the earning of a living in mind when he thought of men of letters. Thus he quoted approvingly remarks about Thackeray's ability to support himself by his pen: 'He then became a regular man of letters — that is, he wrote for respectable magazines and newspapers, until the attention attracted to his contributions in *Fraser's Magazine* and *Punch* emboldened him to start on his own account, and risk an independent publication.'[2] Ordinarily, however, Victorians included as men of letters people like Tennyson, Grote, and Newman, who did not earn a living by their writing. What seems to have bound together all these kinds of writers in the minds of the Victorians was that they shared a market relationship with a general reading public. Their success as writers — in terms of influence and reputation as well as income — depended on the sale of their works to this public. This fact comprised the essential meaning of 'men of letters'.

The size, nature and needs of their public had enormous consequence for the men of letters. The general reading public had come into existence in the early eighteenth century, and by 1800 had almost completely replaced patronage as the means by which writers were supported. Burke believed in the 1790s that the reading public consisted of 80,000 people, most of them in London.[3] With the tremendous economic expansion and population growth of the late-eighteenth and early nineteenth centuries, the reading public grew, so that by 1830 it regularly consumed a huge volume of reading matter and supported a large number of professional writers. Just how large the reading public was in the early Victorian years is impossible to say. Apart from the size of the population itself, the principal limit on its size was literacy, the rate of which is impossible to determine accurately. Some recent estimates put the literacy rate in 1830 or 1840 at 67 per cent of adult males and 50 per cent of adult females.[4] If these estimates are valid, then the reading public in England and Wales might have numbered over 5,000,000 in 1830 and 6,000,000 in 1840. However, these figures seem too high for several reasons. Firstly, the literacy rates have been calculated from the number of people able to sign marriage registers, a method which may overestimate the number of readers, and *certainly* overestimates the number who could do more than simply spell out a wall poster, sound out a ballad hawked in the streets, or scrawl a signature. Secondly, there is some evidence that literacy rates declined in the squalor of the industrial cities of the early nineteenth century and was only beginning to recover in the 1830s.[5] Finally, though the number of schools expanded in the first half of the century, the school 'system' remained incomplete and inadequate at least through 1870, when Forster's education act established the state elementary schools. As late as 1861 it was calculated that only five per cent of all students remained in school after the age of eleven.[6] Thus a reasonable estimate is that in the early Victorian years more than a third of the population was illiterate, and that perhaps another third to a half was only semi-literate.

Another important limitation on the reading public came from the price of books ar d magazines. Even though technological advances were reducing the costs of printing, the price of new publications remained high, partly because of trade agreements among London booksellers.[7] A three-volume novel, the standard form for new fiction, was 31s 6d per set. Such prices represented a significant outlay for early and mid-Victorians, vast numbers of whom earned less than £100 per year. In the first half of the century, men in the lower-middle class earned perhaps £60 to £150 a year, and most fully employed working men took home even less.[8] Portions of the working class enjoyed the opportunity to read expensive literature: skilled artisans like Francis Place sometimes were able to find ways to buy books and periodicals; Mechanics Institutes provided libraries for some workers; tobacco shops and stationers often had small lending libraries; and domestic servants no doubt often had a chance to read their employers' books.[9] But these opportunities cannot have had much impact on the market for expensive, high-brow, publications.

It has often been said that Dickens wrote for all classes, and certainly he was the most widely read of the great Victorian authors. Yet even his public probably did not reach very far down into the working-class population. Dickens apparently was read by some domestics, shopkeepers, and tradesmen and their assistants, as well as by the lower-middle class. One story has it that a London charwoman — and presumably other working people — heard *Dombey and Son* read aloud to non-reading subscribers in a snuff shop.[10] There were readings in some factories and shops, but most workplaces must have been far too noisy to allow such entertainment. Unfortunately, there is no way to know how common such public readings were. What is clear is that Dickens was frequently plagiarized in cheap popular periodicals, and that as Dickens became more serious and less devoted to pure comedy, working-class interest in even the simplistic plagiarisms of his novels dwindled.[11] Even if one assumes that there were as many as 15 readers for every copy of a Dickens novel, then the readership of the serial version of the biggest seller *(The Old Curiosity Shop,* 1840), would have reached no more than 1,500,000 in all of

Britain, at a time when the adult (over 14 years) population of England and Wales stood at about ten million. Thus a sound estimate is that Dickens was read by a very large proportion of the middle and upper classes, but only by a small element of the working class, these more likely being members of the 'aristocracy of labour' interested in self-help and self-improvement.[12]

Thackeray acknowledged the restricted dimensions of the reading public of the men of letters when he said in the early 1840s that the world of the educated was a small part of society, and that there was 'a tremendous society moving around us, and unknown to us — a vast mass of active, stirring life, in which the upper and middling classes form an insignificant speck'.[13] Of course, many people regarded this turbulent, partly literate, partly illiterate working class as dangerous, and they believed that as literacy expanded, they would have to fight for the minds of working men. After all, the first part of Tom Paine's *Rights of Man* had sold 50,000 copies soon after publication in 1791, and one issue of Cobbett's *Political Register* sold 200,000 in 1816.[14] The reaction of the upper class was twofold. Firstly, by means of stamp taxes, they tried to make 'dangerous' working-class literature too expensive for its market. These taxes were not repealed until 1855. Secondly, people in the landed and middle classes made strenuous efforts to reach the working-class public: evangelical tracts, cheap publications by the Society for the Diffusion of Useful Knowledge, penny magazines by the SPCK, for instance. From the 1820s newspapers, magazines, broadsides and tracts poured out a torrent of preventive social doctrines for the working class. But all of the efforts failed. As R.K. Webb has shown, the upper classes could not overcome the problems they faced in reaching the poor — the price of publications, the level of writing and above all their lack of understanding of the working class. The working class preferred, Webb concludes, to 'hammer out their own society, their own culture'.[15]

These remarks are not meant to denigrate the achievement or popularity of the Victorian men of letters, but to stress the relative compactness of their audience. The general reading public through the 1850s was dominated by the middle class. The landed order, less than 2 per cent of the population, and the expanding middle class, perhaps 20 per cent of the population at mid-century, enjoyed 100 per cent literacy and could afford to buy or rent new publications. The middle class grew throughout the century.[16] See Table 2.1.

**Table 2.1:  Middle-class Population of England and Wales**[17]

| Year | Total population | Population over 14 years | Estimated middle class as % of pop. | No. of middle-class adults |
|------|------------------|-------------------------|-------------------------------------|----------------------------|
| 1831 | 13,897,000 | 8,894,000 | 15% | 1,334,000 |
| 1851 | 17,928,000 | 11,574,000 | 20% | 2,315,000 |
| 1867 | 21,000,000 | 13,440,000 | 23% | 3,091,000 |
| 1900 | 32,528,000 | 20,818,000 | 30% | 6,245,000 |

This class, growing in economic and social power as well as in numbers, had a voracious appetite for literature of all kinds. Middle-class people wanted entertainment, diversion, information, social instruction, moral guidance and spiritual reassurance. As members of a relatively new social order, the middle class lacked the traditions and connections that might have satisfied some of these needs, and they turned instead to publications for satisfaction and guidance. Religious literature, fiction, encyclopaedias, newspapers, political commentary and criticism of many varieties were ground out of the presses to meet the new market.[18] Hence the middle class, by their demand for reading matter, created a market for writing and at the same time called into being the man of letters as a social type — a producer of material for the presses.

There was money to be made in writing for the middle-class market. Scott was the great exemplar: the *Waverley* novels brought him thousands of pounds — he got, for example, £1,500 plus half the profits for *Ivanhoe* in 1819. And there were plenty of other models: John Murray paid Byron £600 for the first two cantos of Childe Harold and £2,000 for the third; he also paid Thomas Moore £5,000 for a biography of Byron. In the 1840s and 1850s, a mediocre novelist regularly earned £250 for a novel; while Dickens sold *Barnaby Rudge* for £4,000, and George Eliot sold *Adam Bede* for £800. Other kinds of literature paid equally well: in 1856 Longmans gave Macaulay £20,000 as partial payment for volumes three and four of his *History*. Furthermore, the new quarterly reviews of the early nineteenth century, the *Edinburgh* and the *Quarterly*, established a policy of paying good money for articles, 20 to 25 guineas per sheet of 16 pages.[19] Not everyone, of course, could write for the *Edinburgh* or make large sums of money; and there existed in London a world of hacks trying to eke out an existence on a few articles, sub-editing, and snippets of gossip. When starting out, many writers found support in journalism, which was not, until after the mid-century, sharply separated from other kinds of literature. Hard work and a modicum of talent enabled hundreds of men to survive as professional writers in London by the 1830s. Thackeray, who knew the world of the men of letters intimately, has his character Arthur Pendennis, a completely inexperienced and imperfectly educated young buck, earning almost £400 in his first year of reviewing and general journalism.[20]

The opportunity to make money by writing was powerfully attractive to young men without a set career in life; therefore, it was the chief recruiting device for the trade. No skills were required beyond the ability to read and write. The profession of literature, Trollope rightly observed, required 'no capital, no special education, no training . . . There is no apprenticeship wanted. Indeed there is no room for such apprenticeship. It is an art no one teaches; there is no professor who, in a dozen lessons, even pretends to show the aspirant how to write a book or an article.'[21] The universities did not recruit for the ranks of the men of letters; still less did a person need a post in a university to have a career as a man of letters. As a result of this open opportunity, men of letters were recruited from a wide range of social strata, but mostly from middle-class families. Richard Altick has calculated that for 600 literary writers of the nineteenth century whose fathers' occupations can be identified, 77 per cent came from the middle class:

**Table 2.2:  Social Origins of Nineteenth-century British Writers**[22]

|                     | 1800-35      | 1835-70      | 1870-1900    |
| ------------------- | ------------ | ------------ | ------------ |
| Gentry and          |              |              |              |
|   Aristocracy       | 26 (12.7%)   | 26 (11.3%)   | 13  (7.9%)   |
| Middle class        | 144 (70.2%)  | 185 (80.0%)  | 130 (79.3%)  |
| Working class       | 35 (17.1%)   | 20  (8.7%)   | 21 (12.8%)   |
| Totals              | 205          | 231          | 164          |

But the fact that a career as a man of letters was open to people from other than the middle class meant that the group as a whole formed a kind of social anomaly, not easily placed in the class structure of the nation.

This observation accounts for the ambiguous social status of the early and mid-Victorian men of letters. There is no question that the public's appreciation for their products and the increased income of successful writers improved the standing of professional authors. This fact applied even to journalists, who had held the lowest rung on the ladder of men of letters. In the 1830s and 1840s no one was yet sure where men of letters stood in the social scale. Plainly the men of letters were not professionals in the sense that barristers, clergymen and physicians were. They were not as such adjuncts of the landed orders. Some men of letters, of course, enjoyed incomes from real estate and investments. Yet because all men of letters sold their goods to consumers, they participated in a trade and were accordingly to some degree tainted in social reputation.[23]

Most men of letters readily accepted this aspect of middle-class life — subordination to the market. Many of them gave thoughtful advice to beginners in the trade, stressing self-discipline, hard work, methodical habits and temperate living.[24] Such middle-class values implictly rejected the romantics' notion of the artist as a genius seized by an uncontrollable inspiration. Trollope especially was open in his assertion of the respectability of writing for money: while he admittedly desired fame, he wrote:

> I confess that my first object in taking to literature as a profession was that which is common to the barrister when he goes to the Bar, and to the baker when he sets up his oven. I wished to make an income on which I and those belonging to me might live in comfort.[25]

All progress, he said, has derived from the plain desire of people to do their best for themselves and their families and friends. For a writer to pretend to be moved by inspiration is absurd:

> To me it would not be more absurd if the shoemaker were to wait for inspiration, or the tallow-chandler for the divine moment of melting.[26]

And Trollope felt that writers *had* achieved respectability in the Victorian period. The social elite courted writers and exhibited them at parties and banquets like prize trophies. The 'lionizing' of prominent authors became so common as to arouse frequent comment, and to elicit warnings to serious authors to avoid its traps.[27] No door was closed to men of letters by mid-century; Dickens, for example, was received by Queen Victoria, and she asked him for a set of his complete works.[28]

Yet the ambiguity of the social status of men of letters caused chronic discussion as to whether they were 'gentlemen'. The concept of the gentleman was changing during the nineteenth century, so that it came to be based more on moral qualities than on birth; but enough of the older idea that a gentleman did not work for a living remained to cast doubt on the status of men of letters. Naturally, the men of letters liked to claim gentle status, and so they promoted ideas of gentlemanliness that would allow them to qualify. In his biography of Thackeray, Gordon Ray contends that Thackeray's high standing in contemporary estimation came from his redefinition of the gentlemanly ideal towards a middle-class standard.[29] Clearly, the novel *Barry Lyndon* concerns the harm that can result from following an old-fashioned and false standard of gentlemanly behaviour.[30] To cite only one other example, Mrs Gaskell in *North and South* has her heroine Margaret Hale, daughter of a clergyman, learn that the manufacturer John Thornton, whatever his social origins and occupation, is really a gentleman. By the end of the century, men of letters took their inclusion among gentlemen for granted. In *New Grub Street* (1891) for instance, the starving novelist Reardon and his wife continue to hope he will not have to give up writing, because authorship entitles him to a higher status than that open to clerks and tradesmen.[31]

Another revelation of the status anxieties of the men of letters can be seen in the 'dignity of literature' controversy of the 1840s. In *Pendennis*, which gives a marvellous picture of the rough-and-tumble life of the men of letters as they started out in the 1830s and 1840s, Thackeray comments through one character:

> I deny that there are so many geniuses as people who whimper about the fate of men of letters assert there are. There are thousands of clever fellows in the world who could, if they would, turn verses, write articles, read books, and deliver a judgment upon them; the talk of professional critics and writers is not a whit more brilliant, or profound, or amusing, than that of any other society of educated people. If a lawyer, or a soldier, or a parson, outruns his income, and does not pay his bills, he must go to gaol; and an author must go, too.[32]

Such remarks earned Thackeray criticism from Dickens and others for denigrating the profession of literature. But Dickens himself received criticism from his close friend, the critic John Forster and others on similar grounds when he undertook his amazingly popular and lucrative dramatic readings in the late 1850s and 1860s.[33] The dignity of literature required that authors claimed special attributes but also that they rose above the popular acclamation these attributes won for them.

The central point in the controversy occurred in 1850 when Dickens, John Forster and Bulwer Lytton set out to establish a Guild of Literature and Art. The Guild would control a fund raised by amateur theatricals produced by Dickens, and would use the fund to assist writers when starting out, veteran men of letters who had exhausted their talent, and scholars whose works were too unpopular to sell.[34] The Guild, in fact, was only the latest in a series of organizations, reaching back into the eighteenth century, designed to mitigate the rigours of the market by a plan of collective patronage.[35] Bulwer Lytton and Forster also believed that the Guild would help elevate the status of men of letters, who, in their opinion, were not sufficiently respected by the nation. Lytton wrote a play which was performed a number of times by Dickens' company; and later, Lytton contributed land on his estate on which cottages were built for needy men of letters. However, Thackeray and his circle rejected the whole operation on grounds that society *already* gave adequate protection to men of letters. On the other hand, Thackeray advocated acceptance by men of letters of state honours and pensions, which Dickens and Trollope regarded as degrading the *independence* of the men of letters.[36]

The upshot of all this controversy was that the Guild of Literature was established and some cottages built. But it never became an important source of support for men of letters. Nor did state patronage. The dispute and the limited success of the Guild illustrate that the writers themselves were unsure of the kind of approval their position deserved; but it also shows clearly their market orientation. A few men of letters, most notably John Stuart Mill, advised aspiring writers to take a regular job so that they could escape the pressures of writing for money. But, like Dr Johnson and Scott, most Victorian men of letters valued their independence from patronage, and took pride in honest production for the market. They differed in their estimates of how they as a group stood in public esteem, but on the whole they took a thoroughly middle-class view of the honour of producing for a public. In effect they rejected the principles of patronage or endowment recommended by people like Bulwer Lytton. The organizations by men of letters which *were* effective were conventional trade associations aimed at improving the position of authors within the market systems — organizations with friendly publishers to break the price-setting monopoly of the London booksellers, and the Society of Authors (established in 1883), which worked mainly on copyright law.[37]

The economic operation of the market for the books and articles of men of letters was controlled by certain publishing institutions. In the eighteenth century, support of writing by patronage had given way to publication by subscription and to the development of private booksellers/publishers. This combination of bookselling and publishing had broken down by the nineteenth century, and publishing was mainly in the hands of a number of entrepreneurs who formed an important part of the world of the men of letters — John Murray, Henry Colbourn, Richard Bentley, William Blackwood and Alexander Macmillan, among others.[38] One of their activities was to publish periodicals, most of which in the Victorian period were closely related to newspaper journalism and which carried a remarkable variety of literature — fiction, information, reviews and opinion. Beginning with the *Edinburgh Review* (1802) and the *Quarterly Review* (1809) these journals became key institutions in nineteenth-century English high culture. The middle-class reading public could not get enough of them. Every religious sect, political party and social persuasion needed its own organ. Large numbers were founded each year: between 1830 and 1880, more than 100 were founded each decade.[39] Consequently, though the circulation of any one of them was not particularly big, the total was huge.

**Table 2.3: Circulation of Some Leading Victorian Periodicals**[40]

| | | |
|---|---|---|
| *Edinburgh* | 1820s and 1830s | 12,000-14,000 |
| *Quarterly* | 1830s | 9,000-10,000 |
| *Blackwood's* | 1831 | 8,000 |
| *Fraser's* | 1831 | 8,700 |
| *Household Words* | 1850s | 40,000 |
| *Athenaeum* | 1854 | 7,200 |
| *Westminster* | 1855 | 4,000 |
| *Cornhill* | 1870s | 20,000 |
| *Fortnightly* | 1870s | 14,000 |

Many of these periodicals, like *Bentley's Miscellany* and *Blackwood's* were products of large book publishing houses. These houses were, like most Victorian companies, family firms, in which the owners took a very active part in company activities. Book publishers acted as editors as well as businessmen. Though most of them had readers to whom they turned for opinion on manuscripts, many publishers involved themselves deeply in reading and judging manuscripts for themselves. The risk they took in publishing a book was extremely personal, as were company efforts to recruit good writers. Often, therefore, they had a personal as well as commercial interest in the work of their writers, and the number of close ties between publishers and authors was high — John Blackwood and George Eliot, Dickens and Edward Chapman and William Hall, and Thackeray and George Smith, for example.

But the publishers above all were businessmen, and had to exercise editorial powers with a view as to what the public wanted and would tolerate. Thus publishers in a chronic refrain warned authors to keep their works agreeable and above all within the bounds of decency. John Blackwood, for instance, frequently asked George Eliot to make her novels more cheerful; and Daniel Macmillan took the 'damns' and references to 'beastly' out of Thomas Hughes's *Tom Brown's School Days*.[41] Usually publishers spoke to writers in terms of what the readers wanted; but in fact their own sense of propriety was identical to that of the public. Alexander Macmillan spoke for himself as well as the readers of *Macmillan's Magazine* when he wrote to Caroline Norton about her novel *Old Sir Douglas*:

> You will perceive that we have not inserted the last chapter of this month's supply of your very beautiful novel which is charming us all . . . The effect on the minds of all of us who read it was the same surprise and regret and a strong conviction that it would not do to put it in the *Magazine* under any possible circumstances. You must permit me to say so quite distinctly. There may be . . . very much of pettiness about Court conduct . . . But our Queen who whatever she is in herself (and we are as a nation very thankful for what she is...) is yet the person that does command our loyalty whatever that may mean.[42]

The most powerful institutions in the world of the men of letters were the circulating libraries, which were closely related to the popularity of fiction. The reading public by the 1830s above all wanted fiction, but found new novels expensive. Scott's novels had set the normal form and price for a novel — a three decker at 31s 6d — too much for all but the wealthiest readers to buy. But almost everyone in the middle-class public could pay an annual subscription of one guinea to a lending library for the right to borrow an unlimited number of volumes. Lending libraries had existed since the second half of the eighteenth century, but by far the most important ones in the Victorian period were Mudie's (established 1842) and W.H. Smith's (1858). They became essential parts of the publishing system and powerful forces in the lives of most men of letters. The circulating libraries became the largest buyers of books; and their order could make or break an author. Mudie's for example, bought 960,000 volumes between 1853 and 1862. Mudie's purchased 2,500 sets of the third and fourth volumes of Macaulay's *History of England* — the purchase weighed eight tons! Faithfully reflecting public desires, the libraries wanted more fiction than anything else: in 1858-9, Mudie's bought 42 per cent fiction, 22 per cent history and biography, 13 per cent travel and adventure, and 23 per cent miscellaneous literature, including science and religion. The three-volume novel was perfect for the libraries, for it kept book prices too high for readers to buy books and made it easy for a library to lend a volume at a time. The libraries, therefore, had a stake in the three-volume form and high book prices; and their demand for fiction persuaded many people (including many women) into trying their hands at novel writing, while imposing the triple-decker format on them and their publishers.[43]

Furthermore, the circulating libraries interpreted the views of the reading public to publishers and authors. Both C.E. Mudie and W.H. Smith took an active part in the choice of books for their libraries, and they thought of themselves as protectors of their public. Their 'select lists' of books functioned as a screening mechanism against unpleasant or dangerous subjects. In fact, both Mudie and Smith shared the moralistic views of the Victorian middle class. Mudie was a strong nonconformist who occasionally preached to his congregation and wrote hymns. Smith was an Evangelical Anglican who had thought seriously of entering the clergy. Neither hesitated to speak for the public. In 1850, Carlyle met Mudie and said, 'So *you're* the man that divides the sheep from the goats! Ah! It's an *awfu'* thing to judge a man. It's a *more* awfu' thing to judge a book.' Mudie replied: 'In my business I profess to judge books only from a commercial standpoint, though it is ever my object to circulate good books and not bad ones.'[44]

Working under such common institutions and sharing so many common experiences gave the men of letters considerable group cohesion and identity. After one hilarious party attended by many of the leading authors in London, Jane Carlyle wrote that she doubted that 'there was as much witty speech uttered in all the aristocratic, conventional drawing rooms, thro' out London that night as among us little knot of blackguardist literary people who felt ourselves above all rules, and independent of the universe.'[45] But the men of letters did not become either highly organized or sharply segregated from the rest of society. Their most important collective institutions were informal. In this regard the cultural dominance of the metropolis had heavy influence: as the centre of the largest reading public, the focus of national politics and the home of the English printing and publishing industry, London naturally attracted the overwhelming portion of men of letters, who therefore had many opportunities for personal contact. Writers and publishers patronized the same coffee-houses and taverns, and formed circles of friendship. Those who could afford the fees belonged to the big London clubs — the Reform, the Oxford and Cambridge, the Garrick, the Athenaeum and others. It is important to remember that these clubs had memberships drawn from many elite groups other than men of letters. The Athenaeum, for instance, was more than any other *the* club of eminent writers and learned men, but it also included barristers, physicians and politicians. Similarly, as Noel Annan has pointed out, the families of leading writers and thinkers very often intermarried, but they married with the governing elite — the middle and landed classes — as well.[46] These informal yet strong links provided for men of letters a mutually supportive community, and also helped bind them to the social structure; thus they assisted in preventing the development of an intelligentsia in the Russian model — an alienated elite of the educated.[47]

Perhaps the most important tie binding the men of letters to the established political and social system were their multiple connections with the governing elite — with what Shils calls 'the powers'. The reading public of England was compact and 'reachable', and it included *all* the politicians, the civil service and probably the entire electorate, which down to 1867 was very small: in England and Wales, the electorate was 435,000 (of a population of 13,897,000) in 1831; 800,000 (of 15,914,000) in 1851; and still only 1,057,000 (of a population of almost 23,000,000) in 1871. Given the small size of the electorate before 1867, and given its essentially middle-class composition, it seems likely that an important novel, historical work, or social polemic would have reached a very large portion of the governing elite. Through their newspapers, periodicals and books, the men of letters wrote directly for all the people who counted in decision-making. When Dickens denounced an antiquated part of the administrative system, when Mrs Gaskell reported the poverty of working-class life, or when Carlyle warned of social revolution, they knew that electors, members of parliament, bureaucrats and industrial magnates would get the message. (Lord John Russell is said to have read *David Copperfield* aloud with his wife, after which both wept.)[48] All of them were confident that they could do good and have real effect.

The direct connection between the men of letters and their audience enforced by economic arrangements and strengthened by the particular size and nature of the reading public was essentially a connection of *sympathy,* in the sense of mutual understanding and confidence. The sympathetic relationship held firm even though the greatest Victorian writers were often scathing critics of certain bourgeois attributes and important features of industrial society. The Victorian 'sages' did not earn their popularity and influence by merely mouthing middle-class views. A number of things contributed to the sympathetic relationship. One was that the men of letters shared with their audience fundamental middle-class values — order, progress, a more or less orthodox Christian morality, productivity and self-help. This commonality of values originated partly in the middle-class origins and connections of the men of letters and partly in the writers' acceptance of the disciplines of the market place. The men of letters shared with their audience an ideal of social relations and public order which basically accepted the class structure; thus the men of letters preached social understanding and sympathy but not social revolution. Further, the fact that they exhorted their readers to strive for mental and moral improvement implicitly complimented the capacities of the middle class. The men of letters knew who made up their audience, they respected the character of their readers, and they understood how their ideas and rhetoric would resonate in their readers' minds.[49] As Ian Watt has remarked about eighteenth-century authors of fiction, the growth of a middle-class reading public ensured that men of letters need only consult themselves for standards, forms and content to be sure of a wide audience.[50]

The most important reason for the sympathetic relationship between men of letters and their audience was mutual agreement on the proper function of the men of letters. The public expected them to be *useful,* either as entertainers, providers of an anodyne, or most significantly, as moral leaders or guides. Whether novelist, poet, historian, philosopher, or social critic, the man of letters was expected to help the audience through the troubles of economic, social and religious change.[51] It is not difficult to understand why this was so. In the early and mid-Victorian years, the English people felt that they were experiencing change at a pace and scale new to human society: it was no accident that they took the railroad to be the symbol of their time. Victorians felt keenly the seriousness of the issues they faced and the newness of their position. Economic, social, political and spiritual upheavals generated in Englishmen a powerful need for guidance and support. To some extent, these needs were still being met by the churches — remnants of an Ecclesiastical cultural system — but increasingly the literate public turned to secular sources. In this process of secularization, the public encouraged the men of letters to act as preachers, moralists, critics and sages, with essentially didactic and prophetic functions. And although this role as preachers sometimes forced on the men of letters uncomfortable moralistic or utilitarian aesthetic standards, it also gave them high status and a strong sense of being at one with the society as a whole.

The men of letters talked openly about accepting the utilitarian function thrust upon them. Harriet Martineau recalled that she was sustained by her desire to be useful when struggling to write her *Illustrations of Political Economy*: 'I thought of the multitudes who needed it, — and especially of the poor, — to assist them in managing their own welfare.'[52] J.S. Mill decided upon a life as a man of letters in order to propagate the utilitarian doctrine he felt his society needed.[53] Dickens, Mrs Gaskell, Charles Kingsley and Disraeli all wrote 'propaganda' novels to draw attention to the condition of England in the 1840s and 1850s. But the desire to be useful did not require the writers to address only practical subjects, for *moral* usefulness was even more important. There was a relationship between the role of the men of letters as moralists and social critics and the willingness of the middle class to listen to Evangelical sermons about sinfulness. Thackeray, who was among the least pretentious novelists, wrote that,

> Morals and manners we believe to be the novelist's best themes; and hence prefer romances which do not treat of algebra, religion, political economy, or any other abstract science.[54]

He wrote to a friend in 1847:

> What I mean applies to my own case & that of all of us — who set up as Satirical-Moralists — and having such a vast multitude of readers whom we not only amuse but teach. And indeed, a solemn prayer to

God Almighty was in my thoughts that we may never forget truth & Justice and kindness as the great ends of our profession. There's something of the same strain in Vanity Fair. A few years ago I should have sneered at the idea of setting up as a teacher at all, and perhaps at this pompous and pious way of talking about a few papers of jokes in Punch — but I have got to believe in the business, in many other things since then. And our profession seems to me to be as serious as the Parson's own.[55]

Another good example of a man of letter's acceptance of the role of moral teacher can be found in *David Copperfield*. In young manhood David becomes a journalist, then a general writer and critic. He treats his work as a business, applying steady work habits but exercising no special insights. But when his wife Dora dies, he is distraught, for he realizes that it had been his 'undisciplined heart' which caused their unhappy marriage. However, the good Agnes helps him recover from his depression and find his true function as a writer:

She was sure that in my every purpose I should gain a firmer and higher tendency, through the grief I had undergone . . . As the endurance of my childhood days had done its part to make me what I was, so greater calamities would nerve me on, to be yet better than I was, and so, as they had taught me, would I teach others.[56]

Unquestionably the most exalted statement of the moral utility of the men of letters came from the greatest prophet of them all, Thomas Carlyle. In his lecture, 'Hero as Man of Letters', Carlyle tied the function of the men of letters to his own transcendental philosophy and prophetic social criticism. For Carlyle, a descendant of Scottish calvinists who had drunk deeply of German idealist philosophy, the one great truth was that there existed a divine reality behind material phenomena. To him the grievous problem of the nineteenth century was that the 'steam intellect' prevented people from seeing this underlying truth. What England needed was something ancient societies had produced more easily — men of godlike insight — 'a Prophet or Poet to teach us'. The person who can 'discern the loveliness of things,' Caryle said, 'we call him Poet, Painter, Man of Genius, gifted, lovable'. Hero, Prophet, and Poet are all names for these great men. The most modern form of hero is the 'Hero as a Man of Letters', one who 'must be regarded as our most important modern person'. 'What he teaches,' Carlyle declared, 'the whole world will do and make.' Thus his function is to do what heroes always have done: to make manifest the 'Divine Idea of the World' underlying mere 'Appearance'. Men of letters were far more important than universities, because once printing had spread, literature had made universities obsolete: 'It depends on what we read, after all manner of Professors have done their best for us. The true University of these days is a Collection of Books.'[57]

The response of the reading public testifies to the effectiveness of the men of letters in communicating their message and to the general acceptance of their *preaching* function. It was not just a matter of relatively huge sales of serious works of literature, social criticism, and history, but one of a close community between writers and audience. Poets and novelists were especially able to establish an amazing intimacy with their public. Wordsworth and Tennyson were very widely read, and their readers interpreted them as teaching an elevating philosophy of the immaterial in a materialist age as well as showing the beauty in the commonplace.[58] *In Memoriam* gave consolation to countless Victorians, including the Queen. J.A. Froude recalled:

> Tennyson's Poems, the group of poems which closed with *In Memoriam,* became to many of us what *The Christian Year* was to orthodox Churchmen. We read them, and they became part of our minds, the expression, in exquisite language, of the feelings which were working in ourselves.[59]

Thackeray was praised for the personal intimacy he established with his audience in *Pendennis.*[60] Serial publication of novels made public participation in the fortunes of the characters a kind of national emotional event. Scarcely an eye in the English reading public remained dry when Dickens killed off Little Nell in *The Old Curiosity Shop.* Daniel O'Connell, the Irish nationalist MP, wept as he read the fatal issue: 'He should not have killed her! — he should not have killed her! — she was too good!'[61]

Such emotional experiences, heightening the deeper message of moral exhortation and spiritual comfort, inspired public veneration of the leading men of letters. Dickens, for example, received demonstrations of affection approaching adulation from his audiences at his public readings.[62] During the publication of *Middlemarch,* George Eliot was praised for her treatment of the corrupt Bulstrode; one clergyman declared in a sermon:

Many of you no doubt have read the work which that great teacher George Eliot is now publishing and have shuddered as I shuddered at the awful dissection of a guilty conscience. Well, *that* is what I mean by the prophetic spirit.[63]

And in 1874, George Eliot received this heartfelt letter from Boston:

I feel the most intense desire to know you. I care for you as the embodiment of my highest principles, and after reading your books with me, my husband shares my enthusiasm. If we may never see you, we have much true married happiness to thank you for.[64]

Dependence on the market, close relations with the public and agreement on the 'preaching function' worked many crucial effects on the production of ideas in Victorian England. Some of these effects were unfortunate. The institutional connection with journalism impressed on much of the writing a sense of immediacy and urgency and contributed to the rise of the great realist style in fiction; but it also contributed to hastiness and partisanship. Serial publication and the three-volume format for the novel also led to hastiness and structural weaknesses; but the worst effects of journalism occurred in magazine writing. The arena of the periodicals down through mid-century was fiercely competitive and often ferociously partisan. Political polemics and personal vituperation coloured much of what was published. Partisanship and private vendettas passed as authoritative teaching. Further, the connection between periodical and book publication caused much 'puffery', as publishers planted articles in order to push their books.[65] Irresponsibility was encouraged by the prevailing practice of anonymity in periodical publication, a policy defended on the grounds of enhancing the freedom of authors and the authority of their articles.[66] Reviewing became the most prominent form of periodical writing, because the public craved evaluation of the flood of works that were produced for consumption. Since professional writers had to turn out pages on a staggering variety of subjects in order to earn a living, as well as to defend their own political or literary cliques, many of the reviews were shallow and ill-informed. Thackeray admitted as much in his description of the young Pendennis:

By the help of the 'Biographie Universelle' or the British Museum, he would be able to take a rapid *résumé* of a historical period, and allude to names, dates, and facts, in such a masterly, easy way, as to astonish his mamma at home, who wondered where her boy could have acquired such a prodigious store of reading, and himself too, when he came to read over his articles two or three months after they had been composed, and when he had forgotten the subject and the books which he had consulted.[67]

Not all the effects of the economic, social, and conceptual relations of the world of the men of letters were so clearly bad. Indeed, many effects contributed to a shared culture of knowledge and discourse. For instance, the conditions combined to assure that the man of letters was a generalist. He could not afford to be, nor did he want to be, a specialist. Like the journals in which they published, writers covered politics, theology, philosophy, literature, history and popular science. It is often thought today that specialization is a response to the overwhelming volume of literature that is produced. In the first half of the nineteenth century, however, the response was different. Victorians frequently observed that the amount of knowledge was increasing at a bewildering pace, but they saw this as emphasizing a need for synthesis, generalization, and evaluation. The good had to be separated from the bad, and the parts related to the whole. For the man of letters, the ability to assimilate and interpret rated as a higher quality than the ability to report special knowledge. As John Morley noted of J.S. Mill, the better the generalist, the greater the man of letters. Mill's work shows that:

> our object in the study of each subject should be to rise from its special facts to its general ideas. The best educated man is he who has mastered the largest conceptions which belong to the greatest number of subjects. In a country where there is a characteristic leaning to the narrowest specialism . . . the popularity of an author so far removed from this as Mr Mill is must be eminently useful.[68]

Another effect of great consequence was that the men of letters did not value knowledge for its own sake. Victorians were 'fact-oriented', but for them knowledge had to be geared to practical purpose. Mill produced his *System of Logic,* for example, less as a contribution to philosophy than to destroy the intellectual basis for conservative political ideologies.[69] And Macaulay wrote history to help the present: 'No past event has any intrinsic importance. The knowledge of it is valuable only as it leads us to form just calculations with respect to the future.'[70]

By the same logic, the institutional and conceptual context established moral-utilitarian and 'extrinsic' norms for imaginative literature. Early and mid-Victorians tended to evaluate literature according to effects and standards external to itself and its formal qualities. M.H. Abrams has contended that during the eighteenth century, the desire of the leisured classes to distinguish themselves in virtuosity and connoisseurship established at the philosophical level the theory of 'art as such', consisting of three propositions: (1) the fine arts are *sui generis;* (2) art is to be contemplated disinterestedly; and (3) a work of art is autonomous.[71] But early and mid-Victorians broke with this theory of 'art as such'. For them, as G.H. Lewes put it, 'the object of literature is to instruct, to animate, or to amuse'.[72]

This stricture applied even to poetry. Most literate Victorians believed the poet to be the most elevated and serious kind of writer; yet the poet's skills do not absolve him of the need to be useful. To Bentham, poetry could never be useful because as associative language it necessarily misrepresented reality. But the more common view was that poetry's specially powerful language, in fact, obligated it to be of service. J.S. Mill learned this view of poetry from his father.[73] Later, the younger Mill deliberately used poetry to develop his emotions.[74] And the concept of poetry as the highest instructor prevailed among a much wider audience than the utilitarians. According to Sir Henry Taylor, poetry ought 'to thread the mazes of life in all its classes and under all its circumstances, common as well as romantic, and, seeing all things, to infer and instruct . . .'[75] Bulwer Lytton stated the same thing more grandly:

> if the vice of the time leans to the Material, and produces a low-born taste and an appetite for coarse excitement, — Wordworth's poetry is of all existing in the world the most calculated to refine — to etherealize — to exalt; to offer the most correspondent counterpoise to the scale that inclines to earth. It is for this that I consider his influence mainly beneficial. His poetry has repaired to us the want of an immaterial philosophy — nay it *is* philosophy, and it is of the immaterial school. No writer more unvulgarizes the mind.[76]

Bulwer Lytton's observation reveals the Victorian assumption that poetry constitutes a form of communication. To instruct, so thought the Victorians, poetry must emphasize the content; it must satisfy the readers' understanding as well as their emotions. What is most important in poetry is the message. Taylor wrote: '. . . no man can be a very great poet who is also not a great philosopher'.[77] Mill believed Shakespeare to be the greatest poet, 'because he was one of the greatest of philosophers'.[78] W.H. Smith, reviewing Tennyson's poetry in 1849, observed that poets in his day tended to seize upon the 'elements of passion and reflection', to add 'a greater liberty of imagination' and so indulge in the 'mere intellectual luxury of imaginative thought'. This tendency he thought bad, for poetry must contain 'substantial thought, the broad passions of mankind, or a deep reflection'.[79] Accordingly, poetry, like all art, must communicate to a wide public. The Victorians did not like difficult or 'coterie' poetry — or any such art. As one critic said, a work of art 'which fails to interest the great mass of spectators cannot be one of a high class, nor can it possess real merit'.[80]

While the domination by a middle-class public shaped the norms of poetry, it also made the novel the most popular and influential form of literature. Readers found novels easier to understand than poetry and more convenient vehicles for information and for moralization of everyday life. Hence the number of novels grew rapidly during the century: one estimate holds that about 26 new novels were published in Britain in 1820, about 100 in 1850, and 300 in 1864.[81] Moreover, the needs and interests of the public contributed heavily to two of the most important features of the Victorian novel — realism and moral didacticism.[82] From the 1830s, Gothic novels and romances were supplanted by novels that conveyed information about the social structure and social status; about the nature of the working class and social relations; and about new forms of gentlemanliness. Others explored moral and intellectual problems resulting from religious turmoil. Perhaps the most typical Victorian novel was one which embodied a consideration of vast social and cultural change in the life-history of its leading characters.

In judging all these kinds of novels, the Victorians applied the test of accurate observation, or truth to life. Thackeray, for example, won praise for his realistic portraits; and this was precisely what he hoped to do.[83] George Eliot struck her readers as the most acute and subtle observer of all. When she published her 'Amos Barton' in *Scenes of Clerical Life,* it was so realistic that one reader believed the author to be 'a man of Science' — and indeed George Eliot *had* been influenced by habits of scientific observation.[84] Even Dickens, whose rich imagination and sense of satire pushed his novels towards symbolism and caricature, often asserted that the characters and events of his works were rooted in fact; and he often defended himself on grounds of the strict accuracy of his reporting.[85]

The aesthetic standard of realism sometimes clashed with the demand for moral instruction. Middle-class Victorian readers required characters and events to be probable and recognizable; but they did not want to read about things they regarded as highly disagreeable, immoral, or degrading — sexual desire, prostitution, or wicked behaviour going unpunished, for instance. All the leading Victorian novelists met with difficulty in their readers' prudery, although the authors' intention rarely went beyond realistically exposing some evil behaviour or institution. Dickens probably lost readers when he wrote about fallen women in *Oliver Twist* and *David Copperfield,* even though he intended to rouse public sympathy so that the fallen would not be prevented from returning to virtue.[86] Thackeray declared in a famous preface to *Pendennis:*

> Since the author of Tom Jones was buried, no writer of fiction among us has been permitted to depict to his utmost power a *MAN.* We must drape him, and give him a certain conventional simper. Society will not tolerate the Natural in our Art.[87]

However, most Victorian novelists found that realism and moral elevation were mutually necessary and compatible. George Eliot wrote to Blackwood:

> The moral effect of the stories of course depends on my power of seeing truly and feeling justly; and as I am not conscious of looking at things through the medium of cynicism or irreverence, I can't help hoping that there is no tendency in what I write to produce those miserable mental states.[88]

But Trollope put it best:

> I have always desired to 'hew out some lump of the earth', and to make men and women walk upon it just as they do walk here among us, — with not more of excellence, nor with exaggerated baseness, — so that my readers might recognise human beings like to themselves and not feel themselves to be carried away among gods or demons. If I could do this, then I thought I might succeed in impregnating the mind of the novel-reader with a feeling that honesty is the best policy; that truth prevails while falsehood fails;

that a girl will be loved as she is pure, and sweet and unselfish; that a man will be honoured as he is true, and honest, and brave of heart; that things meanly done are ugly and odious, and things nobly done beautiful and gracious.[89]

## Notes

1. For a sense of who were the men of letters, see John Gross, *Rise and Fall of the Man of Letters* (London, 1969), *passim*.

2. Quoted in Anthony Trollope, *Thackeray* (London, 1879), p. 29.

3. A.S. Collins, *The Profession of Letters* (London, 1928), p. 29. On the emergence of the reading public, see also A.S. Collins, *Authorship in the Days of Johnson* (London, 1927); Ian Watt, *The Rise of the Novel: Studies in Defoe, Richardson and Fielding* (Berkeley, 1962), Ch. II; and W.J. Saunders, *The Profession of English Letters* (London, 1964), Chs. VII-IX.

4. R.K. Webb, *The British Working Class Reader, 1790-1848* (London, 1955), Ch. I; Richard Altick, *The English Common Reader* (Chicago, 1957), Ch. 7; R.S. Schofield, 'The Measurement of Literacy in Pre-Industrial England', in Jack Goody (ed.), *Literacy in Traditional Societies* (Cambridge, 1968), pp. 311-25.

5. Lawrence Stone, 'Literacy and Education in England, 1640-1900', *Past and Present* (February 1969), p. 126; Michael Sanderson, 'Literacy and Social Mobility in the Industrial Revolution', *Past and Present* (August 1972), pp. 75, 86-8.

6. Brian Simon, *Studies in the History of Education, 1780-1870* (London, 1960), p. 347. See also G.A.N. Lowndes, *The Silent Social Revolution,* 2nd edn (Oxford, 1969), Chs. I-III.

7. James G. Barnes, *Free Trade in Books: A Study of the London Book Trade since 1800* (Oxford, 1964); Gordon Haight, *George Eliot: A Biography* (Oxford, 1969), pp. 109-10.

8. G. Kitson Clark, *The Making of Victorian England* (New York, 1967), pp. 113-21.

9. Louis James, *Fiction for the Working Man, 1830-1850* (London, 1963), Ch. I.

10. Edgar Johnson, *Charles Dickens: His Tragedy and Triumph* (2 vols., New York, 1952), II, p. 613.

11. James, *Fiction for the Working Man,* Ch. 4.

12. George H. Ford, *Dickens and His Readers: Aspects of Novel-Criticism since 1836* (New York, 1965), pp. 78-80.

13. Quoted in Gordon Ray, *Thackeray: The Uses of Adversity, 1811-1846* (New York, 1955), p. 214.

14. Louis James (ed.), *Print and the People, 1819-1851* (London, 1976), pp. 28-33.

15. Webb, *British Working Class Reader,* pp. 160-2.

16. For the literature of the working class, see James (ed.), *Print and the People;* Martha Vicinus, *The Industrial Muse: A Study of Nineteenth Century British Working-Class Literature* (London, 1974); and P.J. Keating, *The Working Classes in Victorian Fiction* (London, 1971), pp. 2-3.

17. Sources: B.R. Mitchell and Phyllis Deane, *Abstract of British Historical Statistics* (Cambridge, 1962); G.D.H. Cole, *Studies in Class Structure* (London, 1955), pp. 55-7; E.J. Hobsbawm, *Industry and Empire* (New York, 1968), Diagram 10.

18. Altick, *English Common Reader, passim.*

19. Royal Gettmann, *A Victorian Publisher: A Study of the Bentley Papers* (Cambridge, 1960), pp. 4, 6-7; Edgar Johnson, *Sir Walter Scott* (2 vols., New York, 1970), I, pp. 652-3.

20. W.M. Thackeray, *Pendennis* (2 vols., London, Everyman's Library, 1959), I, pp.

362-3. For the close relationship between journalism and literature, see also Louis Dudek, *Literature and the Press: A History of Printing, Printed Media, and their Relation to Literature* (Toronto, 1960), pp. 25, 46-8. Dudek offers as an example the *Morning Chronicle,* for which Charles Lamb, S.T. Coleridge, Sir James Mackintosh, Henry Brougham, David Ricardo, William Hazlitt, James and John Stuart Mill and Charles Dickens all worked.

21. Trollope, *Thackeray,* pp. 10-11.

22. The figures in this table are drawn from Richard D. Altick, 'The Sociology of Authorship: The Social Origins, Education and Occupations of 1,100 British Writers, 1800-1935', *Bulletin of the New York Public Library* (June 1962), pp. 389-404.

23. Ray, *Thackeray: Uses of Adversity,* pp. 194-5. See also Alan J. Lee, *The Origins of the Popular Press in England, 1855-1914* (London, 1976), Ch. 4; and A. Aspinall, 'The Social Status of English Journalists at the Beginning of the Nineteenth Century', *Review of English Studies* (July 1945), pp. 216-32.

24. Anthony Trollope, *An Autobiography* (London, 1950; first published 1883), pp. 121-2; Harriet Martineau, *Autobiography* edited by Maria Weston Chapman (2 vols., Boston, 1877), I, p. 144; and John Morley, *Recollections* (2 vols., New York, 1917), I, pp. 32-3.

25. Trollope, *Autobiography,* pp. 107-8.

26. Ibid., p. 121.

27. Gordon Ray, *Thackeray: The Age of Wisdom, 1847-1863* (New York, 1958), p. 35; Harriet Martineau, 'Literary Lionism', *The London and Westminster Review* (April 1839), pp. 261-81.

28. Johnson, *Dickens,* II, pp. 1146-7.

29. Ray, *Thackeray: Uses of Adversity,* pp. 13, 215, 418.

30. Ibid., p. 345.

31. George Gissing, *New Grub Street* (2 vols., Leipzig, 1891), I, pp. 251, 292, 298.

32. Thackeray, *Pendennis,* I, pp. 334-5.

33. Johnson, *Dickens,* II, pp. 904-5, 914-16.

34. Ibid., II, pp. 723-4; 736-9; Ray, *Thackeray: Age of Wisdom,* Ch. 5.

35. A 'Society for the Encouragement of Learning' had been established in 1736, to enable authors to escape the power of booksellers. By 1748 it had failed. See Collins, *Authorship in the Days of Johnson,* pp. 20-1. The Royal Society of Literature was founded in 1820-1 to patronize good literature, but it had only small success. See William Jerdan, *The Autobiography of William Jerdan* (4 vols., London, 1852-3), III, Chs. X-XI. And Jerdan tried in 1838 to set up a 'National Association for the Encouragement and Protection of Authors, and Men of Talent and Genius', but the effort failed. See his *Autobiography,* IV, pp. 347-50; and *Illustrations of the Plan of A National Association . . .* (London, 1838). Bulwer Lytton's views in favour of patronage can be found in *England and the English,* 3rd edn., (2 vols., London, 1834), I, pp. 135-42, 235-9; and II, pp. 112-18 and Ch. VII.

36. Ray, *Thackeray: Age of Wisdom,* p. 137; Trollope, *Thackeray,* pp. 34-8; Ford, *Dickens and His Readers,* p. 21.

37. On the development by authors of pride in independence, see Collins, *Authorship in the Days of Johnson,* pp. 196-7, 211; and *Profession of Letters,* p. 249. For the authors' trade associations, see Barnes, *Free Trade in Books;* Johnson, *Dickens,* I, p. 450; and Walter Besant, *Autobiography of Sir Walter Besant* (New York, 1902), Ch. VII.

38. Gettmann, *A Victorian Publisher,* 'Introduction', and Ch. I; Collins, *Profession of Letters,* pp. 155-69.

39. Alvar Ellegard, 'The Readership of the Periodical Press in Mid-Victorian Britain', *Gotesborgs Universitats Arsskrift* (1957), p. 4. See also, Altick, *English Common Reader,* Chs. 14 and 15; and Walter Graham, *English Literary Periodicals* (New York, 1966), Chs. VIII-XI.

40. Sources: Ellegard, 'Readership of the Periodical Press', pp. 22-40; Altick, *English Common Reader,* Appendix C.

41. Gordon Haight, *George Eliot: A Biography* (Oxford, 1968), pp. 221-2, 233-4, 296-7; Simon Nowell-Smith (ed.), *Letters to Macmillan* (London, 1957), pp. 30-2. For the publishing business in general, see F.A. Mumby and Ian Norrie, *Publishing and Bookselling*, 5th edn, (London, 1974), Part One.

42. Quoted in Nowell-Smith (ed.), *Letters to Macmillan*, p. 78.

43. This paragraph and the next rely on the excellent book by Guinevere Griest, *Mudie's Circulating Library and the Victorian Novel* (Bloomington, Ind. 1970).

44. Quoted in ibid., p. 35.

45. Quoted in Johnson, *Dickens*, I, p. 468.

46. Noel Annan, 'The Intellectual Aristocracy', in J.H. Plumb (ed.), *Studies in Social History* (London, 1955), pp. 241-87.

47. On the intelligentsia, see Richard Pipes (ed.), *The Russian Intelligentsia* (New York, 1961).

48. Ford, *Dickens and His Readers*, p. 22.

49. See John Holloway, *The Victorian Sage* (New York, 1965); and Kathleen Tillotson, *Novels of the Eighteen-Forties* (Oxford, 1965), pp. 33-6.

50. Watt, *The Rise of the Novel*, p. 59.

51. There are many discussions of this point. See, for example, Holloway, *Victorian Sage;* Tillotson, *Novels of the Eighteen-Forties;* Richard Stang, *The Theory of the Novel in England, 1850-1870* (New York, 1959); and Alba H. Warren, Jr, *English Poetic Theory, 1825-1865* (Princeton, 1950).

52. Martineau, *Autobiography*, I, p. 130.

53. J.S. Mill, *Autobiography* (Library of Liberal Arts edn. New York, 1957), pp. 44, 54-5.

54. Quoted in Ray, *Thackeray: Uses of Adversity*, p. 327.

55. Quoted in ibid., pp. 385-6.

56. Charles Dickens, *David Copperfield* (Signet Classic edn, New York, 1962), p. 810.

57. Thomas Carlyle, *On Heroes, Hero-Worship and the Heroic in History* (Everyman's Library edn, London, 1965), especially pp. 246-7, 384, 390.

58. Amy Cruse, *The Victorians and Their Books* (London, 1935), Ch. IX; Altick, *English Common Reader*, pp. 386-7, for sales of poetry; and Bulwer Lytton, *England and the English*, II, Book 4, Ch. II.

59. Quoted in Cruse, *Victorians and Their Books*, p. 187.

60. Ray, *Thackeray: Age of Wisdom*, p. 126.

61. Quoted in Cruse, *Victorians and Their Books*, p. 166.

62. Johnson, *Dickens*, II, pp. 941, 951.

63. Quoted in Haight, *Eliot*, p. 445.

64. Quoted in ibid., p. 447.

65. Gettmann, *A Victorian Publisher*, Ch. III.

66. Walter E. Houghton, 'Introduction', *The Wellesley Index to Victorian Periodicals* (Toronto, 1966), pp. xvi-xix.

67. Thackeray, *Pendennis*, I, p. 358.

68. John Morley, 'Review of J.S. Mill's *Dissertations and Discussions'*, *Fortnightly Review* (July 1867), p. 123. See also (Anonymous), 'The London Catalogue of Books Published in Great Britain', *Edinburgh Review* (April 1849), pp. 149-68; and (Anonymous), 'Review of Humboldt's *Kosmos* and Chambers' *Vestiges of the Natural History of Creation'*, *Westminster Review* (September 1845), pp. 152-3.

69. Mill, *Autobiography*, pp. 144-5; Michael St John Packe, *The Life of John Stuart Mill* (New York, 1970), pp. 251-72.

70. T.B. Macaulay, *The Works of Lord Macaulay*, edited by Margaret Trevelyan (8 vols., London, 1866), V, p. 155.

71. M.H. Abrams, 'Art as Such: Origins of the Modern Aesthetic', public lecture delivered at Northwestern University, 1979.

72. G.H. Lewes, 'The Principles of Success in Literature', *Fortnightly Review* (May 1865), p. 90.

73. Mill, *Autobiography*, pp. 11-12; 72-3.

74. Ibid., pp. 93-7.

75. Sir Henry Taylor, 'Preface to Philip Van Artevelde' (1834), republished in Walter E. Houghton and G. Robert Stange (eds.), *Victorian Poetry and Poetics* (Cambridge, Mass., 1959), p. 813.

76. Bulwer Lytton, *England and the English*, II, p. 97.

77. Taylor, 'Preface', p. 814.

78. J.S. Mill, 'Review of *Poems, Chiefly Lyrical*, by Alfred Tennyson', *Westminster Review* (January 1831), p. 213. This also was Carlyle's view: see *Heroes and Hero Worship*, 'The Hero As Poet', especially pp. 333-8.

79. W.H. Smith, 'Tennyson's Poems', *Blackwood's* (April 1849), pp. 455-6.

80. W.E. Aytoun, 'The Royal Scottish Academy', *Blackwood's* (May 1855), p. 592. See also Margaret Oliphant, 'Modern Light Literature—Art', *Blackwood's* (December 1855). Victorian poetics are clearly discussed in Warren, *English Poetic Theory, 1825-1865.*

81. Ford, *Dickens and His Readers*, p. 27. See also Tillotson, *Novels of the Eighteen-Forties*, pp. 13-16.

82. Stang, *Theory of the Novel*, Chs. II and III, discusses these two aspects. See also Watt, *The Rise of the Novel*, Chs. I, II and X.

83. Ray, *Thackeray: Uses of Adversity*, pp. 227, 266, 388, 397.

84. Haight, *Eliot*, pp. 201, 219. For George Eliot's advocacy of realism, see her article, 'The Natural History of German Life', *Westminster Review* (July 1856), pp. 51-79.

85. Stang, *Theory of the Novel*, pp. 156-8; Ford, *Dickens and His Readers*, Chs. 6 and 7, especially pp. 129-33.

86. Ford, *Dickens and His Readers*, pp. 39-42.

87. Thackeray, *Pendennis*, I, xvi.

88. Quoted in Haight, *Eliot*, p. 240.

89. Trollope, *Autobiography*, p. 145.

# 3 THE WORLDS OF SCIENCE AND THE UNIVERSITIES

The men of letters and the institutions which disseminated their work dominated the terrain of English intellectual life in the early and mid-Victorian years, partly because of the needs of the middle-class reading public and partly because the men of letters accepted the role of cultural leadership. In the work of the men of letters, the emphasis lay on articulation and diffusion of interpretations of experience to a general public, rather than on production of new knowledge. Both in functions and in means of support, the men of letters stood apart from the other prominent features on the map of intellectual life — the cultivators of science and the professors and dons of the universities. This is not to argue that scientific institutions and the ancient universities played insignificant roles in the culture of Victorian England, or even that the men of science and the university professors and dons lacked personal connections with men of letters. Rather, it means simply that the cultural functions of science and the universities differed from those of the men of letters, and that in certain vital ways neither science nor university activity was integrated with the work of the men of letters.

In a survey of English science in the 1830s and 1840s the first phenomenon to catch the eye is the 'decline of science' controversy which sputtered and flared among Victorian cultivators of science. In 1830, Charles Babbage, Lucasian Professor of Mathematics at Cambridge and inventor of an early computer, published his *Reflections on the Decline of Science in England,* which split the English scientific community for the rest of the decade. Babbage asserted that English science had in fact declined, by which he meant that England was falling behind other European nations in scientific discoveries and in the nurturing of a set of people devoted to the pursuit of science for its own sake rather than for profit. Babbage cited in support of his view, a long passage in the *Encyclopaedia Metropolitana* by John Herschel, the eminent astronomer and theoretician of the scientific method. In England, Herschel had written:

whole branches of continental discovery are unstudied, and indeed almost unknown, even by name. It is vain to conceal the melancholy truth. We are fast dropping behind. In mathematics we have long since drawn the rein, and given over a hopeless race. In chemistry the case is not much better ... There are, indeed, few sciences which would not furnish matter for similar remark.[1]

Babbage offered several explanations for this alleged decline of science. English schools and universities, he said, taught little science, devoting themselves instead to classics and mathematics. More important, science in England had not become a 'profession'. People go into professions, he contended, expecting successful careers; but in science they could not. Yet the professions — the church, medicine and law — are beneficial, in that they maintain for themselves high standards of performance, which the public cannot do for them. Likewise, the public lacks the mastery over the required knowledge for distinguishing between the truly talented and the second-rate men of science. Babbage tied the issue of professionalization to the fact that the English government gave little tangible encouragement to science. He correctly observed in this connection the overriding importance of free enterprise ideology: the English believed that the public as consumer would provide sufficient rewards and incentives through purchase of scientific commodities. But Babbage felt that this assumption overlooked a crucial difficulty, namely that 'all abstract truth is entirely excluded from reward under this system'. Primary research in science finds no immediate market; therefore, the government ought to encourage men of science by awarding government posts, honours, and university professorships to research scientists.[2]

Babbage saved most of his ammunition for a salvo against the Royal Society, which for some time he had regarded as failing to promote and direct English science. He argued that because its membership was much too large, election to the Royal Society was not a high honour; and further that the membership included far too many men who did no scientific work at all. To him the inclusion of aristocrats, whatever the intended benefits to the social status of the Royal Society, degraded the identity and integrity of the active cultivators of science. Moreover, the officers of the Society won election through a system that allowed self-selection by an irresponsible and unscientific coterie. That clique had mismanaged English science for years by its misuse of the honours, medals, funds and other resources of the Society, and by its opposition to the growth of other learned societies. Only if the Royal Society came into the hands of the active practitioners of science could English science again flourish.[3]

In retrospect, Babbage's attack was both misleading and revealing as to the state of English science in the 1830s. One way in which it was misleading is that Babbage seriously underestimated both the vitality of English science and its integration into the culture of the upper classes. Humphrey Davy and Michael Faraday had, through their research and lecturing, made the Royal Institution (founded 1799) a leading centre for science in Europe. John Dalton had done likewise at the Manchester Literary and Philosophical Society. Adam Sedgwick, William Buckland, and Charles Lyell had made England the home of the most important advances in geology; and they had made natural history a subject for intense debate by the literate public.[4] Furthermore, as a number of recent scholars have shown, science played a variety of important roles in early Victorian England. It was a popular recreation for amateur scientists in the landed orders. It provided for 'improving landlords' a number of useful methods and tools in husbandry, agricultural chemistry and farm implements.[5]

Moreover, despite what later myths may have said, science played an important part in industrialization. Many early English industrialists took an active interest in science; they did not create their industries by primitive rule of thumb.[6] In many new industrial cities, scientific institutions provided some technical services — chemical analyses, for instance — and opportunities for middle-class people to participate in the respectable, gentlemanly activities of scientific study. English public opinion attributed much of the enormous economic growth of the day to science.[7] The literate public consumed popular expositions of science, and the great quarterly reviews tried to keep abreast of new scientific works of general interest.[8] Amateur botanists, zoologists and geologists, including John Ruskin, George Eliot and G.H. Lewes, roamed the seashores and countrysides observing and collecting.

Even more important, scientific data formed an essential part of the generally accepted view of the world. Before publication of *Origin of the Species* in 1859, Victorians normally did not see science as opposed to religion or theology but as a vital element in natural theology.[9] The advocates of natural theology held that a benevolent Deity had designed the world for the benefit of His highest creation — humanity — and He had granted human beings the power to understand the universal machine. For the early Victorians, Newton stood as the heroic figure in human progress, for they saw him, as had their predecessors in the eighteenth century, as having demonstrated the perfection of the divine plan. Newton, wrote Henry Brougham, was 'certainly by far the most extraordinary man that ever lived', for he had shown that all the seeming irregularities of the universe are actually 'subject to a certain fixed rule'.[10] Natural theologians held that God had not only designed the universe but also actively supervised and sustained its operation. To study nature is to study God's work, to participate in the divine scheme and to prove the existence of the designer. Natural philosophy formed a bulwark against unbelief; it would not refute revelation. Hence natural theology for the early Victorians provided the main impetus for scientific study. It even gave a splendid rationale for applied science: because humans are His highest creatures, God gave them science as the means by which they could master creation. In natural theology, pure science and applied science stood equally blessed. According to the geologist Robert Bakewell:

> The value of every science must ultimately rest on its utility; but in making the estimate we ought not to be guided alone by motives of narrow gain. The objects of nature appear destined to answer two purposes; the one, to supply the physical wants of the various inhabitants of the globe; and the other, to excite our curiosity, and stimulate our intellectual powers to the discovery of . . . the contrivance of the Divine Artist, and the ends and uses of the various parts.[11]

Natural theology had received its definitive statement from the Reverend William Paley, whose *Natural Theology; or Evidences of the Existence and Attributes of the Deity collected from the Appearances of Nature* (1802) was required reading for all students at Oxford and Cambridge through the first half of the century.[12] In addition, natural theology was propagated widely through the *Bridgewater Treatises,* a set of eight popular books published in the 1830s, each summarizing a branch of science with the intent of supporting the argument from design. The outlook of natural theology appeared everywhere in the early Victorian period, perhaps most notably in Henry Brougham's *Discourse on the Objects, Advantages, and Pleasures of Science,* published first in 1826 by the Society for the Diffusion of Useful Knowledge as part of the 'march of intellect'. Like many of the statements in support of natural theology, this remarkable volume preached a kind of 'cosmic Toryism' — whatever is, is right — even though Brougham was a reform-minded Whig.[13] The book was meant to be useful in stabilizing the social order. Scientific knowledge, wrote Brougham, 'elevates the faculties above low pursuits, purifies and refines the passions, and helps our reason to assuage their violence'.[14] All objects in nature have properties designed by Providence, and these properties can be known only through scientific enquiry. The perfection of the Providential design is everywhere evident. For example, if one were to arrange an object so that it would have the least possible resistance to air or water, he would arrive at a shape resembling the head of a fish: the Divine Author, therefore, 'has fashioned these fishes so that, according to mathematical principles, they swim most easily through the element they live and move in'. The whole natural order, including social relations, is the best possible:

> So it may be with man in the universe, where, seeing only a part of the great system, he fancies there is evil; and yet, if he were permitted to survey the whole, what had seemed imperfect might appear to be necessary for the general perfection, insomuch that any other arrangement, even of that seemingly imperfect part, must needs have rendered the whole less perfect.[15]

Whatever the piety of such views, certain extreme conservative defenders of Christian orthodoxy worried that natural science eroded the basis of theology. This was an old concern, for even the Newtonians had been accused of contributing to atheism by allegedly eliminating belief in divine intervention in the universe. In the early-nineteenth century, some high churchmen, whose strongholds stood in the ancient universities, contended that science was another way in which modern people were extending the writ of reason into areas where it had no jurisdiction. This became the position of the Oxford movement: science must be combatted on the same grounds as liberalism. The controversy between conservative theologians and natural science focused on geology and biology, because the discoveries of men of science in these areas seemed to question the Biblical account of creation. For instance, the 'Vulcanist' explanation of geological phenomena, first set out by James Hutton in 1795, met with fierce criticism because it rejected the ideas of the recent creation of the earth and of change through great watery cataclysms, both of which were thought to be essential to the Mosaic account. In the 1820s and 1830s, 'catastrophists' combatted 'uniformitarians' with the intent of squaring geology with revelation; yet clerical critics like E.B. Pusey, Professor of Hebrew at Oxford, and William Cockburn, Dean of York, found both sides dangerous to true religion. Robert Chambers' *Vestiges of Creation* (1844) horrified the extreme churchmen and natural theologians alike, since Chambers' uniformitarian explanation of the progress of all organic life apparently removed the Deity from moral as well as physical developments on earth. But such opposition must be kept in perspective: the position of natural theology, associated with the broad church movement within Anglicanism, was the main stream.[16]

Natural theology pictured science as a divine gift, obviously one that could do no wrong yet could read the secrets of the universe. This picture of science made the scientist something of a romantic hero and accounts in part for the extraordinary renown of men like Humphrey Davy and Michael Faraday, whose lectures at the Royal Institution did a tremendous amount to popularize science. Davy, who had powerful social ambitions, certainly helped cultivate the image of scientist as romantic hero as well as spreading the philosophy of his friend Coleridge.[17] Faraday was a much less worldly and more saintly man, but he too appeared as a heroic figure. In the 1830s and 1840s Faraday, probably more than any other living Englishman, was the exemplar in the public eye of the scientist.[18] His marvellously clear lectures, beginning with some observations on an ordinary object, proceeding with carefully chosen and staged demonstrations, and ending in remarks on the wonders of science, established the British tradition for popular science.

Faraday, it is true, always kept science and religion separate; but not because of any antipathy to religion. In fact, his religion even went beyond natural theology. According to his biographer, L. Pearce Williams, Faraday's 'deepest intuitions about the physical world sprang from this religious faith in the Divine origin of nature'.[19] Those intuitions, for instance, underlay Faraday's belief in the unity of natural forces; and this belief led to his great work in relating electricity and magnetism. Faraday was a devout Sandemanian, whose Christianity taught him that the world is beautiful and knowable because God is benevolent.[20] Faraday rejected the argument from design because it seemed pretentious; the existence of God is known through faith. Yet Faraday believed that science does allow people to know God's works and to enter into the divine.[21] In keeping with this attitude, while Faraday did a back-breaking amount of technical advising for businesses and government, he gave most of his earnings to charity and deliberately turned away many opportunities to make himself wealthy through science. He frequently preached the moral superiority of pure research over science for profit. The consequent image was potent. The Duke of Somerset remarked to Babbage in 1835:

The story of Faraday is just one that is sure to make a great noise. There is something romantic and quite affecting in such a conjunction of Poverty and Passion for Science, and with this and his brilliant success he comes out as the Hero of chemistry.[22]

Science, then, was very much a part of early-Victorian high culture, though one could not know that from Babbage's *Decline of Science*. Another way his book was misleading is that it ignored the wide variety of institutions which supported scientific activities. It is true that England in the 1830s and 1840s had no unified system of institutions offering well-defined career patterns for a large number of scientists — nothing like the career structures in the centralized, bureaucratic advanced schools in France or the universities in Germany. But English science did receive support in a number of institutions, mostly voluntary, each of which was connected to particular segments of society. The Church of England, odd as it may now seem, provided some support for science, though not deliberately and not in the sense of maintaining laboratories for pure or applied research. Many a country parson cultivated botany and natural history, in a charming if haphazard way, under the umbrella of natural theology. It was not unusual for the young Darwin to think of a comfortable career as a rural clergyman as a means by which he could pursue his beloved beetles. As Prime Minister in the 1840s, Sir Robert Peel remarked that he had no way to reward achievements in science and scholarship except clerical preferment.[23] The government patronized science in a small way by means of a few posts in government agencies, by an occasional pension to an eminent scientist, by infrequent financial contributions to the publication of scientific books and by signing on young naturalists as scientific members of naval expeditions — the means by which Darwin, Huxley and others got a post-graduate education in geology and biology.[24]

The official view in the 1830s and 1840s was that the government should do nothing for science (or any other economic activity) that private enterprise could do for itself; and as Babbage knew, this policy severely limited government activities in support of science. The ancient universities might have done more, since the natural theology cherished by Oxbridge sanctioned science and since many of the colleges of the universities were wealthy foundations. But Oxford and Cambridge supported science only through a handful of professorships. The list of eminent scientists at Cambridge in the 1830s was fairly impressive: Charles Babbage, Lucasian Professor of

Mathematics; William Whewell, Professor of Mineralogy and Knightbridge Professor of Moral Philosophy; George Airy, Plumian Professor of Astronomy and Astronomer Royal; Adam Sedgwick, Woodwardian Professor of Geology; George Peacock, Lowndean Professor of Astronomy; John Henslow, Professor of Botany; and John Herschel, Fellow of St John's. The list from Oxford was much less imposing: William Buckland, Professor of Mineralogy and Geology; Charles Daubeny, Professor of Chemistry; Baden Powell, Savilian Professor of Geometry; and H.W. Acland, Lee's Reader in Anatomy (after 1846). The fact that one can name in a small space the active scientific workers at the two ancient universities shows that science was not central to their functions. There was no corps of junior scientists at either place. At both universities the honours examinations (mathematics at Cambridge and classics at Oxford) diverted students from lectures in natural science. Moreover, the non-honours courses of study called for classics, divinity and moral philosophy, but not natural science. As late as 1852, Daubeny testified to a Royal Commission that the average attendance at his lectures was only twelve.[25] Practically no scholarships or fellowships went to students of science. Nor did the colleges or the universities provide much in the way of laboratories or apparatus. At Oxford, for instance, F.W. Donkin, Savilian Professor of Astronomy, received a grant of £200 for instruments, which he set up at the top of his house. Otherwise he had no observatory for teaching or research.[26]

The disinclination of the government and Oxbridge to give much support to science contributed heavily to the sense that science was declining, but disguised the fact that a growing number of voluntary associations *did* give impressive assistance to scientific activities. Unlike the men of letters, cultivators of science flourished in the provincial towns as well as in the metropolis. In many provincial cities — Birmingham, Manchester, Leeds, Leicester, Newcastle, York and many others — 'Literary and Philosophical' societies encouraged both the cultivation and the dissemination of scientific knowledge. Although England before the 1860s had no industrial laboratories or provincial university research operations, the literary and philosphical societies provided employment, laboratories and audiences for some full-time scientists — rarely more than one per society, a 'professor' who supported himself by lecturing, private coaching and scientific consulting. By the 1830s, the Manchester Literary and Philosophical Society was the most active and important. In the late-eighteenth century it had been a kind of club for the recreation of gentlemen — all amateurs in science. During the early-nineteenth century, the Society changed to reflect the commercial and industrial leadership of the city.[27] These men wanted to acquire some of the gentlemanly status that scientific pursuits could bestow, but they also meant to use the Society to promote the advancement of industry through applied scientific research. The Literary and Philosophical Society, therefore, formed part of the provincial middle-class culture and economy. By the 1840s the city of Manchester had attracted a large number of men who sought to combine a devotion to science with industrial employment, and these 'devotées' assumed leadership of the Literary and Philosophical Society. They confirmed the close attachment of the Society to local industry and also the Society's impressive tradition in chemistry, the branch of science most useful to Manchester's textile mills.[28] The outstanding figure among these devotées before the 1850s was John Dalton, who was allowed by the Society a room for teaching and experiments, and so was able to devote all his time to scientific research and teaching. He was resolutely middle-class, provincial and a full-time scientist.[29]

In London, a variety of institutions rendered support to science. The Royal Society was the oldest and most prestigious, but it had remained very much a part of the patronage system of the eighteenth century. Indeed, the desire for aristocratic patronage had turned the Royal Society into a grand gentleman's club.[30] Its fellows often won election not according to principles cherished in industrial England — competition and merit — but by social prestige. Babbage calculated that only 106 of the 685 fellows in 1830 had contributed to the *Transactions*.[31] Until the reform of the Royal Society in 1847, it was eclipsed in terms of scientific achievement by another London organization, the Royal Institution, which operated on principles roughly midway between those of gentlemanly patronage and the bourgeois market-place. The Royal Institution had been established in 1799 by members of the landed classes who hoped to stave off political revolution by employing the poor and by disseminating information about practical inventions.[32] The RI originally was to offer lectures to the working class and to display models of the latest industrial technology. However, the idea of teaching working-men ran afoul of fears on the part of certain members of the upper class that workers with a little information might be dangerous beings. And the proposal for a repository of machinery met absolute refusal by manufacturers to share their secrets.

The Royal Institution, therefore, in the early-nineteenth century used its resources mainly in lectures to its members and others in its fashionable London audience.[33] But the RI also supported a laboratory and a professor of chemistry — Davy from 1801 to about 1820, and Faraday from 1825 to 1861. They had great success as lecturers, and the RI, which had been founded by aristocratic subscription, came increasingly to depend on the fees collected by the lecturers. Davy and Faraday in this way came the closest of any early Victorian men of science to resembling the men of letters: they sold their knowledge to a general public. They also did a large volume of technical analysis and consulting for business and the government. In fact, the load of work caused Faraday to break down physically and mentally in 1839.[34] In its technical activities, the RI looked forward to a modern pattern of the scientific laboratory supported by contract work.

Finally, also located in London were a number of specialist societies which had been founded since the early-nineteenth century — for example, the Geological Society (1807), the Astronomical Society (1820), the Zoological Society (1826), the Meteorological Society (1836), and the Chemical Society (1841).[35] An elite based on technical merit in each field dominated these societies, though there existed considerable overlap among their memberships; hence the active practitioners of science found them more satisfactory than the Royal Society. Further, they provided a supportive network for men of science. Lyell, for instance, belonged to the Geological, Linnean, Zoological and Geographical societies, as well as to the Royal Society and the Athenaeum. For him, as for other devotées, these specialist societies offered congenial and competent peer groups for exchanging ideas; libraries, specimens and apparatus for scientific research; and audiences of high social standing for scientific lectures. Perhaps most important, the London societies, like the provincial literary and philosophical societies, published journals in which the results of research appeared. Such journals did not operate commercially but were subsidised by the members of the societies. Articles for the journals were refereed by experts without regard to the saleability of the information conveyed, and in this way they sheltered scientific authors from the rigours of the market place.[36] They also gave powerful support to the tendency in science for the central questions to be set out by the practitioners of a branch of science rather than by a general public. The more general observations on the philosophical meaning of scientific works could go in the quarterly reviews; reports of research, with some exceptions in natural history, went into the specialist journals.

The proliferation of scientific organizations, and their domination by men who regarded science as their vocation, if not their source of income, pointed to a growing self-consciousness of the early Victorian scientific community. It was in showing the sense of identity among men of science that Babbage's book was revealing. Other organizational activities showed the same development. In the Royal Society, for example, the active cultivators of science staged a successful campaign to take power. During the 1820s, Babbage and other reformers had tried to reduce the membership from more than 600 to 400, to ensure that only those who had actually distinguished themselves in science would gain admission. This proposal was rejected by the Council of the Royal Society, and in reaction the dissidents put up John Herschel for president. Though Herschel lost to the Duke of Sussex, the reformers had scored an important point, and they continued to make headway. In the 1830s, the Council consistently had a majority composed of active men of science. In 1845, R.W. Grove, a distinguished physicist and judge, led the reformers to success. Under his influence, a committee proposed that elections to membership should be held only once a year, so that the candidates could be scrutinized; and that no more than fifteen candidates could be put forward. The Council approved these proposals in 1847, with the result that thereafter active men of science dominated the membership. The Royal Society lost its dilettante image and became an organization of, for and by full-time practitioners of science.[37]

Meanwhile, the problems in the Royal Society and the multiplication of devotées of science, especially in the provinces, led to the founding of the British Association for the Advancement of Science.[38] A growing number of men who regarded scientific research as their chief work in life, even if they earned a living by some other means, did not feel that the Royal Society was their kind of organization or served their purposes. Herschel, for instance, had a private income and so felt no need for financial support; none the less he complained that no audience of experts existed to consider reports of original research in England. England needed a forum of masters of the sciences who could understand and integrate into the whole body of science the latest discoveries.[39] Other cultivators of science, like Babbage and David Brewster, an eminent publisher in Edinburgh and a researcher in optics, believed that the Royal Society had failed to win tangible financial and honorary rewards for scientific investigators. Furthermore, they believed that there should be an organization to bring the men of science together, concentrate their abilities, stimulate their efforts, and, in Brewster's words, 'bring the objects of science before the public eye'.[40] In the industrial towns, particularly of the North, there simmered middle-class, provincial resentment of the tone and privileges of the Royal Society. And in the provinces men like William Vernon Harcourt, Canon of York, amateur chemist and member of the Yorkshire Philosophical Society, knew that scientific enquiry was being done by two sorts of people: one, the interested amateurs, who together could make countless useful observations without being masters of any branch of science; and two, the experts, the devotées, people who committed themselves fully to scientific work, mastered a field, and sometimes even found a way to make a living from science. These two sets needed to be co-ordinated, so that the masters could direct, systematize, and interpret the work of the enthusiastic amateurs.[41]

In the event, the BAAS, founded in 1831, satisfied some of these objectives but not others. Mainly it gave organizational expression to the emergent identity of men of science. It did not become a research centre employing a team of scientists. Nor did it come into being as a central agency to direct scientific work, though it very soon began giving small grants to applicants to support their research.[42] Men like Herschel, and others associated with Oxford and Cambridge, refused to allow science, which they felt advanced through the work of individual geniuses, to be subordinated to any central agency.[43] The BAAS took as its principal official functions the facilitation of communication among men of science, and the promotion of science in the eyes of the general public.

Psychologically, the BAAS functioned to satisfy a herding instinct that was a product of the emerging sense of identity in the scientific community. This can be seen in its provisions for membership. Membership in the BAAS was closed to those with only a casual interest in science. The first meeting decided that anyone could be a member of the BAAS providing he was a member of a 'chartered society' — a specialized scientific society — or an *officer* of a literary and philosophical society, or was recommended by the officers of such a society. The ruling body of the BAAS also reserved the right to bestow membership on anyone else.[44] This ruling body, the General Committee, itself would be restricted to those 'who appear to have been actually employed in working for science', that is, people who had published a paper with any scientific society.[45] Further, the BAAS thereafter met each year, first in specialized divisions dominated by masters of the branch of science, and then in a general meeting to hear a presidential address often directed on behalf of science to the nation at large. Lyell ably expressed its function best when he wrote to Darwin:

> But I am convinced, although it is not the way I love to spend my own time, that in this country no importance is attached to any body of men who do not make occasional demonstration of their strength in public meetings. It is a country where, as Tom Moore justly complained, a most exaggerated importance is attached to the faculty of thinking on your legs, and where, as Dan O'Connell well knows, nothing is to be got in the way of homage or influence, or even a fair share of power, without agitation.[46]

The BAAS initially received some criticism from people who considered these annual bouts of scientific papers and mutual declarations of support to be inappropriate or ridiculous. Dickens, who had no antipathy to science and in the 1840s invited Faraday to contribute popular articles on science to *Household Words,* satirized the BAAS in *Bentley's Miscellany* as the 'Mudfog Association for the Advancement of Everything'. More seriously, some high church Anglicans expressed grave concern about the fact that science would be pursued and considered in an organization that was not a monopoly of the Church of England and even open to dissenters.[47] Nevertheless, the membership of the BAAS grew remarkably from 96 after the 1831 meeting to 1,377 after the meeting of 1833.[48] These figures reflect the existence of a substantial body of people who identified themselves primarily as cultivators of science.

Another reflection of the same development appeared in a switch in terminology, from words like 'philosopher', 'natural philosopher', or 'man of science' to 'scientist'. By about 1830 in England, 'science' was separating from the older, more general term 'philosophy'. Furthermore, the expansion of the number of people who specialized in a particular branch of science and who identified themselves primarily as investigators of the natural world, made older terms like 'men of science' obsolete. In the 1830s and 1840s 'scientist' came into use to refer both to specialization and to full-time devotion to scientific work.[49] By the 1840s, then, natural science was being pursued by people who were specialized, self-conscious, and organized thoroughly in various kinds of societies for individual and collective support. These constituted some important ways in which they stood apart from the men of letters.

They also stood apart from the men of letters by their ideas of knowledge and its acquisition. These ideas formed the conceptual context underlying the institutions of scientific work. In early Victorian England, it is true, Idealist philosophies of science (best represented by William Whewell) competed with empiricist philosophies (best represented by J.S. Mill).[50] Nevertheless, the vast majority of English scientists, Idealists and empiricists alike, agreed on certain fundamental points about scientific knowledge and scientific method. First, they agreed that science is a research activity. They insisted that their primary task was to discover new knowledge, and this required rigorous procedures of observation and reasoning. Precision and clarity in method counted for everything; consequently, early Victorian scientists often paid tribute to Bacon for his insistence on disinterestedness, meaning non-partisanship and a willingness to abandon unsuccessful hypotheses or inductions.[51] Secondly, science is progressive, in the sense that it actually gets somewhere by retiring falsehoods to the dustbin and adding individual truths to the stockpile.[52] Thirdly, science goes forward through specialization. Because of the tradition of natural theology, early Victorian scientists assumed that ultimately all knowledge is one. This led some to regret the tendency towards specialization, but all the leading theorists acknowledged that specialization inevitably characterizes scientific work; and not even the Idealists thought that specialization distorts or destroys the truth.[53] Fourthly, their orientation towards the 'frontiers' of knowledge required for at least part of their work a special audience of fellow experts. Fifthly, scientists admitted that scientific research may not be marketable, and they asserted that it should not be limited by that standard. Indeed, the highest and most important kinds of scientific work are precisely those that would not be supported by the consuming public, and so would require endowment. Finally, most early Victorian scientists asserted the value of knowledge for its own sake. Here the context of natural theology was crucial. Of course, all scientists believed that scientific discoveries contribute to material progress, and they would have found it inconceivable that any practical product of this divine gift could be harmful. But the early Victorian scientists also believed that the highest level, most abstract generalizations are the most important, for which point they invariably cited Newton; and they believed that the greatest utility of science lay in its ennobling and edifying effects. Hence, they insisted that scientific knowledge is good in itself — 'eternal and imperishable', as William Whewell put it.[54] On all these points, scientists differed from men of letters about mental work. Darwin, recently returned from his voyage in HMS *Beagle,* recorded his sense of the difference in his notebook:

> Mention persecution of early astronomers. Then add chief good of individual scientific men is to push their science a few years in advance of their age (differently from literary men).[55]

Because scientific work went forward in a framework of natural theology, and therefore was seen as contributing to moral strength, and because it added to the material welfare of the nation, men of letters rarely took objection to it. Most of them failed to see that scientists represented a way of thinking that would destroy their own cultural hegemony. Carlyle was the great exception. In his magnificent essay 'Signs of the Times' (1829), Carlyle recognized that the early-nineteenth century in England was an 'Age of Machinery' in thought as well as industrial production. While the 'Metaphysical and Moral Sciences are falling into decay', he wrote, 'the Physical are engrossing, every day, more respect and attention'. The consequence was that Englishmen assumed 'what cannot be investigated and understood mechanically, cannot be investigated and understood at all'.[56] But Carlyle himself admired the wonderful capacity of science and its offspring, industry, to work productively, and so to do God's will. In this view he was joined by all the early and mid-Victorian men of letters.

They felt very differently about Oxford and Cambridge. Carlyle believed that the universities had been made obsolete by the spread of printing and books.[57] Dickens expressed his criticism of Oxbridge in praising American colleges, which, he said,

> disseminate no prejudices, rear no bigots; dig up the buried ashes of no old superstition; . . . exclude no man because of his religious opinions; above all, in their whole course of study and instruction, recognize a world, and a broad one too, lying beyond the college walls.[58]

In so attacking the ancient universities, men of letters spoke for many people in the new middle class, who believed that Oxford and Cambridge lacked proper connections with the real business of England — economic progress. Further, one aspect of the charges against the universities amounted to an assessment of their role in

English intellectual life. Here again the evaluation was negative: according to the *Edinburgh Review*, Oxford and Cambridge 'cease to lead the intellect of the country'.[59] Sir William Hamilton, the Scottish academic philosopher, wrote that:

> *there is to be found among those to whom Oxford confides the business of education, an infinitely smaller proportion of men of literary reputation, than among the actual intructors of any other university in the world.*[60]

Such an assessment sustained the acid judgement of Edward Gibbon:

> The schools of Oxford and Cambridge were founded in a dark age of false and barbarous science; and they are still tainted with the vices of their origin. Their primitive discipline was adapted to the education of priests and monks; and the government still remains in the hands of the clergy, an order whose manners are remote from the present world, and whose eyes are dazzled by the light of philosophy.[61]

By these views, Oxford and Cambridge clearly stood at the periphery of the intellectual tasks of the English people. But they must not be taken at face value, for such judgements measure the universities by performance in the secular worlds of writing and scientific investigation, circles of activities of which they did not intend to be part. The old universities in their unreformed state did not mean to produce secular men of letters or knowledge for the urban industrial world. Therefore, it is not surprising that, as Professor Altick has found, Oxbridge did not function either as essential recruiting or training institutions for men of letters, or as means of their support.[62] The old English universities in the 1830s and 1840s remained part of the church, and consequently had religious functions: the training of the clergy of the Church of England and the education of the nation's social elite in Christian discipline and morality. They were relics of a medieval social order, in which the church had been almost the sole agent of civilization, and which had reached the population at large through parish priests, their sermons and paternal advice, and through the influence of the landed gentry and aristocracy. As John Lonsdale has remarked, the church was the liturgical expression of the wholeness of society; and the universities worked within that context.[63] As we shall see, certain institutional developments may have kept them from fulfilment of this role; but in the early-Victorian period, it probably still was true that more people got their world view from the church than from any other source.[64] The universities were peripheral to the world of the men of letters and the men of science, but not to English culture in general.[65]

Coleridge made the most profound and comprehensive statement of the role of the universities in that medieval social outlook in his *On the Constitution of Church and State* (1830). This remarkable book was Coleridge's most popular and influential work.[66] In his later years, Coleridge turned towards orthodoxy in religion and conservatism in politics; thus in the *Constitution of Church and State* he adopted an *estate* theory of society. A state, he wrote, has three estates: the landed, which provides 'permanence'; the 'Personal Interest', which provides progress; and the 'national Church', which promotes 'the harmonious development of those qualities and faculties that characterize our humanity'.[67] Part of the fixed wealth of the nation properly goes to the landed proprietors; but part ('the Nationality') must be reserved to the national Church, which would support the universities as elements in an integrated cultural system:

The Nationality, therefore, was reserved for the support and maintenance of a permanent class or order with the following duties. A certain smaller number were to remain at the fountainheads of the humanities, in cultivating and enlarging the knowledge already possessed, and in watching over the interests of physical and moral science; being, likewise, the instructors of such as constituted, or were to constitute, the remaining more numerous classes of the order. The members of this latter and far more numerous body were to be distributed throughout the country, so as not to leave even the smallest integral part or division without a resident guide, guardian, and instructor; the objects and final intention of the whole order being these — to preserve the stores and to guard the treasures of past civilization, and thus to bind the present with the past; to perfect and add to the same, and thus to connect the present with the future; but especially to diffuse through the whole community and to every native entitled to its laws and rights that quantity and quality of knowledge which was indispensable both for the understanding of those rights, and for the performance of the duties correspondent: finally, to secure for the nation, if not a superiority over the neighbouring states, yet an equality at least, in that character of general civilization, which

equally with, or rather more than, fleets, armies, and revenue, forms
the ground of its defensive and offensive power. The object of the
two former estates of the realm, which conjointly form the State;
was to reconcile the interests of permanence with that of
progression — law with liberty. The object of the national Church,
the third remaining estate of the realm, was to secure and improve
that civilization, without which the nation could be neither
permanent nor progressive.[68]

The members of this third estate Coleridge named 'the clerisy'. He
recognized that in England the national Church, the civilizing agency,
was 'by a blessed accident' historically imbedded in the Church of
England; but he insisted that the two are not identical. He knew that the
commercial and professional classes had detached themselves from the
clergy of the church. But he asserted that they did not thereby cease to
be parts of the clerisy, which still, as in its

original intention, comprehended the learned of all denominations,
the sages and professors of the law and jurisprudence, of medicine
and physiology, of music, of military and civil architecture, of the
physical sciences, with the mathematical as the common organ of
the preceding; in short, all the so-called liberal arts and sciences, the
possession and application of which constitute the civilization of a
country, as well as the theological.[69]

Similar social views underlay the central elements in the
conservative idea of the universities. Defenders of Oxford and
Cambridge said that the universities were elements of the Church and
existed for the moral and religious welfare of the nation. Given this
purpose, the universities should function primarily as educational
institutions rather than as factories for new knowledge. The teachers
properly should be clergymen of the Church of England, because, as
Edward Pusey put it, clergymen were more likely 'to *train* the young
more religiously than the average of other men'; they would teach any
subject 'religiously' rather than 'irreligiously'.[70] Further, the tutorial
(or 'catechetical', as it was revealingly called) method of Oxbridge was
the best teaching style since it actively engaged the minds of the
students. The professorial (or lecture) method valued in Germany and
Scotland served only to convey information to passive minds. Like
other academic conservatives, Pusey believed that the professorial
system, which he had observed first hand in Germany — to him the

home of irreligious scholarship — would lead to rationalism and the destruction of belief in authoritative texts:

> We have abundance of theories about the professorial system. We have no facts of its having produced any but evil fruits. The training of our youth, the intellectual, moral, religious formation of their minds, their future well-being in this world and the world to come, are not matters upon which to try experiments.[71]

It followed that the domination of Oxbridge by the colleges comprised the best constitution for the universities: the colleges and their tutors served best the purposes of moral training.

The idea of a liberal education formed an integral part of the orthodox concept of a university. In the eighteenth century, liberal education had been supposed to produce the *beau ideal* of a gentleman: a person with the attributes of independence, civility, sociability and paternal generosity.[72] In the early-nineteenth century the onset of Evangelicalism and fear of the French revolution added strong measures of moral discipline to the ideal, without displacing the virtues of breadth inherited from the Augustan age. Thus a liberal education — essentially classics at Oxford and mathematics at Cambridge — was defended on grounds of breadth, even though in fact it constituted very narrow curricula. The defenders of Oxbridge reasoned that classics or mathematics did not prepare a student for any trade or profession but gave a mental and moral discipline which served as a foundation for any vocation, indeed for life as a whole. Further, the rationale for a liberal education stressed its inutility. Liberal education was explicitly posed against the 'servile' world of trade and industry. To Edward Copleston, Provost of Oriel College, any education that would train a young man for a particular career would be selfish and degrading. The classics, on the other hand, while not preparing a person for 'any of the employments of life . . . enriches and ennobles all'. For people such as Copleston, mental and moral elevation were more important in life than material progress:

> Never let us believe [Copleston wrote], that the improvement of chemical arts, however much it may tend to the augmentation of national riches, can supersede the use of that intellectual laboratory, where the sages of Greece explored the hidden elements of which man consists, and faithfully recorded all their discoveries.[73]

At Cambridge, William Whewell, Master of Trinity as well as an eminent scientist, gave a similar defence of mathematics. Whewell knew as much about as many subjects as anyone alive; in fact it was said of him that 'science is his forte; omniscience his foible'. Yet he stoutly defended mathematics as the basis for the Cambridge curriculum. He considered all subjects of study to be divided into 'permanent' and 'progressive' types. The progressive types were worthless unless a person had first mastered the permanent types — that is, those subjects like classics and mathematics that have become fixed and accepted bodies of knowledge. Classics, he said, taught the language skills necessary for reasoning; while mathematics taught 'habits of strict reasoning, of continuous and severe attention, and of constant reference to fundamental principles'. For Whewell and other defenders of Cambridge, mathematics was an 'indispensable preparation' alike for all areas of further education and for dealing with all the problems of life.[74]

During the first half of the century, the confinement of the Oxbridge curricula to classics and mathematics came under severe pressure; but even the consequent broadened theories of liberal education sought to retain the old connection with a gentlemanly style of life. Thus they continued to emphasize the importance of study for no 'useful' purpose. John Henry Newman gave the best expression to such an ideal. In his lectures *On the Scope and Nature of University Education* (1852), Newman declared that a university 'is a place of *teaching universal knowledge*'.[75] A university exists for 'the diffusion and extension of knowledge rather than the advancement', for which other kinds of institutions were better suited. All branches of knowledge should be taught, but the students should be helped to see the whole, the relations of the various branches; and that wholeness constitutes 'liberal' education. Liberal education, he said, should not be taught for moral purposes, but for intellectual. It produces a 'habit of mind' which is equitable, calm, moderate and wise. Further, such an education has no external purpose, for it is 'its own end'. As such, it satisfies a primary need of our nature. Knowledge acquired for itself Newman called 'gentleman's knowledge' as well as liberal knowledge. Teaching of gentleman's knowledge, the philosophical habit, comprises the scope for the university's function.[76]

So much for the ideas of the university. What did Oxford and Cambridge *actually* do? Both were very small, very expensive, and open in practice only to members of the Church of England. (At Oxford, students had to subscribe to the Thirty-Nine Articles at matriculation; at Cambridge, they subscribed just before taking the BA.) The universities had fallen into low esteem during the eighteenth century, because they were suspected of being strongholds of Jacobitism. Numbers of students declined, especially from the lower social orders, so the universities became more socially exclusive than ever before. With the return of the universities to political orthodoxy at the end of the eighteenth century, the number of students began to increase, but the social exclusiveness remained.

**Table 3.1: Number of Oxford and Cambridge Students, 1800-50[77]**

| Date | Oxford | | Cambridge | |
| | Average no. freshmen | Total student body | Average no. freshmen | Total student body |
|---|---|---|---|---|
| 1800-9 | 236 | 700-800 | 180 | 350-700 |
| 1810-19 | 328 | 900-1100 | 291 | 800-950 |
| 1820-9 | 410 | 1200-1500 | 440 | 1300-1600 |
| 1830-9 | 384 | 1100-1400 | 427 | 1300-1600 |
| 1840-9 | 410 | 1200-1500 | 453 | 1350-1650 |
| 1850-9 | 389 | 1100-1500 | 436 | 1300-1600 |

Though the student bodies of the two universities grew during the first two decades of the century, they still represented a smaller proportion of the university-age population than ever before: .24 per cent in 1835, as contrasted to 1.18 per cent in the 1580s, .96 per cent in the 1660s, and .31 per cent in 1750.[78]

As Bulwer Lytton noted in 1830, many parents sent their sons to public schools and universities not for education itself but for social advancement and connections. They hoped their sons would mix with aristocrats, who attended as Fellow Commoners or Gentlemen Commoners.[79] But the intent of both parents and students became more serious about the education itself during the early-nineteenth century, as shown by the fact that larger numbers of young men stayed for their degrees. At Oxford, for instance, the proportion of a freshman class who obtained the BA degree rose from about 50 per cent in 1800 to more than 70 per cent in the 1850s.[80] Most students came from families associated with the landed orders — the gentry, the clergy and the military. Together, such families provided for about 80 per cent of all students between 1752 and 1886.[81] Furthermore, most of the students after graduation returned to vocations in the same social strata, with the largest proportion by far going into the clergy — almost 60 per cent during the first half of the nineteenth century.[82] The law, next to the clergy, was the most popular career for Oxbridge graduates, with about 10 per cent choosing legal careers, even though only about 2.5 per cent had come from the families of lawyers. Oxford and Cambridge, therefore, did not function as agencies of social mobility enabling men to move from one class to another; instead, they served as the means for families to consolidate and maintain their status in the landed orders.[83] They were particularly important for younger sons, channelling young men from all elements of landed society into the clergy.

Also associated with Oxford and Cambridge were the fellows and professors — about 540 fellows and 25 professors at Oxford and 356 fellows and 24 professors at Cambridge.[84] They came exclusively from the ranks of the graduates of the two universities; indeed, most fellows came from their own undergraduate colleges. Not all the fellows, or even professors, resided in the universities, as very few fellowships carried any requirements beyond that of taking holy orders after a period of time, normally seven years. By 1830 most professors had given up teaching. Only a small number of fellows — perhaps 20 per cent — taught, a number which had been adequate for the rare serious students in the eighteenth century. The other fellows, having received their fellowships as prizes for undergraduate performance, felt entitled to collect their emoluments while occupying themselves as they pleased — preparing for the bar, studying for ordination, or waiting for a parish living in the gift of the college to open up. For the latter group, longevity was the essential qualification. Practically none of the fellows felt any obligations towards the world of secular high culture. Mark Pattison got to the heart of the matter when he recalled the Oxford of the 1830s:

Oxford was, at the time I write of, *de facto,* though not *de jure*, a close clerical corporation, and . . . therefore talent was much scarcer here than it now is [the 1880s], since the secularisation of the University. A very little literature, and a modicum of classical reading, went a long way. Sermons were almost the only public appearance to which the teachers of all the arts and sciences ever committed themselves. Any one then who ventured upon the broad ocean of general literature, and could speak to the intelligence of England so as to be attended to, was a more conspicuous person in the place than he would now be.[85]

This separation from the world of secular thought may be seen as one of the consequences of clerical assumptions about the functions of a university. Another was the fact that there existed no career structures in either teaching or learning at Oxbridge. Career patterns for the fellows at both places led *out* of the university rather than *up* within them. The fellowships of the colleges, from whose holders the tutors were chosen, were regarded as temporary subsidies to be held by young men while they waited for Church livings or prepared for the bar. Moreover, few of the fellowships were open to genuine competition, since most of the vacancies were restricted by their endowments to candidates from particular localities, preparatory schools, or kinship of the founders. Of the 542 fellowships at Oxford, only 22 were open to all candidates.[86] It might be thought that the professorships would have functioned as the top rung on a career ladder for the tutors; but they did not. For one thing, there were not enough professorships to serve that way and for another, many of the chairs carried such small endowments that they were not nearly as attractive as a good parish living or higher Church office. As John Conington told the Oxford University Commission in the early 1850s, 'Education is not likely, at least for some time to come, to become so definite and substantive a profession that men will be unwilling to combine it with orders, especially if College livings continue to exist.'[87] Finally, the professorships could not be career attractions for aspiring professionals because they stood in very low repute; the business of Oxbridge was education of undergraduates, and the professors had little to do with teaching them.

This final point stemmed from the fact that, at both the ancient universities, the examinations dominated the lives of students and teachers alike. Exams had not always been so central to the activities of the universities, but with the establishment of honours examinations by which students might distinguish themselves, they increasingly defined the lives of all university people. The first honours examination (the mathematical tripos) was established at Cambridge in 1747; the classical honours school at Oxford in 1801, the latter in an effort to discipline the unruly student body.[88] In the early-nineteenth century, the spread among students of evangelical and middle-class values of seriousness, earnestness, work and competition, turned ever larger numbers of students towards the race for honours. By the 1830s, about one-half of all Oxbridge students were opting for honours courses.[89] Their lives were devoted to cramming for examinations, since one's place on the honours list constituted a principal avenue to fellowships, clerical careers and even political appointments. By the same token, the college tutors inevitably became examination crammers, and they had to restrict their teaching to a small set of standard, frequently-examined texts. At both universities, and especially at Cambridge, much of the cramming was done by private coaches, who formed an impressive cottage industry and became an integral part of the educational system. These men, many of whom were preparing for fellowship examinations themselves, or who had been forced to forfeit fellowships because of marriage, developed much demanded skills in cramming and so tended to eclipse the college tutors; yet they could not look ahead to careers as coaches, for the years brought no prestige, only dreadful repetition of the same lessons.

These conditions discouraged high quality teaching by the tutors and professors. The professors found themselves squeezed out of teaching by the examination system. The tutors controlled the examinations and through the catechetical method were able to contribute at least something to a student's preparation. But the professors gave only lectures, which students invariably found useless in cramming. Consequently, many professors simply stopped lecturing. According to the *Edinburgh Review,* in 1831 only nine of 23 professors at Oxford were giving any lectures at all.[90] As for the tutors, they found that since each college taught all the required subjects to all the college's students, they could not master any particular subject. Many tutors, not being devoted to teaching as a career in the first place, resorted to elementary handbooks of translations and commentaries to keep up. Dedicated teachers felt themselves pulled in so many directions that they could barely stay ahead of the students. Mark Pattison, for example, found that if he read up on, say, Herodotus, he had to leave Sophocles, Livy, *et al.* badly done.[91] Under such conditions, tutorships could not provide careers for men who may have wanted to do original work in classics and theology, not to mention other subjects of secular scholarship or science. This institutional context provided for a static idea of knowledge: everything worth knowing and teaching had been established long before, either by the ancients or the great mathematicians. This was an idea of knowledge quite different from that of either the men of letters or the scientists.

These attributes of the ancient universities were of great importance for the Victorians because of the overwhelming social prestige of Oxbridge; and because down through the 1850s, Oxford and Cambridge were almost the only universities in England. The

University of Durham was established in 1833 (chartered in 1837), by the Bishop, Dean and Chapter of Durham, out of cathedral property; but it remained an ecclesiastical backwater through the mid-century. The only other English university — the University of London — was more successful than Durham but did not approach Oxbridge in importance. The exclusiveness and expense of the two old universities had led a number of non-conformists, Whigs, and Benthamites to establish in 1828 the 'London University' (later University College) on the model of Scottish and German universities — professorial and non-resident. In response to this perceived threat, churchmen founded King's College, London; and a charter of 1836 joined the two colleges in the University of London. This new university offered a much broader curriculum than Oxbridge, and even declared the intent of preparing young men for particular careers. It attracted a small number of distinguished professors, including some in the natural sciences. But London did not for many years compete with Oxbridge in terms of prestige; and in 1858 it was converted into a purely examining body. Its great development would come only in the twentieth century.

Oxford and Cambridge, then, were by a wide margin the most important English universities. The sad state of learning there, the restriction of teaching to classics and mathematics, and the detachment of the dons from what the middle class thought of as useful and productive work, all contributed to a remarkably low opinion among men of letters about scholars and scholarship. The Victorians, of course, had no objections to deep learning *per se,* but they almost always thought of it in connection with classical languages and literature, and therefore in terms of the narrow isolation that such studies at the time actually entailed. Thus early and mid-Victorian writers often regarded scholars as amusingly eccentric or worse.[92] De Quincey had found that his scholarly education earned him the rank of gentleman, and scholarship throughout the century continued to carry the high social status associated with gentility. But with the onset of Victorian values like hard work and productivity, many Victorians considered the 'useless' accomplishments of scholarship wanting. For instance, Frederic Harrison wrote in his *Memoirs* that scholars 'suppress spontaneous expression' and were often 'ignorant and mindless men'.[93] The novels of university life published in the early and mid-Victorian periods — Thackeray's *Pendennis,* 'Cuthbert Bede's' *Verdant Green* and Thomas Hughes's *Tom Brown at Oxford* are the best examples — all heaped scorn on the dons for their isolation and pedantry.[94] Carlyle expressed such views most forcefully: he said that universities had been made obsolete by books and authors; and Dr Johnson had been a scholar *but* lived and spoke the truth.[95]

The two most famous examples of scholars in Victorian fiction — Trollope's Josiah Crawley and George Eliot's Edward Casaubon — show very clearly the unfavourable image of scholars in the minds of men of letters. Crawley, the splendidly complex protagonist of *The Last Chronicle of Barset,* is in some ways a sympathetic character: his love of classical learning is genuine and contrasts sharply with Archdeacon Grantley's purely superficial attachment to books. Crawley likes to occupy himself with composing Greek iambics and solving problems in trigonometry. But Trollope, who considered Crawley to be one of his best creations, shows firmly that Crawley's scholarly orientation towards life interferes with his ability to get along in the world and causes trouble for his innocent and long-suffering family.[96] In *Middlemarch,* which was published in 1873 but set in the 1830s, George Eliot uses Casaubon's scholarship as a symbol of stunted emotional growth. His scholarship is wholly traditional and out of touch with the achievements of German university scholars. It is for Casaubon self-indulgent, aimless and sterile. The refuge of a second-rate mind, Casaubon's scholarship acts not as a path to genuine understanding, but as a barrier to real intellectual pleasure and sympathetic contact with other people. For George Eliot, failure to break out of one's own egocentric universe is the gravest of sins.

This survey of the worlds of the men of letters, the scientists and the universities reveals a complex relationship among them. In some ways, the actors in each of these worlds shared basic attitudes as well as personal connections; in other ways, they moved in different intellectual and social galaxies. All three groups had tendencies towards 'generalism' in their intellectual work: the men of letters had not only to write in many different fields but also to give general interpretations of experience to the broad literate public; the scientists interpreted scientific data in terms of natural theology and set the highest value to the most general conclusions; the university dons viewed their teaching in classics and mathematics as a most general preparation for life. One can argue that the generalist education of the public schools and universities in the first half of the century was well suited for the men of letters. A liberal education prepared them to be generalists, and it gave them and their wide public the same basic body of knowledge — the classics and the scriptures. Further, the world of the upper and middle classes, from which all three groups came, was relatively small; consequently, many of these people had personal inter-connections. None of the groups felt itself to be alienated, since all believed they were doing important work and all had access to political, social or economic power. Yet despite these factors of cohesion within and among them, the three sets of people neither saw themselves nor were seen by the general public as combined in a class. There were two main reasons for this curious fact: first, the links each had with its own 'public' were more important than the links it had with the other groups; and secondly, the ideas that each group, and the larger society, had of its own functions, including the acquisition and uses of knowledge, differed from those of the others. High culture among the early and mid-Victorians was remarkably cohesive; but the producers of high culture were oddly disconnected.

## Notes

1. Quoted in Charles Babbage, *Reflections on the Decline of Science in England* (London, 1830), pp. viii-ix. The original remarks appeared in Herschel's article on 'Sound', in the *Encyclopaedia Metropolitana*, 2nd edn, (London, 1849).

2. Babbage, *Reflections on the Decline of Science*, Chs. I and II.

3. Ibid, Ch. IV.

4. For the public debate in natural history, see C.C. Gillispie, *Genesis and Geology* (New York, 1959). I have also benefited from reading a copy of an unpublished paper by Robert M. Young, 'Natural Theology, Victorian Periodicals, and the Fragmentation of the Common Context', presented to the King's College Research Seminar on Science in 1969. See also Robert M. Young, 'The Historiographic and Ideological Contexts of the Nineteenth-Century Debate on Man's Place in Nature', in Mikulas Teich and Robert Young (eds.), *Changing Perspectives in the History of Science* (London, 1973), pp. 345-438.

5. Morris Berman, *Social Change and Scientific Organization: The Royal Institution, 1799-1844* (Ithaca, 1978), Chs. 1 and 2; Susan Faye Cannon, *Science in Culture: The Early Victorian Period* (New York, 1978); George A. Foote, 'Science and Its Function in Early Nineteenth Century England', *Osiris*, vol. XI (1954), pp. 438-54.

6. A.E. Musson and Eric Robinson, *Science and Technology in the Industrial Revolution* (Manchester, 1969).

7. Cannon, *Science in Culture*, pp. 17-20; Foote, 'Science and Its Function', pp. 441-2; Arnold Thackray, *John Dalton: Critical Assessments of His Life and Science* (Cambridge, 1972), p. 8.

8. For a few examples of the kind of scientific articles that appeared in the leading reviews, see John Herschel, *Essays from the Edinburgh and Quarterly Reviews, with Addresses and Other Pieces* (London, 1857); [David Brewster], 'Memoir and Correspondence of the Late Sir James Edward Smith', *Edinburgh Review* (April 1833), pp. 39-69; [John Crosse], 'Review of A. von Humboldt's *Kosmos* and the 4th edn of Chambers' *Vestiges of the Natural History of Creation*', *Westminster Review* (September 1845), pp. 152-203.

9. Gillispie, *Genesis and Geology, passim*; Cannon, *Science in Culture*, Chs. 1 and 2; Young, 'Historiographic and Ideological Contexts', *passim*.

10. Henry Brougham, *A Discourse on the Objects, Advantages, and Pleasures of Science* (New York, 1855), p. 69.

11. Quoted in Gillispie, *Genesis and Geology*, p. 89; from Bakewell's *Introduction to Geology*, 2nd edn (London, 1815).

12. For a recent analysis of Paley, See Daniel LeMahieu, *The Mind of William Paley* (Lincoln, Nebraska, 1976).

13. 'Cosmic Toryism' is Basil Willey's term. See his *Eighteenth Century Background* (London, 1940), Ch. III.

14. Brougham, *Pleasures of Science*, p. 38.

15. Ibid., pp. 86-7.

16. Gillispie, *Genesis and Geology*, Chs. II-VI; Cannon, *Science in Culture*, Chs. 1 and 2.

17. David M. Knight, 'The Scientist as Sage', *Studies in the History of Romanticism* (Winter 1967), pp. 65-88. For Davy's views as to the primary functions of science, see his *Consolations in Travel* (London, 1830). See also George A. Foote, 'Sir Humphrey Davy and His Audience at the Royal Institution', *Isis* (April 1952), pp. 6-12.

18. Cannon nominates others for the exemplar of science: Alexander von Humboldt and John Herschel (*Science and Culture*, Chs. 2 and 3). But they seem more influential among other scientific investigators than in the general public. For Faraday, see Berman, *Social Change and Scientific Organization*, Ch. 5.

19. L. Pearce Williams, *Michael Faraday* (London, 1965), p. 4.

20. Ibid., pp. 2-6, 64.

21. Ibid., p. 104.

22. Quoted in Berman, *Social Change and Scientific Organization*, p. 174.

23. Cannon, *Science in Culture*, p. 249.

24. For discussions of government support of science, see D.S.L. Cardwell, *The Organisation of Science in England* (London, 1957), Chs. III and IV; and G.W. Roderick, *The Emergence of a Scientific Society* (London, 1967), Chs. 1 and 2. The main government posts in the 1830s and 1840s were in the Greenwich Royal Observatory; the Museum of Economic Geology (founded 1839); and the Royal College of Chemistry (founded 1845). The government subsidized, for example, books by Darwin, Huxley, Andrew Smith and Herschel. See J.W. Robertson Scott, *The Story of the Pall Mall Gazette* (London, 1950), p. 35.

25. *Royal Commission on Oxford University* (1852, c. 1482, vol. XXII), p. 268.

26. Ibid., p. 261.

27. Robert Kargon, *Science in Victorian Manchester: Enterprise and Expertise* (Baltimore, 1977), 'Preface' and Chs. 1 and 2; J.B. Morrell, 'Individualism and the Structure of British Science in 1830', *Historical Studies in the Physical Sciences*, vol. 3 (1971), pp. 183-204; Steven Shapin and Arnold Thackray, 'Prosopography as a Research Tool in the History of Science: The British Scientific Community, 1700-1900', *History of Science*, Vol. II (1974), pp. 5-9.

28. Kargon, *Science in Victorian Manchester*, Ch. 2.

29. Thackray, *Dalton, passim*; Kargon, *Science in Victorian Manchester*, pp. 11-13.

30. My remarks on the Royal Society rely heavily on Dorothy Stimson, *Scientists and Amateurs: A History of the Royal Society* (London, 1949).

31. Babbage, *Decline of Science in England*, Appendix 3.

32. U.J. Sparrow, *Knight of the White Eagle: A Biography of Sir Benjamin Thompson, Count Rumford (1753-1814)*, (London, 1964), pp. 107-20; Berman, *Social Change and Scientific Organization*, Chs. 1 and 2.

33. Sparrow, *Count Rumford*, pp. 123, 125, 131; Foote, 'Davy and His Audience at the Royal Institution', pp. 6-12.

34. Williams, *Faraday*, pp. 106-9; Berman, *Social Change and Scientific Organization*, pp. 49-72, 130, 162-7.

35. See J.B. Morrell, 'London Institutions and Lyell's Career: 1820-41', *The British Journal for the History of Science* (July 1976), pp. 132-46; and M.J.S. Rudwick, 'The Foundation of the Geological Society of London: Its Scheme for Cooperative Research and Its Struggle for Independence', *The British Journal for the History of Science* (December 1963), pp. 325-55.

36. Morrell, 'London Institutions and Lyell's Career', p. 136.

37. Stimson, *Scientists and Amateurs*, pp. 191-219. On the self-consciousness of men of science, see Everett Mendelsohn, 'The Emergence of Science as a Profession in Nineteenth Century Europe', in Karl Hill (ed.), *The Management of Scientists* (Boston, 1964), pp. 23-31.

38. For the founding of the BAAS, see: O.J.R. Howarth, *The British Association for the Advancement of Science: A Retrospect, 1831-1921* (London, 1922), Chs. I-VII; L. Pearce Williams, 'The Royal Society and the Founding of the British Association for the Advancement of Science', *Notes and Records of the Royal Society* (November 1961), pp. 221-33; A.D. Orange, 'The Origins of the British Association for the Advancement of Science', *The British Journal for the History of Science* (December 1972), pp. 152-76; George A. Foote, 'The Place of Science in the British Reform Movement, 1830-1850', *Isis* (October 1961), pp. 192-208; and Cannon, *Science in Culture*, Chs. 6 and 7.

39. John Herschel, 'Sound', *Encyclopaedia Metropolitana*, 2nd edn (London, 1849).

40. David Brewster to John Phillips, February 23, 1831, quoted in Howarth, *British Association*, pp. 13-14. See also [David Brewster], 'Decline of Science in England and Patent Laws', *Quarterly Review* (October 1830), pp. 305-42.

41. The provincial origins of the BAAS are stressed in Cannon, *Science in Culture*, Ch. 7. Vernon Harcourt's views are fully stated in his opening remarks at the founding meeting in York in 1831. His address is reprinted in George Basalla, William Coleman and Robert Kargon (eds.), *Victorian Science: A Self-Portrait from the Presidential Addresses of the British Association for the Advancement of Science* (Garden City, NY, 1970), pp. 29-44.

42. A complete list of grants paid by the BAAS from 1834 to 1921 is provided in Howarth, *British Association*, Appendix I.

43. Cannon, *Science in Culture* pp. 194-95.

44. Ibid., p. 208. For Harcourt's proposals regarding membership, see his 'Address', in Basalla *et al.*, *Victorian Science*, pp. 39-40.

45. Harcourt, 'Address', in Basalla *et al.*, *Victorian Science*, p. 40.

46. Quoted in Howarth, *British Association*, p. 38.

47. A.D. Orange, 'The Idols of the Theatre: The British Association and Its Early Critics', *Annals of Science*, vol. 32 (1975), pp. 277-94.

48. Cannon, *Science in Culture*, p. 216. The number who attended the annual meetings reached 3,138 at Manchester in 1861.

49. Sydney Ross, '*Scientist:* The Story of a Word', *Annals of Science* (June 1962), pp. 65-85.

50. J.S. Mill, *A System of Logic, Ratiocinative and Inductive; Being a Connected View of the Principles of Evidence and the Methods of Scientific Investigation* (Collected edn, Toronto, 1973), vols. VII-VIII; and R.E. Butts (ed.), *William Whewell's Theory of Scientific Method* (Pittsburgh, 1968), contain the major statements of the dispute. A good discussion of the conflict is E.W. Strong, 'William Whewell and John Stuart Mill: Their Controversy about Scientific Knowledge', *Journal of the History of Ideas* (April 1955), pp. 209-31. See also Alvar Ellegård, *Darwin and the General Reader* (Göteborg, 1958), Ch. 9; G.N. Cantor, 'Henry Brougham and the Scottish Methodological Tradition', *Studies in the History and Philosophy of Science* (May 1971), pp. 69-89; Richard Olson, *Scottish Philosophy and British Physics, 1750-1880. A Study in the Foundations of the Victorian Scientific Style* (Princeton, 1975); and L. Pearce Williams, 'The Physical Sciences in the First Half of the Nineteenth Century', *History of Science* (1962), pp. 1-15.

51. William Whewell, *Novum Organon Renovatum* (3rd edn, 1858) in Butts (ed.), *Whewell's Theory of Scientific Method*, especially pp. 148, 155-64, 171, 269-70; John Herschel, *A Preliminary Discourse on the Study of Natural Philosophy* (London, 1832), pp. 10-11, 14, 76, 79-80; and Ch. IV; Brougham, *Pleasures of Science*, pp. 56-7.

52. Progress is central to Bacon's goals for science in *The Novum Organon:* see Book I, Aphorisms I-IX, XVIII-XIX, LXXXI-LXXXIV. See Herschel, *Preliminary Discourse*, p. 43, 73; and Mill, *Logic*, especially vol. VII, p. 283 and vol. VIII, pp. 833-5.

53. Herschel, *Preliminary Discourse,* Part III; Whewell, *Novum Organon Renovatum,* pp. 166-7; Prince Albert, Presidential Address to the BAAS in 1859, in Basalla *et al., Victorian Science,* p. 51.

54. For this and the preceding point, see: Babbage, *Decline of Science in England,* pp. 14-23; Herschel, *Preliminary Discourse,* pp. 10-11; Herschel, 'Review of Mrs. Somerville's *Mechanism of the Heavens',* in *Essays from the Edinburgh and Quarterly Reviews,* p. 46; Brougham, *Pleasures of Science,* pp. 35-6, 38, 119-24.

55. Quoted in Gertrude Himmelfarb, *Darwin and the Darwinian Revolution* (Garden City, NY, 1962), p. 153.

56. Carlyle, 'Signs of the Times', reprinted in Herbert Sussman (ed.), *Thomas Carlyle: Sartor Resartus and Selected Prose* (New York, 1970), pp. 1-30, especially pp. 6-13. 'Signs of the Times' first appeared in the *Edinburgh Review* (June 1829).

57. Carlyle, *Heroes and Hero Worship,* pp. 389-90.

58. Quoted in Johnson, *Dickens,* I, p. 373.

59. [William Empson and F.W. Newman], 'Oxford University Statutes', translated by G.R.M. Ward; D.C. Heron, *The Constitutional History of the University of Dublin,' Edinburgh Review* (July 1848), p. 86.

60. Sir William Hamilton, 'On the State of the English Universities, with More Especial Reference to Oxford' in *Discussions on Philosophy and Literature* (New York, 1855), pp. 397-8. This essay first appeared in the *Edinburgh Review* (June 1831).

61. Edward Gibbon, *The Autobiography of Edward Gibbon* (London, 1911), pp. 40-1.

62. Altick, 'Sociology of Authorship', pp. 398, 401. Of the 587 authors from 1800 to 1870 on whom he could find biographical information, Altick found that only 140 had Oxbridge degrees and only 21 were teachers or professors.

63. John Lonsdale, public address at Northwestern University, 1977.

64. For the continuing importance of sermons and other types of religious publications, especially Keble's *Christian Year,* see Cruse, *Victorians and Their Books,* Chs. I, II, IV and VI.

65. See G. Kitson Clark, *The English Inheritance* (London, 1950); and *The Making of Victorian England,* Ch. VI.

66. Basil Willey, *Samuel Taylor Coleridge* (New York, 1973), p. 236. See also David P. Calleo, *Coleridge and the Idea of the Modern State* (New Haven, 1966).

67. S.T. Coleridge, 'On the Constitution of Church and State According to the Idea of Each' in Professor Shedd (ed.), *Complete Works of Samuel Taylor Coleridge,* vol. VI (New York, 1853), p. 51.

68. Ibid., pp. 51-2.

69. Ibid., p. 53.

70. Quoted from Pusey's 'Evidence' before the Hebdomadal Board in 1852, in H.P. Liddon, *Life of Edward Bouverie Pusey* (4 vols., London, 1894), III, p. 385.

71. Quoted in ibid., p. 384.

72. The idea of a liberal education is brilliantly analyzed in Sheldon Rothblatt, *Tradition and Change in English Liberal Education: An Essay in History and Culture* (London, 1976), Chs. 1-8; and in Robert G. McPherson, *Theory of Higher Education in Nineteenth-Century England* (Athens, Ga., 1959), *passim.* There are brief but incisive comments in Michael Sanderson (ed.), *The Universities in the Nineteenth Century* (London, 1975), 'Introduction'.

73. Edward Copleston, *A Reply to the Calumnies of the Edinburgh Review, Containing an Account of Studies Pursued at that University* (Oxford, 1810), pp. 133-4. There is a short excerpt from this work in Sanderson (ed.), *Universities in the Nineteenth Century,* pp. 36-8.

74. William Whewell, *Of A Liberal Education,* 2nd edn (London, 1850), pp. 1-7, 95-109; and 'Study of Mathematics', in *English University Education* (London, 1837), *passim.*

75. J.H. Newman, *On the Scope and Nature of University Education* (Everyman's edn, London, 1915), p. xxix. Italics in the original.

76. Ibid., 'Discourse IV; Liberal Knowledge Its Own End', especially pp. 82, 84, 91.

77. The table is constructed from Lawrence Stone, 'The Size and Composition of the Oxford Student Body, 1580-1909', in Lawrence Stone (ed.), *The University in Society* (2 vols., Princeton, 1974), I, Tables 1A, 1B and 4.

78. Ibid., Table 12.

79. Bulwer Lytton, *England and the English*, I, pp. 212-14.

80. Stone, 'Size and Composition of the Oxford Student Body', Table 4.

81. C.A. Anderson and Miriam Schnaper, *School and Society: Social Backgrounds of Oxford and Cambridge Students* (Westport, Connecticut, 1952), pp. 5-6.

82. Ibid., pp. 7-8.

83. See Michael Sanderson (ed.), *Universities in the Nineteenth Century*, pp. 16-19.

84. For the numbers of fellows and professors, see the *Royal Commission on Oxford University* (1852), evidence of Frederick Temple, pp. 127-32, and 'Part II: Professorships'; *Royal Commission – Cambridge University* (1852-3), pp. vi, 156; and Arthur Engel, 'Emerging Concepts of the Academic Profession at Oxford', in Stone (ed.), *The University in Society*, I, p. 305.

85. Mark Pattison, *Memoirs* (London, 1885), pp. 69-70. The fellows and fellowships have been discussed in a number of works: see, for instance, Sheldon Rothblatt, *The Revolution of the Dons: Cambridge and Society in Victorian England* (London, 1968); Engel, 'Emerging Concepts of the Academic Profession', especially pp. 305-20; E.W.G. Bill, *University Reform in Nineteenth-Century Oxford: A Study of Henry Halford Vaughan, 1811-1885* (Oxford, 1973), pp. 75-7; John Sparrow, *Mark Pattison and the Idea of A University* (Cambridge, 1967), Ch. 3; W.R. Ward, *Victorian Oxford* (London, 1965), pp. 9-19; and D.A. Winstanley, *Early Victorian Cambridge* (Cambridge, 1940). Two contemporary works contain priceless descriptions of the fellows: W. Tuckwell, *Reminiscences of Oxford* (New York, 1908), especially Chs. I-VI; and Charles A. Bristed, *Five Years in An English University*, 3rd edn (New York, 1873), especially pp. 186-99, 207-37, 347-56.

86. *Royal Commission on Oxford* (1852), pp. 129-30.

87. Ibid., p. 118.

88. Sheldon Rothblatt, 'The Student Sub-culture and the Examination System in Early 19th Century Oxbridge', in Stone (ed.), *University in Society*, pp. 247-303; Rothblatt, *Tradition and Change in English Liberal Education*, pp. 119-22; Engel, 'Emerging Concepts of the Academic Profession', pp. 309-10. The degree to which the exams dominated student life is well revealed in Bristed, *Five Years in An English University;* and J.W. Adamson, *English Education, 1789-1902* (Cambridge, 1930), pp. 73-81.

89. Bristed, *Five Years in An English University*, p. 309; Adamson, *English Education*, p. 77.

90. Ward, *Victorian Oxford*, p. 16.

91. Pattison, *Memoirs*, pp. 215-17.

92. See, for example, the views cited in Myron Brightfield, *Victorian England in Its Novels* (4 vols., Los Angeles, 1968), III, pp. 405-9.

93. Harrison, *Memoirs*, I, p. 36.

94. Mortimer Proctor, *The English University Novel* (Berkeley, 1957), discusses these novels very nicely.

95. Carlyle, *On Heroes and Hero-Worship*, pp. 408-9.

96. For instance, Trollope remarks about Crawley: 'The intellect of the man was as clear as running water in all things not pertaining to his daily life and its difficulties.' *The Last Chronicle of Barset* (3 vols., New York, 1915), I, p. 48.

# 4 THE IMPACT OF SCIENCE ON VICTORIAN INTELLECTUAL LIFE

Thus far I have mapped for analytical purposes a static landscape of early and mid-Victorian intellectual life. However, even in the 1830s and 1840s, and then steadily throughout the century, a number of forces were working to change the topography of intellectual life. The most important of these were: (1) the expansion of science; (2) the university reform movement; and (3) the growth of culturally-based criticism of industrial society. Theoretically, these forces could have operated independently of each other, for they were not even the same *kinds* of forces; in actuality they were intimately bound together. By the last thirty years of the century, their combined strength was radically transforming the conceptual and institutional relations of intellectual activity in England.

Of these three forces perhaps the primary was the expansion of science. It is a truism that science grew in importance during the nineteenth century, in England as elsewhere. One need only think of the great impact of Darwin's theory of evolution, the struggle between science and theology and the growing acceptance of science's claims to jurisdiction in almost all the realms of human understanding to recognize the influence of scientific thought on Victorian ideas — not to mention the enormous consequences of science and technology on material civilization. In her autobiography, Beatrice Webb observed of the last half of the nineteenth century:

> [W]ho will deny that the men of science were the leading British intellectuals of that period; that it was they who stood out as men of genius with international reputations; that it was they who were the self-confident militants of the period; that it was they who were routing the theologians, confounding the mystics, imposing their theories on the philosophers, their inventions on capitalists, and their discoveries on medical men; whilst they were at the same time snubbing the artists, ignoring the poets, and even casting doubts on the capacity of politicians?[1]

Given the influence of science, it is not surprising that scientists had a powerful impact on both the conceptual framework and the economic and social organization of intellectual life. Yet there are larger complexities in understanding *how* science changed intellectual life than one might predict. It is not easy to say, for example, what the institutional consequences of the 'victory' — if we call it that for a moment — of science over orthodox theology were. In addition, while the scientists themselves took the initiative in advancing the institutional claims of science, the reshaping of English intellectual life according to their desires or practices was neither automatic nor complete. The scientists disagreed among themselves on many issues, and they also protested throughout the century that the intellectual and material achievements of science were not matched by institutional alterations in English society. Certain themes from the 'decline of science' controversy were played by the advocates of science well into the twentieth century. Further, the great paradox of the history of Victorian science had become apparent by the end of the century: while England was the locale of revolutionary discoveries in many scientific fields, England also was falling behind in the industrial and military application of science. The economic, social and political elites of England remained remarkably committed to values and attitudes discouraging to science, even while science advanced in knowledge, organization and professional status.

To begin to understand the ways in which science did, and did not alter the conceptual and institutional contexts of intellectual activity in England, it helps to distinguish between three types of impact. First, the triumph of science over theology: science contributed to the shrinking of the boundaries of theology, and thus to the secularization of thought. Second, the institutionalization of science: the rise of science embodied the establishment by scientists of particular kinds of organizations in which intellectual activity went on, including both the founding of new institutions and the alteration of old ones. And third, the dissemination of the scientific paradigm for intellectual activity: science provided a model for the acquisition and cultural functions of knowledge, and the rise of science spread this model into many areas. (A discussion of this last process will be reserved for the next chapter).

The relations among these kinds of impact, and between them and Victorian society as a whole, were complex. Propagandizing of the scientific model of intellectual activity, a model firmly established by the 1840s, went forward as part of the campaign for the institutionalization of science. At the same time, both the advocacy of scientific thinking and the campaign for institutional support of science were imbedded in the context of the break from theology. Hence the conflict between science and theology was part of the formative background for specific aspects of the impact of science on Victorian intellectual activity. Finally, both the ideas of good scientific work and of the proper institutional support for it were shaped in part by the ideals and organizations of the wider society. Scientists and their work were not immune to the power and influence of well-established Victorian institutions.

The conflict between science and theology was itself part of that very complex phenomenon known as the decline of religion or the secularization of thought. Natural science did not by itself cause this phenomenon. If one looks to the issue of the decline of *popular* religious belief and attachment to organized sects, then the explanation must in large part be social. Growing numbers in the working class, for example, became unbelievers and separated themselves from the churches because they saw those churches and their doctrines as upper-class instruments of social control.[2] The Church of England failed to maintain contact with large sections of the working class by its inability or unwillingess to make parish churches available to the urban workers.[3] If one considers the issue of the growing doubts about religion in the minds of educated people, then again science was not the only effective force. For educated people, there were several major contributors to doubt: an ethical reaction to certain doctrines of orthodox Christianity; an increasing awareness and acceptance of historical criticism of the scriptures; and the assimilation of the assertions of natural science about the origins and nature of the world and man's place in it.[4]

The ethical reaction against the harshness of certain Christian teachings probably prepared the way for acceptance of historical and scientific criticism by many educated Victorians. In this regard, as in so many others, the evangelical revival of the eighteenth and early-nineteenth centuries was crucial to the Victorian frame of mind. Evangelicalism dramatically heightened the intensity of the individual conscience and of the drive for personal morality. It taught the radical separation of people from God by original sin, but also the unfathomable goodness and mercy of God in offering salvation to all who would accept it. Evangelicalism did not teach salvation for an elect only. Instead it taught salvation for all those who would recognize their sinfulness through a severe examination of conscience and who would accept Christ as a personal redeemer. It also taught the therapeutic value of good works — social reform as well as methodical religious behaviour — in the process of sanctification. When combined with the genuine economic and administrative capacity of the British nation to do good across the whole of the society, evangelical beliefs made for a potent meliorism.[5] Yet by the 1840s, many Victorians were finding this meliorist conscience inconsistent with orthodox doctrines of hell, everlasting punishment and the atonement. For them it did not seem right to believe on the one hand that a loving God could so easily condemn people to an eternity of suffering, or on the other hand that the sacrifice of Jesus was adequate compensation for the sins of millions of people over the ages.

Historical criticism of the scriptures, which the popular mind often confused with the assertions of natural science, led to doubt about the claims to historical truth made in both the Old and New Testaments. German scholars led the development of Biblical historical criticism, and by the 1830s and 1840s word of these advances had come to England. D.F. Strauss's *Life of Jesus* caused much debate on its publication in 1835, though a full translation was not published in England until 1846 (by Mary Anne Evans). The translation of Renan's *Life of Jesus* in 1863 and the publication of J.R. Seeley's *Ecce Homo* in 1865 caused even greater disturbance. Such works undermined orthodox belief by arguing that the scriptures ought to be understood as the works of real men in particular historical circumstances, and therefore not as the words of God, at least in the literal sense. The most conservative English Christians resisted the new historical criticism, but by the 1880s even main-stream theologians had come to terms with it, largely by accepting that the word of God is *in* the Bible, while rejecting the belief that the word of God *is* the Bible.[6] The big historical question is why so many educated Victorians in the 1850s, 1860s and after chose to adopt the new historical interpretation of scripture rather than to retain the orthodox. This is one of those enormous historical problems to which no one will ever know the answer; but the explanation surely has to do with the revulsion from *what* the literal interpretation taught, with the early Victorians' acute sense of their own historicity — of existing at a unique historical moment — and with their growing preference for natural accounts of worldly phenomena.

It was in connection with this last point that natural science played its part. Science was not the only body of knowledge or method of knowing things that caused the spread of unbelief among the Victorians; yet it contributed heavily to both the ethical reaction against orthodoxy and the acceptance of historical criticism. Scientific knowledge and the methods of scientific reasoning contributed powerfully to the economic expansion which enabled the Victorians to think that melioration of earthly suffering was in fact possible.[7]

Rational approaches to social problems, even the approaches that were religiously motivated, assumed that naturalistic explanations of social phenomena existed. Science and its parent, reason, made these explanations seem credible. Likewise, science added its weight to the preference for natural explanation of Biblical events, and so to the frame of mind that made historical studies of the Bible seem convincing. Similarly, Newtonian physics and 'modern' geology made uniformitarian assumptions about the operation of natural forces believable, and thus made belief in miraculous events difficult if not impossible. Hume's definition of miracles — that they are violations of natural law — was made possible by the scientific revolution and powerfully advanced among the educated public by Lyell's *Principles of Geology* (1830).

To be more specific, science in the 1860s and after contributed to the Victorian religious crisis by delivering severe blows to natural theology, both as a theological position and as the umbrella for scientific knowledge. Uniformitarian geology made it difficult to accept the natural theological position, which held that science supported the revealed account of the origins of the world, and it also worked against the doctrine of the special creation of each species. Yet uniformitarianism by itself was not enough to refute the argument from design for the existence and benevolence of God: Lyell himself held to the position of natural theology. The mortal damage to natural theology came from Darwin's hypothesis of evolution by the mechanism of natural selection, an account of the development of species which many Victorians found compelling because it conformed to their experience of a changing, progressive, and highly competitive world. The evidence of the operation of chance, brutality, suffering and extinction changed the view of the universe for many Victorians and destroyed the reverent attitude and sacred image of the world necessary for natural theology. It is true that many scientists remained active Christians. In his survey of English men of science, Francis Galton found in 1874 that seven of ten distinguished professional scientists were members of the Establishment.[8] But even the Christians among the scientists, like Whewell and Faraday, believed that they had to assert the separation of science from theology: physics and geology say nothing about religion; and theology says nothing about the natural world.[9]

Theologians in general inclined in the same direction, for they too concluded that science and religion had to be regarded as addressing different spheres of human experience. This primary act of specialization was illustrated by the famous volume of articles published in 1860, *Essays and Reviews.* This remarkable book, very much a sign of the times, was written by six Anglican clergymen and one devout layman. Two of the authors, C.W. Goodwin and Baden Powell, addressed directly the conflict between science and orthodoxy; but plainly all of them had the issue on their minds. The main point made by Goodwin and Powell was that since the scriptural explanation of natural events such as the origin of the world differs from that given by modern science, modern people should accept that the Bible was not meant to teach truths about the physical world. 'Matters of clear and positive fact,' Powell declared, 'investigated on critical grounds and supported by exact evidence, are properly matters of knowledge, not of faith.'[10] All of the essayists believed that while truth may ultimately be one, the truth of revelation is known by moral experience and not by historical or scientific verification.[11] Hence, theology in the late-Victorian period increasingly became, as Owen Chadwick has observed, 'immanentist' — God is 'within the world', rather than apart from it and intervening in it.[12]

The damage done to natural theology and the separation of science from theology were, for the specialization that came to characterize intellectual activity, necessary but not sufficient events. It is hard to imagine that the division of intellectual work into specialities, each deeply concerned with developing distinct methods and vocabularies, and with boundary-keeping to maintain its distinctiveness, could have occurred under the umbrella of natural theology. Yet the separation of science from theology did not *cause* further acts of specialization, or even end the early and mid-Victorian concern to have intellectual activity address the general literate public.[13] Specialization was inspired and legitimated by the deeply-ingrained principle of the division of labour articulated by Adam Smith and accepted as essential to material progress by Victorian political economy. The parting of science and theology *did* help to erode what Robert Young and others call the 'common context' of public discourse in England, and it served as a model for later steps towards specialization in other fields. This process will be discussed further in the next chapter; here it is necessary only to point out that after the 1860s, theology ceased functioning as the umbrella for all branches of knowledge and took its place as one of them.

Newman, for instance, accepted this 'specialist' idea of theology in his lectures on university education in 1852, while trying to retain something of the older idea of theology as above all other branches of knowledge. He argued, first, that theology *is* a branch of knowledge; secondly, that any branch of knowledge is incomplete without the others; and thirdly, that theology is especially needed by all other branches for completeness. 'In a word,' he said, 'religious truth is not only a portion, but a condition of general knowledge.'[14] In the latter half of the century, his first point was retained and the second and third discarded. Oxford established an honours school in theology in 1870 and Cambridge a theological tripos in 1871; but divinity dropped out of the other schools and triposes. Professors of divinity, theology and ecclesiastical history multiplied in both universities. Increasingly, such scholars of theology saw themselves as being 'scientific' — that is, as careful and diligent research scholars within a distinct discipline. In 1899, the *Journal of Theological Studies,* which displayed high scholarly standards, was founded.[15]

There was another important consequence of the conflict between science and theology. The reaction of conservative churchmen against scientific and historical criticism of Christian teachings often looked like attempts to quash the truth. Conservative Anglicans tried, for instance, to force the clerical authors of *Essays and Reviews* to recant or resign their orders. Convocation condemned the book, and nearly 11,000 of the 25,000 Church of England clergymen signed a paper reaffirming against *Essays and Reviews* the doctrine of the divine inspiration of the Bible.[16] Similarly, when a synod of bishops in South Africa removed Bishop Colenso of Natal from his post for publishing a critical study of the Pentateuch, many conservative Anglicans in England approved of his removal. Such reactions allowed the advocates of science to shift the grounds of their argument to defending the quest for truth itself — a position conforming to and emphasizing the element of disinterestedness in existing Victorian scientific ideology. Hence in the classic confrontation of 'science versus religion' — T.H. Huxley's defence of Darwinism against Bishop Samuel Wilberforce at the BAAS meeting at Oxford in 1860 — Huxley scored a sensational hit, not by refuting Wilberforce's scientific information, but by pointing out that Wilberforce was using his considerable talents to obscure the search for truth.[17] With a conflict on those grounds, scientists easily made themselves seem more moral than the theologians, and they found the way well prepared for the extension of their ideas about knowledge and its acquisition.

This conflict between science and theology contributed to the breadth and complexity of the effort by scientists to improve the position of science. They wanted nothing less than to move science from the periphery to the centre of English life. They wanted England to become a 'scientific nation'. They wished to establish a national system of education and to base it on natural science; they wanted to establish elementary and advanced schools of technical instruction for the working and middle classes; they intended to stimulate the desire for, and create opportunities for, scientific research; and they wanted to open the ancient universities to scientific knowledge and teaching. Science may not necessarily have been opposed to religion, but a 'scientific culture' *was* inherently opposed to a religious culture. And the scientists' general desire for a scientific culture was only half the story; the other was their powerful impulse towards the professionalization of science.

Most Victorian scientists were quite explicit about their professional ambitions: while they wanted to win institutional support for scientific activity, they also wanted to be able to devote their lives to science, to combine their avocational with their vocational interests; and they wanted to enjoy high economic and social status while doing it. By the 1850s and 1860s, scientists had a strong sense of identity *qua* scientists. Their extensive organizational activity gave expression to their collective identification and helped promote their intellectual and material interests. Leone Levi found that there were 11,922 members of specialist societies alone, in 1869 — a significant number of more or less active scientists.[18] In his survey of distinguished men of science, Galton found that most of them came from middle-class families — commercial, industrial and professional people.[19] In Victorian middle-class families the value of the self-made man and the drive towards upward social mobility were powerful forces, and the aspiring scientists shared these potent urgings. They valued hard work, productivity and achievement by merit. But they also desired to achieve the status of gentry and its ancillary troops, the professions. The scientists meant to be professionals in both major senses: they wanted to make a living doing science, and they wanted the attributes and standing of the professions.

Inevitably the impulses towards self-identity as scientists and towards professional status combined to affect profoundly the institutional claims and achievements of English science. Together these impulses required that the scientists distinguish themselves as a community apart from the rest of society — a community thought of as necessary to, but not accountable to, the nation. Moreover, they led the scientists to seek places in the kinds of institutions that could confer status — the universities. This orientation towards universities was strengthened by the interaction between the scientists' outlook and prevailing ideas of political economy. Most advocates of science accepted the Victorian liberal principle that the state should do nothing, even to promote science, that private effort could do. Further, the common notion that governmental expenditures should remain minimal put limits on what scientists would ask for, and what the government would grant. However, scientists could without damage to *laissez-faire* principles look to the resources of universities for the means of support. In addition, scientists tended to see Oxford and Cambridge as bulwarks of an older, 'unscientific' culture; consequently, they believed that if a scientific culture was to be promulgated then the training grounds of the elite would have to be altered. Most scientists, therefore, wanted to penetrate and reform Oxford and Cambridge because the old universities were the strongholds of theology, because they could bestow high status and because they possessed vast financial resources which the scientists hoped to turn to their own purposes.

Reform of Oxbridge proved to be only one of the routes taken by scientists towards gaining a university habitat. The other led towards establishing provincial or technical universities. This second route grew out of the general upper-class concern to promote technical education and out of the industrial connections of provincial, literary-and-philosophical-society science. In these new universities — the red bricks — the utilitarian functions of science were stronger than at Oxbridge. Yet even here the tradition of the higher functions of science came to be emphasized.

The two routes of English science towards institutionalization in universities are best understood by illustration. The train of development in technical education is clearly illuminated by the careers of Lyon Playfair, perhaps the leading politician-scientist of the Victorian period, and other Manchester scientists. Playfair was a Scotsman of good family, educated at St Andrews and at the Andersonian College in Glasgow, where he received a strong preliminary training in research chemistry from Thomas Graham. Playfair intended to become a doctor, but he was unable to stand the dissection laboratory. In 1839, on Graham's suggestion, Playfair decided to pursue the study of chemistry. There being no adequate facilities in England, he went to the University of Giessen to study with the eminent organic chemist, Justus von Liebig. There, like a number of other young British chemists, Playfair imbibed not only the chemical knowledge of Liebig but also his ideals of original research and of *Wissenschaft.* Liebig inspired in his students a remarkable *élan* built upon his direction of their research and his ideal of science as both disinterested and useful. He taught that science, and especially organic chemistry, is crucial to modern agriculture and industry, but that the individual scientist should not pursue scientific research for motives of personal advantage.[20] Science should be for public service.

When Playfair return to England with his doctorate in 1841, he had already won a reputation in organic chemistry. He translated Liebig's new work applying organic chemistry to agriculture, and he presented papers by Liebig and himself to the BAAS meeting in 1840. He was made secretary of the chemical section of the British Association and established useful contacts with influential English scientists. In the early 1840s chemistry more than any other science played an important role in industry, largely because of the importance of dyes in the production of textiles. Playfair went to work for a calico printer in Lancashire, thereby beginning an association with the growing scientific community in Manchester, and with industry in the most important of all English manufacturing centres. Liebig wrote to him:

> In all that you do, do not forget science and keep fresh and vigorous your taste for mental work, for unless a man is making progress in that which gives nourishment and life to industry he is scarcely in a position to fulfil the demands of his times . . . After satisfying the claims which Mr. Thomson makes on your attainments for his business, you ought not to trade on your experience and your chemical knowledge, but to give advice and help where they are useful . . . You will have sufficient time for this, and it will raise you higher in the eyes of sensible men and be more really beneficial to your interests than if you tried to make money. Be true to yourself and true to science — This is all I wish to ask of you.[21]

Playfair took this lesson to heart. He pointed out to James Young, another former student of Graham's, the commercial possibilities of oil in a pit in Derbyshire, but he did not make money from it himself. And in 1844, Playfair and the German chemist, R.W. Bunsen, analyzed the composition of blast-furnace gases in the iron industry, thereby enabling manufacturers to use fuel more efficiently; yet his attitude remained one of using science in public service.[22]

In 1842, Playfair experienced the difficulty common to English scientists: unemployment. He foresaw that the calico firm for which he worked was doomed to failure, and resigned. For several years thereafter, Playfair searched unsuccessfully for permanent employ-ment. The experience confirmed his high ideal of science — as similar experiences did for many English scientists. In 1844, speaking to the Royal Manchester Institution, Playfair denounced the 'class of men who cannot see why years should be spent investigating laws which may after all lead to no practical end. Such are the men who can only see beauty in the infinity of divine wisdom when it shows how to cheapen the yard of calico by a diminution of labour'.[23] Playfair did not become anti-business, but he felt that a great industrial nation should be willing to provide support for scientists even if their work did not lead to immediate profits. Meanwhile, he was able to use his scientific skills in public service.

Fortunately for Playfair, he had very good connections, including Sir Robert Peel, who was an improving landlord as well as Prime Minister. Peel knew of Playfair's role in advancing agricultural chemistry and wanted to keep him in England. Peel appointed him to the Royal Commission investigating the public health in large towns in 1843, and then to tasks in several other practical investigations for the government.[24] Eventually, a post was found for him in the Museum of Geology in London, which became part of the Government School of Mines in 1851. But Playfair's main occupation and reputation came through his role as a member of Royal Commissions and investigatory committees, and as adviser to successive governments. He was asked to report on sanitation arrangements at Buckingham Palace, the state of graveyards, the use of coal by the navy, and the potato blight in Ireland. In the latter 1840s, then, Playfair was increasingly involved in the utilization of science for direct public benefit. He was a professional, and he was an *expert*.

In 1850, Peel recruited Playfair to work with the Prince Consort, Henry Cole and the Royal Commission planning the Great Exhibition for 1851. This assignment not only gave Playfair enviable influence through his friendship with Prince Albert, but also it re-emphasized for him the crucial connection between research science and industry. Like the Prince Consort, Playfair thought that the evident superiority of British industry was due to the British headstart in industrialization, and not to leadership in science or education. They knew that headstarts were not durable and drew the conclusion that technical education was needed for further industrial progress. They believed that as industry advanced, the relative importance of raw materials to the productive process declined, while that of skill and intelligence increased. Britain, therefore, needed to do what Germany already had done: alter the educational system so as to make manufacturing more efficient. They had in mind technical education at all levels, including technical colleges for the manufacturers.[25]

The Great Exhibition made a profit, with which Playfair and the Prince Consort hoped to establish a permanent institution to continue the work of the Exhibition in promoting technical and industrial progress. Albert's plan was to establish four institutions in South Kensington to exhibit industrial, technical and artistic items, to provide the rooms for conferences and lecturing, and to house the various scientific societies.[26] Playfair thought more in terms of central technical colleges supplementing, but not replacing, existing educational institutions. He dreamed of establishing two central institutions, both meant to maintain British industrial pre-eminence — a 'University of Mines and Manufactures', incorporating the Geological Museum and the Government School of Mines; and a college for the textile industry. Albert, however, had long emphasized the international character of the Great Exhibition, and he was set on using the profits for the benefit of *all* nations. He refused to accept any plan for a scientific establishment such as existed on the continent, because this kind of plan would favour Britain, which had no such institutions. As Albert's secretary wrote to Playfair:

> In projecting, therefore, modes for the disposal of the surplus, the object must not be so much the founding of institutions through which Great Britain may be raised to equality, or maintain her superiority over other nations, as the foundation of some establishment in which, by the application of science and art to industrial pursuits, the industry of all nations may be raised in the scale of human employment . . .[27]

Given this concept, it was impossible for the advocates of central technical colleges to mobilize public opinion in favour of their project. Such mobilization would have been an uphill task in any case, for the general public had concluded from the Great Exhibition that British manufactures already were the wonder of the world and were likely to go on from triumph to triumph. For most Englishmen, the Great Exhibition showed that the relations of science to industry in England were optimal. In the end, the profits from the Exhibition were used to buy land in South Kensington on which was founded a Museum of Science and, in the 1870s, a Royal College of Science. Even the new Science College fell below Playfair's ideal. Disputes within the faculty of one of its components, the School of Mines, as to whether their institution should remain a technical college closely tied to the mining industry or should become a more general, and elevated, college of science, reduced the actual impact of the new Science College. For many years it functioned as a relatively small normal school for training science teachers.[28]

Playfair continued his efforts on behalf of scientific and technical education, but it was not until 1867 that he and his fellow advocates were able to win a wide hearing. In that year, Playfair served as juror at the Paris Exhibition, and he was among those who interpreted the exhibits as revealing that Britain had fallen behind in technical innovation.[29] This perception caused considerable concern in Britain, especially among scientists, and gave a strong impetus to the technical education movement. In 1868, for example, many chambers of commerce, in answer to a circular from the government, remarked on recent losses in British trade and called for more technical education as one solution.[30] In May 1867 Playfair wrote to Lord Taunton, chairman of the Royal Commission on the public schools, 'That as an inevitable result of the attention given to technical education abroad and of its neglect in England, other nations must advance at a greater rate than in our own country . . . this result has already arrived for some of our staple industries.'[31] Whatever their individual enthusiasms and specialisms, all British scientists could agree with this proposition; consequently, the scientific community supported the technical education movement steadily throughout the rest of the century — indeed more steadily and enthusiastically than the businessmen themselves.[32] There were modest advances but no revolutions in British support to technical education through the end of the nineteenth century.

It was in the context of his ideas of scientific research as a disinterested public service and of support for technical education that Playfair recommended changes in English colleges and universities. He testified to the Select Committee on Provision of Scientific Instruction to the Industrial Classes (1867-8) that 'increasing skill and intelligence in manufactures become more important than any advantage which this country may possess in the abundance of its raw materials'.[33] At the level of post-secondary education, Playfair urged the establishment of technical colleges and the alteration of existing colleges and universities into technical schools — but, significantly, not Oxford and Cambridge. These universities, he acknowledged, were obligated to give all their students 'a liberal education'; and he assumed the truth of what was to be an increasingly important proposition in England, namely that disinterested research is more compatible with liberal education than is technical education or applied research. 'It would be better for those universities [Oxbridge]', he said, 'to prosecute pure science rather than applied science.' Honours examinations in the natural sciences had been established at Oxford and Cambridge in 1850 and 1848 respectively, but each required a heavy dose of 'liberal education' subjects before a student could opt for the natural sciences — mainly classical literature and languages at Oxford, and classics, mathematics and divinity at Cambridge. With this scheme Playfair essentially agreed. In his judgement, *all* students of science at Oxbridge should be examined in Latin, Greek (or two modern languages instead of Greek), English, logic, arithmetic and other mathematics, and mechanics, as well as the natural sciences.[34]

For him the other side of the coin of liberal education was that all students in the old universities ought to receive some education in the sciences — as indeed, everyone in Britain should. In his presidential address to the British Association in 1885, Playfair reiterated his message of technical education as the means of national survival. But by then he felt that because of the establishment of a national system of elementary education in 1870 and the proliferation of science classes offered by the Department of Science and Art, diffusion of scientific knowledge among the working class was progressing, while the scientific training of the middle and upper classes lagged behind. Like almost all the scientists of the day, he felt that science should form part of the education of all students in the endowed schools and universities. It was, he said, because the middle and upper classes (from which industrial owners and managers were drawn) were deficient in the scientific knowledge that 'whole branches of manufactures' were passing from Britain. The state should do much more, as in Germany and Switzerland, to support scientific teaching in the universities. If the English universities, he said, 'created that love of science which a broad education would surely inspire, our men of riches and leisure who advance the boundaries of scientific knowledge could not be counted on the fingers as they now are', England could have an army as well as generals in science, and the nation could survive industrial competition.[35]

Encouragement of students in their appreciation of science, however, was not all that universities should do. Like most scientists of his day, Playfair assigned to new and old universities alike the function of scientific research: 'Universities are not mere storehouses of knowledge; they are also conservatories for its cultivation . . . The widening of the bounds of knowledge, literary or scientific, is the crowning glory of university life.'[36] Scientific progress was necessary for industrial progress, but it ought not to be done mainly *because* of industrial progress. He declared to the School of Mines in 1851: 'Science is too lofty for measurement by the yard of utility; — too inestimable for expression by a money standard.'[37] Here, of course, Playfair was drawing on the model of the German university, which he had seen first hand, and which had been idealized for him by Liebig. The German universities, it should be noted, developed not out of a need for industrial progress but out of a bureaucratic rationalization of ranks in social status. In nineteenth-century Germany, high status came from holding degrees awarded by the elite educational institutions, the *gymnasia* and the universities, and from displaying the general and 'useless' culture they bestowed. The German university professoriate, with its research orientation, ranked as high-level civil servants, for they were above all others the products and propagators of disinterested culture. German science professors shared the values of non-utilitarian culture with their colleagues in the mandarinate.[38] Hence even for Playfair, with his concern about industrial competition and technical education, the German example meant that while the universities should become centres of scientific research, they ought to do so in the spirit of 'higher', non-utilitarian culture.

Playfair believed that assigning the national effort in research to the universities, and keeping university research in science *abstract*, was the way to support science in order to ensure British industrial progress. He agreed with the prevailing concept of scientific activity that 'when the seeds of science are sown, technics as its fruit will appear at the appointed time'. *Abstract* science is what the university researcher should pursue, even though industrial advance is one of its ends, and even though abstract research requires a deliberate ignoring of utility:

> Abstract discovery in science is then the true foundation upon which the superstructure of modern civilisation is built; and the man who would take part in it should study science, and, if he can, advance it for its own sake and not for its application.[39]

The scientific community in Manchester, which Playfair left in 1845 for his career in London, meanwhile advocated a role for science more closely attached to industry. One of the essential features of provincial scientific institutions — connections between the scientific community and industrial leadership — was preserved in new scientific institutions. Yet it was of crucial importance that this development was not towards industrial or state laboratories, but towards provincial universities. In the latter half of the century, the 'red brick' universities replaced the old literary and philosophical societies as the principal locations of professional science and scientists in the provinces; the 'lit. and phils.' were left to the amateurs, for the new professional scientists wanted to be seen on a larger stage.[40] The new universities — established initially as university colleges — all emphasized science as the basis of higher education. They followed the example of Owens College, Manchester, founded in 1851 by a bequest from a prominent man of commerce. Perhaps because chemistry was the most important industrial science in the Manchester area, the chemistry department dominated the new university college and provided its first claim to eminence. The key figure in Owens College chemistry was Henry Enfield Roscoe, appointed Professor of Chemistry in 1857. Trained in Germany under Bunsen, Roscoe did a great volume of consulting for the local manufacturers and diligently canvassed them to support Owens College, not least by sending their sons there.[41]

For all their connections with industry, it must be noted, Owens College and the other provincial colleges did not become German-style technical high schools. As they developed towards university status, they became more like Oxbridge. They emphasized a broad liberal education as well as science for their students. It was impossible for them to resist pressure from the traditional English ruling elite towards non-vocational higher education. Speaking for the Oxbridge-bred upper class, the *Saturday Review* observed:

> all work and no play, especially if that work has to be done in a very large and smoky town, will certainly make Jack a dull, and probably make him a vicious boy.[42]

Further, the research ideal, which all the professional scientists of the provinces shared, led to some restraint on any tendency towards a technical orientation in higher education. Edward Frankland, the first professor of chemistry at Owens College, declared in his inaugural address:

I am far from coinciding with those persons who urge upon you the study of chemistry merely on the ground of its numerous applications to the arts and manufactures. I would take much higher ground than this, and recommend the science for its own intrinsic excellence, for the intellectual delight which every student must find in its pursuit and for the bright glimpses of the Deity which it discloses at every step.[43]

Arthur Schuster, Langworthy Professor of Physics at Owens College, declared in 1889 that original research was the most important activity of the College: practical applications would only be possible if scientists had done 'theoretical researches . . . without a view to commercial application.'[44] For such people, to be a *professional* in science required emphasis on disinterested research and not on domestic service in industry.

The idea of science, its proper functions and locale, expressed by Lyon Playfair and the founders of Owens College were the *most* utilitarian to be found in mid and late-Victorian England. Yet even for these men the notion that scientific research is best pursued for its own sake was of great importance. Thus in the thought of the scientists who most approved of close connections between science and industry, and who were most concerned about German competition, the purist ideal of science and the tradition of liberal education remained influential. For them, professional impulses tended to preserve the elements of abstract, disinterested research embedded in the older traditions of natural theology and early-Victorian science. In the ideas of other mid and late-Victorian advocates of science — those of the other scientific route to the universities — these themes played an even more important role.

The most prominent of these scientific spokesmen who were not *primarily* industrially oriented was the great biologist and publicist, T. H. Huxley. His ideas, which did more than any other individual's to define science for the literate public, show how the conflict between science and theology, in combination with the impulse to obtain respectable careers for scientists, dictated enormous changes in the ancient universities. Like most Victorian scientists, Huxley was neither an Oxbridge man nor a well-to-do amateur man of science. He was part of a growing corps of professional scientists aspiring to improve their status. For him, as for Playfair and the provincial scientists, these aspirations included both major meanings of 'professional': Huxley wanted to make a living doing science and also to enjoy the high status accruing to the existing professions. But

Huxley was also 'Darwin's bulldog', the great agnostic, the most effective basher of bishops in Victorian England. Consequently, his professional aspirations naturally tended towards coveting the places of clerics in the universities, just as his advocacy of scientific culture looked to the replacement of clerics by scientists as the new cultural authorities. The central tendency of his promotion of science, then, led towards the replacement of one priestly class by another, while his concept of scientific thinking itself pulled in the opposite direction.

Huxley's public personality was combative and self-confident. He loved a stiff fight with any representative of Authority, and he viewed science above all as a mode of anti-authoritarian reasoning. But this public aggressiveness masked a contemplative and melancholy side to his personality — a side that had profound religious yearnings. The complexities of his psyche shaped both his concept of science and his specific professional and institutional claims.[45] Huxley's parents were of sturdy, middle-class Evangelical stock, and they reared him in Evangelical Christianity. Huxley never lost the intense moral impulses and the urge to proselytize that Evangelicalism inculcated. Hence for him, as for many young men in the 1840s and 1850s, abandonment of orthodoxy was an extraordinarily painful and guilt-ridden experience. It was also part of the process of achieving an identity independent of the authority of his father, for whom Huxley developed considerable hostility. Like many mid-Victorians, Huxley arrived at the condition of doubt while continuing to recognize the value of religion and devoutly wishing to be able to believe. 'The end of man is to act', he wrote to his fiancée in the 1840s, 'and belief is the source of action.'[46] But he joined the ethical revolt against Evangelical orthodoxy, for he found his parents' faith cruel and intolerant. The authoritarian aspects of Victorian Christianity drove him to unbelief. On this matter, as on others, he liked to quote Luther's phrase: 'God help me, I can do no other'.[47]

For these reasons, Huxley's doubt took the form of the rationalism of the enlightenment. From David Hume, Sir William Hamilton and other thinkers, Huxley adopted the view that one should not believe anything for which he has no evidence in sensory experience.[48] He became a philosophical phenomenalist, but one with a profound speculative bent, trying to overcome doubt and establish a secure basis for moral behaviour. He regarded science as a species of empiricist philosophy: be aware of the limitations of the mind and commit oneself to reason and evidence, not authority. However, Huxley's sense of guilt and isolation resulting from his rejection of Christian orthodoxy did not allow him easily to choose science as a career. Indeed, the tensions that resulted from his Evangelical legacy led him not only to learn from Carlyle and Goethe, but also to suffer a first-class identity crisis when he was in his early twenties. He resolved the crisis by electing to identify himself as a professional man of science, but he found he had to struggle for many years against both the lack of career opportunities and his own religious hankerings to keep the identity intact. Not surprisingly, he tended to think orthodox religion was the source of both of his problems.

Huxley was in large measure a self-made scientist. He had very little formal schooling, and in fact resented his father's failure to provide a better education.[49] Mainly because of family connections and not his own choice, Huxley received training as a physician, but he much preferred the scientific to the clinical side of his work. For want of better employment, he applied to the Admiralty when his training was completed in 1845. Eventually he was assigned as medical officer to HMS *Rattlesnake*, a vessel commissioned to make geographical surveys in the Pacific. It was while on board the *Rattlesnake* in the years 1846-50 that Huxley passed through his identity crisis. He wanted to submit to some calling, as he wrote in his diary:

> There is something noble, something holy, about a poor and humble life if it be the consequence of following what one feels and knows to be one's duty. And if a man do possess a faculty for a given pursuit, if he have talent entrusted to him, to my mind it is distinctly his duty to use that to the best advantage, sacrificing all things to it.[50]

But he had grave doubts whether he did have any ability in scientific research, and he suffered periodically from severe depression.[51]

However, while on the *Rattlesnake*, Huxley began to publish scientific articles and gradually he overcame his doubts about a career in science — and about his own moral worth. He wrote in 1847:

> Opinion is the result of evidence . . . The opinion a man has, once more, neither is nor can be a matter of moral responsibility. The extent to which he deserves approbation or reprobation depends on the mode in which he has formed his opinion — and of this, the Almighty Searcher of Hearts can alone be the efficient judge.[52]

Scientific thinking would prove his moral value; science as a calling would justify his life.[53]

His practical career problems, however, became acute after the voyage of the *Rattlesnake* ended. In Australia, Huxley had become engaged to be married, and he meant to bring his fiancée to England as soon as his career permitted. But he found earning a living as a scientist almost impossible. He wrote to his fiancée:

> The difficulties of obtaining a decent position in England in anything like a reasonable time seem to me greater than ever they were. To attempt to live by any scientific pursuit is a farce. Nothing but what is absolutely practical will go down in England. A man of science may earn great distinction, but not bread.[54]

Huxley's problem was that as a scientist he had no marketable product like that of the men of letters, especially since, as a biologist, he had no immediate conection to industry. He suffered a galling sense that pure science received no rewards commensurate with its moral and intellectual value:

> There are not more than four or five offices in London which a Zoologist or Comparative Anatomist can hold and live by. Owen, who has a European reputation, second only to that of Cuvier, gets as Hunterian Professor £300 a year! which is less than the salary of many a bank clerk. My friend Forbes, who is highly distinguished and a very able man, gets the same from his office of Paleontologist to the Geological Survey of Great Britain. Now, these are first-rate men — men . . . whose abilities, had they turned them into many channels of moneymaking, must have made large fortunes . . . In literature a man may write for magazines and reviews, and so support himself; but not so in science . . . You will naturally think, then, 'Why persevere in so hopeless a course?' At present I cannot help myself. For my own credit, for the sake of gratifying those who have hitherto helped me on — nay, for the sake of truth and science itself, I must work out fairly and fully complete what I have begun.[55]

Given his sense of science as a calling, and given the fact that there was no practical advantage to be gained from his brand of science, Huxley naturally tended to define and justify science by its most abstract qualities. Ironically, these impulses established in Huxley's ideal of science links between the older natural theology and his modern agnostic science. Huxley wrote that he could not give up science because he found 'that the real pleasure, the true sphere, lies in the feeling of self-development — in the sense of power and of growing *oneness* with the great spirit of abstract truth'.[56] In time, Huxley found fortune as well as fame in science, but he never lost either the powerful impulse to improve the position of scientists or the inclination to picture science as a highly moral activity. In his work as a scientific publicist, he always focused on the propositions that scientific work is selfless pursuit of truth; that the pursuit of truth for its own sake is the most noble and virtuous of enterprises; and that such work ought to be rewarded according to its intrinsic value. Thus Huxley and his fellow advocates of science — Tyndall, Hooker and Spencer, for instance — constructed a public image of science emphasizing the moral and intellectual benefits as well as the practical results of scientific thinking and knowledge. Ultimately they valued science as knowledge for its own sake.[57]

Huxley and his immediate circle of scientific friends played an extremely important part in the dissemination of the image of science. In 1864, Huxley and eight others formed the 'X Club' to maintain their friendship and advance the cause of science. The eight were: Thomas Archer Hirst, John Tyndall, George Busk, J.D. Hooker, Herbert Spencer, Edward Frankland, John Lubbock and William Spottiswoode.[58] For two decades this little group dominated English scientific organizations. From 1873 to 1885, for example, every president of the Royal Society was a member of the X Club. Hooker, Huxley, Tyndall, Spottiswoode and Lubbock all served as president of the British Association between 1868 and 1881. The combined output of the X Club in both technical scientific works and popularizations of the scientific message was enormous. Huxley, Spencer and Tyndall led the struggle, as they saw it, against the theologians. They developed a position which has since been called 'scientific naturalism': hostility to supernatural explanations of natural events, devotion to the doctrine of justification by verification, and assertion of the claims of the jurisdiction of science in nearly every part of human knowledge and experience.[59] Huxley won widespread fame (or notoriety) for himself and for science as the expositor of the Darwinian hypothesis of evolution. To be sure, not all scientists in England agreed with the views of the most militant members of the X Club. University scientists tended to be more conservative on the question of the institutional interests of science, and some of them were concerned to maintain harmony between science and revealed religion.[60] But on the whole, the X Club expressed the views of professional scientists, and as far as one can tell, the public took Huxley's expression of those views as that of scientists in general.

Huxley's ultimate valuation of scientific knowledge for its own sake does not mean that he and his colleagues denied the practical utility of science. No one was better than Huxley at proclaiming the material benefits of science. As he said in his marvellous essay 'On the Advisableness of Improving Natural Knowledge', Huxley declared it obvious that the 'material civilisation' of the nineteenth century had advanced as much beyond the seventeenth century as the seventeenth had advanced beyond the first. Because of science, he said, 'our countrymen are less subject to fire, famine, pestilence, and all the evils which result from a want of command of Nature, than were the countrymen of Milton . . .' But he emphasized that what underlay this material improvement were the initial discoveries of pure science. If the first president of the Royal Society could escape the seventeenth century to see the world of the 1860s, Huxley wrote,

> he would need no long reflection to discover that all these great ships, these railways, these telegraphs, these factories, these printing-presses, without which the whole fabric of modern English society would collapse into a mass of stagnant and starving pauperism,—that all these pillars of our State are but the ripples and the bubbles upon the surface of that great spiritual stream, the springs of which only, he and his fellows were privileged to see . . .[61]

The point Huxley always stressed was that science makes many advances in knowledge 'not directly convertible into instruments for creating wealth'. One should not think of science as merely creating useful things. If utility became the governing view, Huxley declared, 'I, for one, should not greatly care to toil in the service of natural knowledge.'[62] The terminology of service to some higher cause gives a clue as to one reason why the doctrine of knowledge for its own sake was so important to Huxley and other scientists. In the first half of the century, when natural theology stood intact, pure scientific research was seen as nothing less than the effort to know God through His works. In the latter half of the century, when natural theology had been eroded, scientists wished to keep the sense of working in a high enterprise, and so they thought of the pursuit of knowledge for its own sake as the lofty cause to which one might sacrifice oneself. Indeed, for Huxley, the pursuit of research because of a simple love of knowledge 'redeems' a man regardless of his personal flaws; the religious function of science could scarcely have been made clearer.[63]

Huxley's notion of the highest justification of scientific labour led him to support liberal education. English educational theorists had long valued liberal education because they regarded non-vocational education as morally superior to vocational training. No doubt generalizing from his own experience, Huxley contended that the great scientists never were attracted primarily by the practical applications of science.

> That which stirs their pulses [he wrote] is the love of knowledge and the joy of discovery of the causes of things sung by the old poet — the supreme delight of extending the realm of law and order even farther towards the unattainable goals of the infinitely great and the infinitely small, between which our little race of life is run.[64]

Science could give to anyone, not just the scientist, the same satisfactions. It could give a correct understanding of the world, a knowledge of the 'secret and wonderful harmony' that pervades all things and thereby could enable people to bear pain and evil. Science, he thought, improves the finer feelings by making people more alert and observant. It has value as a *discipline* as well — 'the training and strengthening of common sense'. In fact, science was to him 'nothing but *trained and organised common sense*, differing from the latter only as a veteran may differ from a raw recruit . . .'[65] In Huxley's view, science and literature together made for a good liberal education, for ideally neither was taught only as useful knowledge.[66]

These views of science carried heavy implications for the kind of institutional support that Huxley and his circle thought science ought to be given. For one thing, the logic of Huxley's idea of science led directly to education. Huxley laboured hard in the technical education movement, and even harder to inject science into the curricula of all schools. For example, in 1867 the British Association adopted the report of a committee on education, which included Huxley and Tyndall, and which argued in favour of making science part of liberal education in schools and colleges. The report offered five reasons for science in education: (1) it provides the best discipline; (2) it stimulates students who are bored by literary education; (3) it offers access to modern philosophy; (4) it brings very great pleasure in later life; and (5) it affects 'the present position and future progress of civilization'.[67] It is significant that utility appears last on the list. Further, although Huxley and his colleagues were quick to point out that England's national power depended on giving more support to science, they did not argue for the establishment of industrial laboratories and were divided about state laboratories devoted to applied science. They *assumed* that scientific discoveries would always eventually find practical application, and that applied science would receive adequate support through normal commercial mechanisms. What needed more respect and support was *pure* scientific research, and the proposition that the location of scientific research should be the universities.

Another factor that directed Huxley's attention to the universities was his view of human history, especially English history, which explained to him why science did not receive the support it deserved. This view he shared with Spencer and other free-thinkers. The problem, as they saw it, was that religion had held on to men's minds long past its serviceability. Huxley, like Spencer, assumed that the desire to understand the world and the universe had been common to all people. In primitive societies, the desire to understand gave rise to religion. Therefore, to him, religion was the result of people's inability to satisfy their desire to understand natural phenomena in conditions of primitive culture. It followed that religion should recede as science progresses — and one of the distinguishing characteristics of science is that it *does* progress. Further, as natural knowledge advances, it reshapes even the 'moral convictions' cultivated by the religious habit of thought: it replaces obedience with scepticism, blind faith with the appeal to experience. This march of intellect, the spread of the scientific mentality as well as the accumulation of knowledge, was the wave of the future, for it was bound to extend itself into every area of thought.[68]

The scientific mentality, then, represented to Huxley both intellectual and moral superiority. But, Huxley thought, science was resisted in its advance by entrenched religious interests. The church resisted fair consideration of evolution, and it tried to muzzle the clerical authors of *Essays and Reviews* and Bishop Colenso of Natal.[69] In England, the resistance thrown up by theologians was, in Huxley's view, particularly powerful because of clerical control over education at all levels. The churches retarded the march of intellect by teaching the barbarous ethic of unquestioning obedience to authority. Until the schools were reformed so that the modern scientific ideal of justification by verification was inculcated, science would not be appreciated and scientists not supported in the style they deserved. Science was the culture of the future, religion the culture of the past; thus it was everyone's duty to remove all institutional — that is, clerical — obstacles to science's advance.[70]

The strongest citadels in theology's line of defence were, in Huxley's judgement, Oxford and Cambridge. Huxley was glad to see provincial universities and university colleges established in England, and he worked hard to make respectable the Royal College of Science in South Kensington; but, like most other university reformers, he had a fixation on Oxbridge. The two ancient universities remained overwhelmingly the most important institutions of higher education in England. They conferred high status on their graduates and fellows, and they transmitted from generation to generation the values and mental habits of the ruling orders. Not only did they train the clergy, but they also shielded the governing elite from the modern scientific style of thought. Through their examinations the universities powerfully influenced the curricula of secondary and even elementary schools. Hence Huxley knew that if the universities could be reformed, the changes would reverberate through the governing orders and the nation's schools.

Reformed in what ways? To Huxley and other scientific propagandists, the reforms required were: (1) destruction of the clerical monopoly on university appointments and curricula; (2) provision of sufficient career opportunities for men of science; (3) introduction of natural science into the studies of all students; (4) broadening of the range of studies offered, so that all branches of knowledge were available for specialised study; and (5) conversion of the universities into great engines for producing new knowledge.

Scientists like Huxley wanted to have professional careers for scientists established at Oxford and Cambridge; but their impulses towards professionalization were related to university reform in a more general, albeit indirect, way. English culture had to be altered so that the elite would become more appreciative of the scientific mentality and therefore more hospitable to scientists. Furthermore, since the scientists defined the scientific enterprise in terms of research, they believed that university appointments should be altered to subsidize research instead of preparation for legal and clerical careers. Thus the scientists wanted to create what for England would be a new kind of university. Yet no more than Playfair did they want to destroy the status-conferring power of Oxbridge; so they did not seek to change them into technical schools or to break their links to the governing elite. These factors combined in Huxley's mind to produce a complicated concept of the universities and university science, in which an expanded number of scientists, enjoying the status and security of professionals, were to pursue pure research in institutions devoted both to the advancement of knowledge and the liberal education of a governing elite.

Huxley usually presented his ideas for university reform by contrasting the ideal with the reality of Oxford and Cambridge. He believed that in their current condition:

> What we call our great seats of learning are simply 'boarding schools' for bigger boys; that learned men are not more numerous in them than out of them; that the advancement of knowledge is not the object of the fellows of the colleges; that in the philosophic, calm, and meditative stillness of their greenswarded courts philosophy does not thrive, and meditation bears few fruits.[71]

The universities were not places for either men of 'learning and research' or 'zealous cultivators of science'. If someone wanted to know about the 'scientific or literary activity of modern England', he would waste his time visiting the universities. Oxford and Cambridge thus stood in sad contrast to German universities:

> And, as for works of profound research on any subject, and, above all, in that classical lore for which the universities profess to sacrifice almost everything else, why, a third-rate, poverty-stricken German university turns out in one year more produce of that kind than our vast and wealthy foundations elaborate in ten.[72]

In the ideal university, Huxley thought, a man should be able to get instruction in all branches of knowledge, and get it from the ablest researchers: 'In such a University, the force of living example should fire the student with a noble ambition to emulate the learning of learned men, and to follow in the footsteps of the explorers of the new fields of knowledge.'[73] This model implied that the main method of teaching would be the lecture (including demonstrations in the natural sciences) rather than the tutorial; a change which alone would have altered the universities significantly. Moreover, the old English universities offered no careers to those interested in learning as such. They offered no pattern of advancement by merit in research, or even promotion by the decision of one's peers. In Germany, Huxley said, the universities were 'corporations of learned men devoting their lives to the cultivation of science, and the direction of academical education'. The judgement of learned men in Germany came from their peers, not from 'a mob of country parsons':

The Germans dominate the intellectual world by virtue of the same simple secret as that which made Napoleon the master of old Europe. They have declared *la carrière ouverte aux talents*, and every Bursch marches with a professor's gown in his knapsack.[74]

In wishing to make the universities operate according to the principle of the career open to talent, Huxley and the other scientist-reformers were applying one of the fundamental tenets of bourgeois liberal ideology to their concept of professionalism. Other principles drawn from liberal ideology also shaped this vision of professional science, research and the universities. One was the division of labour, a phrase used again and again to give positive justification for specialization. Science progresses, they said, partly because each researcher investigates his particular subject without having to know the whole. One did not need to be a genuis to make a contribution; indeed, they thought that above all England needed an institutional structure providing support for the rank and file of researchers — the geniuses seemed to be able to provide for themselves.[75] Another liberal principle was that the state should not provide what private effort was able to do. The scientists disagreed among themselves as to the application of this principle, but they agreed with Huxley that the fabulous endowments of Oxford and Cambridge could be turned to the support of science without violation of political economy.[76]

Yet while Huxley and many of his colleagues imported liberal principles into their ideas about support for science, they also promoted an anti-liberal principle — namely, their drive for professionalization itself. Professions characteristically sought for their members a place outside the dictates of the market-place, a position based on exclusive knowledge and expertise which the public was supposed to respect and need but not understand or question. Professionalization therefore tended to establish new orders of priests, who acted *for* the larger society but who held to themselves the language and procedures of their activities. Huxley promoted professionalization, but he instinctively drew back from its consequence of establishing a new priesthood. His liberal principles, shared widely but not fully by the English scientific community, limited the extent to which he would go towards establishing and endowing professional elites.

The tension between liberal ideals and professionalization in Huxley's thought, and in that of the scientific community in general, was illustrated by certain proposals made in the 1860s and 1870s for endowing research outside the universities. In 1868, Lt Col Alexander Strange made a bold proposal for state support of applied scientific research to the mathematics and physics section of the BAAS. Strange, a retired army officer, had served in the Trigonometrical Survey in India. This post convinced him of the state's need for scientific research and advice. He argued, even more urgently than had Babbage and Brewster, that to survive, all nations must extend and teach physical science. The necessity for teaching science had been recognized, but the 'provision for extending the boundaries of scientific knowledge in England is inadequate and unsystematic'. Modern sciences, he said, require special buildings and costly apparatuses, as well as 'the continuous employment of the highest skill'. Private enterprise cannot meet these requirements; hence 'the State alone can adequately supply the existing want . . .' What he proposed was 'a system of national institutions for the sole purpose of advancing science by practical research, *quite apart from teaching it*'. These national laboratories would be presided over by a body of qualified scientists responsible to a minister of state for science. The council of scientists would direct research and sanction experiments by any qualified member of the scientific public, whether from the universities, industry or elsewhere. Strange believed that this research would be immediately beneficial to the nation, 'whether applied to strictly State purposes, or whether utilized in the public works, the manufactures, and the general necessitites of the nation'.[77]

Colonel Strange's proposal coincided with the longstanding desire of some English scientists to obtain more posts for researchers by way of state support, and with the current concern about the backwardness of British industry. However, the proposal went counter to the orientation towards the universities, towards scientific research as a liberal arts subject, and towards independence from state control. The scientific community, after all, had rejected the old ideas that some agency like the BAAS would direct the research of the rank and file.[78] Thus though the British Association was not ready to accept Strange's proposal, it did appoint a committee to inquire whether there was sufficient provision for scientific research in Britain, and if not, how further provision should be made.[79] The committee, which included Strange, Huxley, Tyndall, Frankland and William Thomson (later Lord Kelvin), were unable to suggest a plan for expanding the provisions for scientific research without having full information as to what provisions already existed. However, they were certain that the existing facilities were 'far from sufficient'. They recommended that a

Royal Commission be appointed to investigate 'the whole question of the relation of the State to science'.[80] The result was a great step in the institutional advance of science and an important index to the growing acceptance of the scientific ideal of knowledge: the Devonshire Commission, which sat for six years and issued eight reports on the conditions of science and scientific research in Britain.

The Devonshire Commission gathered data on practically every agency or institution that supported scientific research or teaching. It heard testimony from the advocates of every way of supporting science. Since the Commissioners assumed that more governmental help was needed for science, they not surprisingly recommended increased support for every variety of scientific activity: technical education at the elementary levels, classes for training science teachers, polytechnics for instruction at the higher levels; universities and university colleges for London and the provinces; professors and facilities at Oxford and Cambridge; individual research grants; and national laboratories for scientific research.[81] Almost all the expert witnesses, including Lords Salisbury and Derby, agreed that somehow more support ought to be given to pure scientific research; that applied research *already* was adequately rewarded; that Britain did not offer enough careers in scientific research; and that Oxford and Cambridge were not the centres of scientific research that they should be.[82] But the general tone of agreement on 'more for science' among the witnesses and the rather indiscriminate recommendations of the Commission masked important differences of opinion in the English scientific community about the role of the state in scientific research, the best location of research institutions, and the question whether scientists ought to teach as well as do research.

Colonel Strange raised all these points of contention in his testimony. In his evidence, given in April 1872, Strange emphasized the need for pure research. He argued that 'science is essential to the advance of civilization, the development of national wealth, and the maintenance of national power'. It followed that 'all science should be cultivated, even the branches of science which do not appear to promise immediate direct advantage'. The state should provide for scientific research whenever private effort did not do so. Not concerned with the establishment of a 'scientific culture', Strange opposed the linkage of scientific research with teaching:

it is one of the opinions on which my mind is convinced that nothing is so wasteful as to employ men highly distinguished for their capacity for investigation in teaching the elements of knowledge. I call that a positively criminal waste of intellect.

Strange had in mind nine national laboratories, to be funded by the state and staffed by state scientists. Other scientists — from the universities, for instance — would also conduct research in the national laboratories; but whoever did the work, the laboratories would be devoted to research in pure science, on which national power ultimately depended. Strange declared that currently the only kind of research done in England was that which led directly to profit; but he was certain that 'A great nation must not act in the commercial spirit.' One cannot predict, he said, the practical applications of fundamental discoveries, though one can be sure that all discoveries will find their applications: 'A civilized people should believe that all knowledge of nature is valuable, and act on that belief.'[83]

One of the most enthusiastic advocates of Strange's various proposals was Norman Lockyer, secretary to the Devonshire Commission, astronomer, promoter of science, former civil servant and editor of the most influential scientific journal of the day, *Nature*.[84] Lockyer had made *Nature*, which he had helped found in 1869, a vehicle for the expression of the interests of professional scientists and the most vigorous voice of 'the claims of Science to more general recognition in Education and Daily Life'.[85] Leading articles in *Nature* argued strongly for the conversion of Oxbridge into research institutions by redirection of their college endowments towards support of research in science and other fields. Lockyer associated *Nature*, and by implication, the whole professional scientific community, with a university group devoted to what was called 'the endowment of research'. This movement, as we shall see in Chapter 6, had much success in publicizing the view that there should be established and endowed in the universities an elite of scholars devoted to the production of knowledge for its own sake. One policy held by some participants in this movement was a withdrawal from teaching, and Lockyer joined Strange in denying that a scientist should teach in order to have his research subsidised:

We believe that powers of teaching and powers of investigation by no means go together, though they are united in some great men like Mr.Huxley; and we believe, further, that on this ground alone the idea of making a man teach in order that he may carry on researches is bad in principle: it is even worse than this, because it is apt to cause the public to underrate research — to think that the end of all research is to teach, while in point of fact the end and aim of the acquisition of all old knowledge is the acquirement of new knowledge.[86]

This vision of autonomous, well-subsidized, full-time research careers located in both national laboratories and universities was extremely attractive to many English scientists, but not to all. Huxley joined the movement to endow research, but the implications of professionalization began to bother him, and he grew concerned about the establishment of a new priesthood. He had argued in public against Matthew Arnold's idea that England needed Academies as authoritative centres of 'correct' thought.[87] He had engaged in hot dispute with English Comtists, partly because he felt that Comte had not shown any real knowledge of natural science, but also because he objected to the authoritarian cast — the secularized popery — of Positivism.[88] In the 1880s and 1890s he used his considerable weight against people like Karl Pearson, who wanted to turn the University of London into a German-style university, dominated by a professoriate accountable to no one. He wrote to a friend: 'That to which I am utterly opposed is the creation of an Established Church Scientific, with a hierarchical organisation and a professorial Episcopate . . .'[89] Huxley had been sensitized by his long struggle with entrenched clerical privilege to the evils of privilege in general. Hence he believed that national laboratories might become 'scientific deaneries', in which the wrong people, through personal favour, might get the appointments. He also thought that there would be no guarantee that a person holding a research appointment would do any work, but that when a scientific appointment was attached to teaching duties, or in some other way was subordinated to public opinion, 'jobbery' was less likely.[90] He agreed wholly with Sir William Thomson and others that the location of research laboratories in universities would contribute to that liberal education which was of benefit to scientists and non-scientists alike.[91]

A second objection to proposals like those of Strange and Lockyer focused on state intervention itself. On this point Huxley did not take the lead, for he had long before decided that in the matter of education the state would have to play an active role. Instead, the case against state subsidy of scientific research was made by a populist element in the scientific community. Some scientists who objected to state intervention were scientific opponents of Lockyer. They considered that Lockyer, who had been equipped by the government with a solar physics laboratory in South Kensington, was working to feather his own nest. Indeed, they thought of the Devonshire Commission as the 'mere tools and catspaws of a needy and designing confederacy', of which the leaders were Strange and Lockyer.[92] Lockyer's principal scientific opponent, Richard Proctor, argued that there was a conflict between pure science and government support, for the state might undermine the disinterestedness necessary to pure science.[93] A more principled case against state support of science came from Alfred Russel Wallace, co-discoverer with Darwin of the evolutionary hypothesis and active political Radical. Wallace opposed any legislation that favoured one class or section of the population over another. He accepted the idea of a state educational system, which was for all, but not that of technical education, which would be for the manufacturers. He wrote to *Nature:* 'The broad principle I go upon is this — that the State has no moral right to apply funds raised by the taxation of all its members to any purpose which is not directly available for the benefit of all.' Scientific laboratories and museums were really of value only to those interested in advanced science. Scientific and technical education ought to be paid for by the manufacturers who benefited from them. Men of science should look to private benefactors for extensive laboratories and apparatus, as they had done in the past. Of course, he admitted, every scientific discovery is 'more or less valuable' to the general public; but like the study of old china or stamps, most scientific research is of interest only to a relatively small circle of students.[94]

The blast that Wallace's views elicited from *Nature* suggests that he had touched a sensitive spot in the self-image of most Victorian scientists.[95] English scientists had throughout the century argued that science is beneficial, directly and indirectly, to everyone. It is safe to say that only a tiny minority at most agreed with Wallace about the proper status and functions of science. Perhaps the best expression of the majority view among English scientists on the subjects of state interference with scientific research and public accountability of researchers came from the BAAS. In March 1876, the Council of the British Association sent two deputations to the government to urge implementation of the recommendations of the Devonshire Commission. The deputations, led by Lyon Playfair and Sir John Hawkshaw (president of the British Association), had as their main objects three matters: (1) the study of scientific subjects in elementary and endowed schools; (2) 'the endowment of research'; and (3) the appointment of a minister of science and art. As to the endowment of research, the British Association took, according to *Nature,* a moderate course: 'There would be no objection to the course of liberally endowing professorships in the several Universities, combining the duty of original research with a moderate amount of teaching to be attached to the professorship . . .'[96] This was a formulation that Huxley and the mainstream of English scientists could agree with, and it nicely summarized the institutional objectives of the professional scientists.

For a variety of reasons in the minds of the advocates of science — reasons partly intellectual, partly social, and partly political — the broad effort to advance the claims of science had potent implications for the national university structure. And the real effect of the 'rise of science' on the universities was by the end of the century very impressive. For one thing, a number of provincial university colleges had been founded, all of them with a pronounced emphasis on scientific training and research. One of them, Owens College, had become the central element in a new university, the Victoria University.[97] For another, the University of London had grown into a large institution with science well established in most of its colleges, and the constituent elements of what would in the twentieth century become Imperial College had been founded at South Kensington, including the Royal College of Science and the Royal School of Mines. At Oxford and Cambridge, honours courses in the natural sciences were introduced at mid-century. The number of scientific professorships grew from 13 in 1850 to 26 in 1900 (not counting those in mathematics and medicine). Oxford got the Science Museum in 1860 and the Clarendon Laboratory in 1872; Cambridge the Cavendish Laboratory in 1874. Clerk Maxwell turned the Cavendish into one of the leading centres of theoretical physics in the world, and Michael Foster, a protégé of Huxley, established at Cambridge a major physiological research laboratory and school of researchers.[98] The scientific posts at both universities by 1900 were all regarded as research positions with some teaching duties attached. Further, Huxley himself was offered the Linacre Chair in Comparative Anatomy in Oxford and the mastership of University College in 1881; he received honorary degrees from Cambridge in 1879 and Oxford in 1885. He enjoyed seeing the evolutionary hypothesis, once so hotly disputed by conservative theologians, accepted at both universities. In 1892, Huxley wrote to a friend to advise him where to send his son to study science: 'A very good scientific education is to be had at both Cambridge and Oxford, especially Cambridge now.'[99] He even sent his own son to Oxford.

Late-Victorian scientific research, then, found its home in the universities. The number of university positions in science and technology grew from about sixty in 1850 to more than four hundred in 1900. A few other forms of support of scientific research made some headway in the last decades of the century — for instance, an annual government grant to the Royal Society for distribution as personal research stipends was increased from £1,000 to £4,000 — but overall the non-university effort was not impressive. This fact, which was in large part the outcome of deliberate choice by the newly professionalizing scientists, had unfortunate effects on English industry. As Roy MacLeod has observed, 'Unwittingly, the endowment of research movement helped drive a barrier between science and its industrial applications.'[100] English industry suffered in competition with German and American industries in the last three decades of the century partly because it failed to integrate scientific research into the productive process; and a major cause of that failure was the aversion of scientists to what they regarded as the taint of applied research. In seeking improved status and support for professional careers, English scientists had been attracted by the old universities and consequently allowed their idea of the functions of science to be shaped by these ancient institutions.

In its detachment from the industrial process, English science was less a part of the general culture in 1900 than in 1830. There were other senses in which that seemingly paradoxical proposition was true. As Professors Shapin and Thackray have observed, it was in the years from 1870 to 1900, the years of the 'triumph' of science, that the divorce was effected between 'natural knowledge and the general culture'.[101] The political and social elite retained their preference for a literary, if not classical, education; thus England did not become a scientific nation. Moreover, the destruction of natural theology by science had removed a vital sanction for amateur botanizing and geological observation; indeed, that destruction removed natural knowledge from the list of essential elements of the generally accepted world view. Educated people in 1900 accepted that science would provide the best understanding of the world and of a wide range of human experience, but they did not have access to the latest scientific knowledge themselves. They had to accept that the scientists possessed the knowledge. The effort of the scientists to elevate themselves professionally grew out of a sense of community among the scientists, and that effort propagated an image of the community for the general public. One aspect of the public image was the desire by scientists to isolate themselves from the economic and social demands of the public — the opting for endowment rather than for support by the market-place. To the extent that this condition of separateness rubbed off on other producers of ideas, they too would become part of an isolated stratum of society.

The ideal of separateness did rub off on other people, and not least in the universities. As Mark Pattison, Rector of Lincoln College, Oxford, observed in 1885: 'It is to the silent permeative genius of science that the growth of a large and comprehensive view of the function of the University and the desire to discharge it has spread among us.'[102] Thus the 'rise of science' involved not only the defeat of religious orthodoxy and the proliferation of scientific posts, but also the spread to other fields of the scientific ideal of knowledge and its acquisition.

## Notes

1. Beatrice Webb, *My Apprenticeship* (London, 1926), pp. 126-7.

2. Susan Budd, 'The Loss of Faith in England, 1850-1950', *Past and Present* (April 1967), pp. 106-25; and *Varieties of Unbelief: Atheists and Agnostics in English Society, 1850-1960* (London, 1977), Ch. 4; Edward Royle (ed.), *The Infidel Tradition from Paine to Bradlaugh* (London, 1976); and Hugh McLeod, *Class and Religion in the Late Victorian City* (London, 1974).

3. K.S. Inglis, *Churches and the Working Classes in Victorian England* (London, 1963).

4. Owen Chadwick, *The Victorian Church* (2 parts, London, 1966 and 1970), I, Ch. VIII; II, Chs. I, II, III, VIII; Josef Altholz, 'The Warfare of Conscience with Theology', in Josef Altholz (ed.), *The Mind and Art of Victorian England* (Minneapolis, 1976), pp. 58-77; and Howard R. Murphy, 'The Ethical Revolt against Christian Orthodoxy in Early Victorian England', *American Historical Review* (July 1955), pp. 800-17.

5. Murphy, 'Ethical Revolt against Christian Orthodoxy', *passim;* Altholz, 'Warfare of Conscience with Theology', pp. 60-5.

6. Chadwick, *Victorian Church,* II, p. 109.

7. Ibid., pp. 1-3.

8. Francis Galton, *English Men of Science: Their Nature and Nurture* (London, 1874), pp. 95-8; Victor L. Hilts, 'A Guide to Francis Galton's *English Men of Science', Transactions of the American Philosophical Society,* vol. 65, part 5, new series (Philadelphia, 1975), p. 30.

9. Robert M. Young, 'Natural Theology, Victorical Periodicals, and the Fragmentation of the Common Context', pp. 13-25 (paper presented to the King's College Research Seminar on Science, 1969); Chadwick, *Victorian Church,* II, pp. 30-1.

10. Baden Powell, 'On the Study of the Evidences of Christianity', in *Essays and Reviews,* by Frederick Temple, H.B. Wilson *et al.,* 8th edn. (London, 1861), p. 128.

11. Chadwick, *Victorian Church,* II, pp. 75-77; Basil Willey, *More Nineteenth Century Studies: A Group of Honest Doubters* (London, 1956), Ch. IV.

12. Chadwick, *Victorian Church,* II, p. 31.

13. This interpretation disputes that of Robert M. Young, in 'Natural Theology, Victorian Periodicals, and the Fragmentation of the Common Content.'

14. J.H. Newman, *Scope and Nature of University Education* (Everyman's edn, London, 1915), p. 54.

15. Chadwick, *Victorian Church,* II, pp. 450-2.

16. Ibid., p. 84.

17. Ibid., p. 11; Altholz, 'Warfare of Conscience with Theology', pp. 62-3, 75-7. The Huxley-Wilberforce debate has been described many times, perhaps most dramatically in William-Irvine, *Apes, Angels, and Victorians* (first published 1955; paperback edn, Cleveland, Ohio, 1959), pp. 3-7.

18. Figures given in Hilts, 'Guide to Galton's *English Men of Science*', p. 14.

19. Galton, *English Men of Science*, pp. 16-18.

20. Robert Kargon, *Science in Victorian Manchester: Enterprise and Expertise* (Baltimore, 1977), pp. 101-8.

21. Quoted in Ibid., p. 108.

22. For biographical information, see Wemyss Reid, *Memoirs and Correspondence of Lyon Playfair* (New York, 1899); and J.G. Crowther, *Statesmen of Science* (London, 1965), pp. 105-71.

23. Quoted in Kargon, *Science in Victorian Manchester,* p. 92.

24. Ibid., pp. 117-20.

25. Reid, *Playfair,* pp. 131-3.

26. Reginald Pound, *Albert: A Biography of the Prince Consort* (London, 1973), p. 236; Roger Fulford, *The Prince Consort* (London, 1949), p. 225.

27. Sir Charles Phipps to Playfair, September 27, 1851; quoted in Reid, *Playfair,* p. 136.

28. D.S.L. Cardwell, *The Organisation of Science in England* (London, 1957), pp. 68-9, 110, 131-2, 143-4; Cyril Bibby, *T.H. Huxley: Scientist, Humanist and Educator* (New York, 1960), pp. 115-22.

29. Cardwell, *Organisation of Science in England,* pp. 84-5.

30. 'Answers from Chambers of Commerce as to Technical Education', *Parliamentary Papers*, (vol. LIV, c. 168,1868).

31. Quoted in Reid, *Playfair,* p. 153.

32. For instance, in the *Royal Commission on the Great Depression in Trade and Industry, First Report* (vol. XXI, c. 4621, 1886), the response to a circular addressed to chambers of commerce rarely mention a lack of technical education as a major cause of economic difficulties. The responses by the chambers of commerce in Leeds (p. 91) and Macclesfield (p. 96) *did* mention technical education.

33. *Report from the Select Committee on the Provisions for Giving Theoretical and Applied Science to the Industrial Classes, Parliamentary Papers*, (vol. XV, c. 432,1867-68), p. 57.

34. Ibid., pp. 63-4.

35. Playfair's Presidential Address is reprinted in Basalla, Coleman and Kargon (eds.), *Victorian Science,* pp. 64-83. See especially p. 80.

36. Ibid., p. 76.

37. Quoted in Kargon, *Science in Victorian Manchester,* p. 135.

38. Joseph Ben-David, *The Scientist's Role in Society: A Comparative Study* (Englewood Cliffs, New Jersey, 1971), Ch. 7; Fritz Ringer, 'Higher Education in Germany in the Nineteenth Century', *Journal of Contemporary History* (July 1967), pp. 123-38; Fritz Ringer, *The Decline of the German Mandarins: The German Academic Community, 1890-1933* (Cambridge, Mass., 1969), Chs. 1 and 2; Alan Beyerchen, *Scientists Under Hitler: Politics and the Physics Community in the Third Reich* (New Haven, 1977), Ch. 1.

39. From his Presidential Address to the BAAS, in Basalla, Coleman and Kargon (eds.), *Victorian Science,* p. 82.

40. Kargon, *Science in Victorian Manchester,* pp. 163-4.

41. Sir Henry Enfield Roscoe, *The Life and Experiences of Sir Henry Enfield Roscoe* (London, 1906), especially, pp. 101-4 and 167; Kargon, *Science in Victorian Manchester,*

Ch. 5; and Michael Sanderson, *The Universities and British Industry, 1850-1970* (London, 1973) Chs. 3 and 4.

42. *Saturday Review* (No. 42, 1876), p. 203.

43. Quoted in Kargon, *Science in Victorian Manchester,* pp. 158-9. For a similar statement by Roscoe, see the quote from his speech to the Chemical Society in 1891, in *Life of Sir Henry Enfield Roscoe,* pp. 172-3.

44. Quoted in Kargon, *Science in Victorian Manchester,* p. 224.

45. I have learned much about Huxley's psychological condition and religious attitudes from David Roos, 'Matthew Arnold, Thomas Henry Huxley, and the Rhetoric of Friendship and Controversy', unpublished PhD thesis, University of Chicago, 1979, Ch. II.

46. Quoted in ibid., Ch. II, p. 39.

47. Ibid., Ch. II, p. 31.

48. See, for instance, his book on *Hume* (London, 1878), later republished as *Hume, with Helps to the Study of Berkeley* (vol. VI of *Collected Essays,* 1894); and 'Agnosticism' in *Collected Essays,* vol. V, pp. 209-62.

49. Roos, 'Arnold and Huxley', Ch. II, p. 9.

50. Julian Huxley (ed.), *T.H. Huxley's Diary of the Voyage of H.M.S. Rattlesnake* (New York, 1936), p. 99.

51. Ibid., pp. 90-3.

52. Quoted in Roos, Ch. II, p. 31.

53. T.H. Huxley, *Autobiography,* in Charles Darwin and Thomas Henry Huxley, *Autobiographies,* edited by Gavin de Beer (London, 1974), pp. 108-9.

54. Quoted in Leonard Huxley, *Life and Letters of Thomas Henry Huxley* (2 vols., New York, 1901), I, p. 72.

55. Quoted in ibid., I, pp. 74-5.

56. To his fiancée, November 7, 1851. Quoted in ibid., I, p. 75.

57. The best discussion of Huxley's efforts on behalf of science is William Irvine's brilliant *Apes, Angels, and Victorians.* See also Bibby, *T.H. Huxley: Scientist, Humanist and Educator;* and Houston Peterson, *Huxley: Prophet of Science* (New York, 1932).

58. J. Vernon Jensen, 'The X Club: Fraternity of Victorian Scientists', *The British Journal for the History of Science* (June 1970), pp. 63-72; Roy MacLeod, 'The X Club: A Scientific Network in Late-Victorian England,' *Notes and Records of the Royal Society* (December 1970), pp. 305-22.

59. Frank Miller Turner, *Between Science and Religion: The Reaction to Scientific Naturalism in Late Victorian England* (New Haven, 1974), Ch. 2.

60. W.H. Brock and R.M. MacLeod, 'The Scientists' Declaration: Reflexions on Science and Belief in the Wake of *Essays and Reviews,* 1864-5', *The British Journal for the History of Science* (March 1976), pp. 39-66. This is an account of the declaration by some scientists that science did not conflict with religion. See also Chadwick, *Victorian Church,* II, pp. 1-8. In 'Resources of Science in Victorian England: The Endowment of Science Movement, 1868-1900', Roy MacLeod discusses some of the disputes within the scientific community (see Peter Mathias (ed.), *Science and Society, 1600-1900* (Cambridge, 1972), pp. 111-66).

61. T.H. Huxley, 'On the Advisableness of Improving Natural Knowledge', *Collected Essays* (New York, 1902), I, p. 25. (First published in 1866).

62. Ibid., p. 31.

63. T.H. Huxley, 'The Progress of Science, 1837-1887', *Collected Essays,* I, pp. 56-7. (First delivered in 1887).

64. Ibid., p. 53.

65. T.H. Huxley, 'On the Educational Value of the Natural History Sciences', *Collected Essays* (New York, 1894), III, pp. 45 and 59. (First delivered in 1859). Italics his.

66. T.H. Huxley, 'Science and Culture', *Collected Essays,* III, pp. 141-3. (First delivered in 1880).

67. 'Report of A Committee of the British Association for the Advancement of Science and Technology, on the Best Means for Promoting Scientific Education in the Schools', *Parliamentary Papers,* (vol. LIV, c. 137, 1867-8), p. 3.

68. Huxley, 'On the Advisableness of Improving Natural Knowledge', pp. 33-40. See also Herbert Spencer, *The Principles of Sociology* (Westminster Edn of the Complete Works, New York, 1896), part VII, 'Professional Institutions', especially pp. 181-4.

69. Lyell, Darwin and Hooker also supported Bishop Colenso. Chadwick, *Victorian Church,* II, p. 95. See also Roos, 'Arnold and Huxley', Ch. III.

70. Huxley, 'On the Advisableness of Improving Natural Knowledge', p. 41. See also Huxley's essays: 'A Liberal Education and Where to Find It', *Macmillan's Magazine* (March 1868), pp. 367-78; 'Scientific Education: Notes of An After-Dinner Speech', *Collected Essays,* III, pp. 111-33; and 'Science and Culture', pp. 134-59.

71. Huxley, 'A Liberal Education and Where to Find It', p. 376.

72. Ibid., p. 377.

73. T.H. Huxley, 'Universities: Actual and Ideal', *Collected Essays,* III, p. 205.

74. Huxley, 'A Liberal Education and Where to Find It', pp. 377-8.

75. See Francis Galton, *English Men of Science: Their Nature and Nurture,* pp. 167-9; the evidence of Henry Enfield Roscoe in *Report of the Select Committee on Scientific Instruction* (1867-68), pp. 284-6; and the evidence of Sir William Thomson, in the *Royal Commission on Science and Scientific Instruction, Minutes of Evidence* (vol. II, c. 958, 1874), p. 111.

76. For example, see the evidence of Henry Enfield Roscoe to the *Royal Commission on Science and Scientific Instruction: Second Report* (vol. XXV, c. 536, 1872), p. 513; and *Nature* (August 28, 1873), p. 354.

77. Lt Col Alexander Strange, 'On the Necessity for State Intervention to Secure the Progress of Physical Science', *Report of the Thirty-Eighth Meeting of the British Association for the Advancement of Science* (1868), (London, 1869), pp. 6-8.

78. Cannon, *Science in Culture,* Chs. 6 and 7.

79. *Report of the Thirty-Eighth Meeting of the British Association,* p. xlviii. See also, 'Science Reform', *Nature* (December 2, 1869), pp. 127-8.

80. *Report of the Thirty-Ninth Meeting of the British Association for the Advancement of Science* (1869), (London, 1870), pp. 213-14.

81. There are accounts of the Devonshire Commission in Crowther, *Statesmen of Science,* pp. 213-33; Cardwell, *Organisation of Science in England,* pp. 92-8; and A.J. Meadows, *Science and Controversy: A Biography of Sir Norman Lockyer* (London, 1972), Ch. IV.

82. See the conclusions by the Commission: *Royal Commission on Scientific Instruction and the Advancement of Science: Third Report* (vol. XXVIII, c. 868, 1873), pp. vii-viii and xxvi-lvii; and *Eighth Report* (vol. XXVIII, c. 1298, 1875), pp. 8-9, 22, and 27-46. For particularly important evidence, see that by Sir William Thomson, *Second Report* (vol. XXV, c. 536, 1872), pp. 160-71; Henry Enfield Roscoe, *Second Report,* pp. 497-514; James Prescott Joule, *Minutes of Evidence* (vol. II, c. 958, 1874), pp. 100-4; Earl of Derby, *Minutes of Evidence* (1874), pp. 338-44; and Marquess of Salisbury, *Minutes of Evidence* (1874), pp. 344-50.

83. *Minutes of Evidence* (vol. II, c. 958, 1874), pp. 75-92.

84. For Lockyer's career, see Meadows, *Science and Controversy: A Biography of Sir Norman Lockyer;* and T. Mary Lockyer and Winifred Lockyer, *Life and Work of Norman Lockyer* (London, 1928).

85. Quoted from the statement of purpose in *Nature* (January 20, 1870), p. 323. For the founding of *Nature,* see the series of centenary articles by Roy MacLeod in *Nature* (November 1, 1969), pp. 423-56.

86. 'Professor Huxley at Aberdeen', *Nature* (March 5, 1874), p. 338. Also see 'Science Reform', *Nature* (December 2, 1869), pp. 127-8.

87. See, for example, Huxley's 'On Coral and Coral Reefs', *Critiques and Addresses* (New York, 1973; first published in *Good Words,* 1876), pp. 111-14. This issue is discussed in Roos, 'Arnold and Huxley', Ch. III.

88. Sydney Eisen, 'Huxley and the Positivists', *Victorian Studies* (June 1964), pp. 337-58.

89. Quoted in Bibby, *Huxley: Scientist, Humanist and Educator,* p. 227.

90. Huxley made these remarks as a member of the Devonshire Commission during the testimony of Lord Salisbury. See *Minutes of Evidence* (1874), p. 348.

91. Sir William Thomson, testimony to the Devonshire Commission, *Second Report* (1872), p. 163.

92. Quoted in MacLeod, 'Resources of Science in Victorian England', p. 155. See also Meadows, *Science and Controversy,* Ch. IV.

93. MacLeod, 'Resources of Science in Victorian England', pp. 155-6.

94. Alfred Russel Wallace, letters to the editor, *Nature* (January 13, 1870), pp. 288-9; and (January 20, 1870), p. 315.

95. 'Government Aid to Science', *Nature* (January 13, 1870), pp. 279-80.

96. 'Scientific Instruction and the Advancement of Science', *Nature* (March 9, 1876), p. 371.

97. For the 'red brick' universities, see W.H.G. Armytage, *Civic Universities* (London, 1955), Chs. 8-10; and Sanderson, *Universities and British Industry,* Chs. 2-4.

98. Gerald L. Gieson, *Michael Foster and the Cambridge School of Physiology: The Scientific Enterprise in Late Victorian Society* (Princeton, 1978).

99. Quoted in Huxley, *Huxley,* II, p. 338.

100. MacLeod, 'Resources of Science in Victorian England', p. 163.

101. Shapin and Thackray, 'Prosopography as a Research Tool in the History of Science: The British Scientific Community, 1700-1900', *History of Science,* vol. XII (1974), p. 11.

102. Mark Pattison, *Memoirs,* p. 305.

# 5 THE IMPACT OF SCIENCE: THE CASE OF HISTORY

Victorian scientists, in pursuit of high status careers, chose to settle in the universities. Moreover, their concept of the scientific enterprise required a re-orientation of the universities from teaching to research and the alteration of at least part of the university faculty from tutors to research professors. The influence of natural science in England by the late-nineteenth century was so great that the presence of an enlarged number of professional scientists by itself would have altered the universities, and this alteration alone would have constituted an important change in English intellectual life. But science had an equally great impact by another route — it deeply affected the nature of almost all the other disciplines. The 'silent and permeative genius' of natural science, more than any other factor, converted many fields of intellectual activity into professional disciplines. Workers in these fields then sought places in the universities and so redoubled the impact of science on university life. Hence, as the workers in each of the crystallizing disciplines came to define their activities as scientific, they developed new ideas of their proper cultural functions and new relations with the society at large.

The emergence of disciplines — that is, the division of profound efforts to understand the world and human experience into separate, self-conscious, and autonomous enterprises — was deeply shaped but not caused solely by the model of natural science. Not even specialization, which was only one aspect of the development of professional disciplines, was caused by science alone. Nor was specialization simply the consequence of the explosion in knowledge. The volume of knowledge most certainly did increase during the first half of the nineteenth century, but the early Victorian response was mainly to put a premium on synthesis, not on specialization, in order to cope with it. Indeed, specialization itself contributed powerfully to the further expansion of knowledge; thus at least at first specialization was more a cause than a consequence of the knowledge revolution of the nineteenth century.

To understand the causes of specialization in England, one has to look not only to the model provided by science, but also to the fundamental sources of the research impulse — the desire to add to knowledge by systematic investigation — and to the basic ideas that provided a rationale for specialized learning. Behind the research impulse lay a number of vast and potent forces in the minds of Englishmen, including: (1) the empirical spirit, the desire propagated during the Enlightenment to know more about physical and human nature through observation of material events; (2) the romantic fascination with details — the unique in nature; and (3) the impulse from natural theology to know God through the study of nature and human history.

The rationale whereby deep and concentrated investigation was focused into specialities came from a reverence for the principle of the division of labour. Together the research impulse and the principle of the division of labour eventually counteracted the powerful Victorian need for synthesis and generalization. From the time of the publication of Adam Smith's *An Inquiry into the Nature and Causes of the Wealth of Nations,* the division of labour was widely regarded as the key to England's power and prosperity.[1] Darwin's evolutionary hypothesis seemed to show the universal applicability of the division of labour for each individual and species adapted to its special circumstances. Herbert Spencer, the most sweeping and influential evolutionary philosopher, offered a complete — and to the Victorians, a very satisfying — account of social development in terms of the division of labour. As societies progress from primitive to advanced levels, they change by a process of differentiation: all professions have differentiated out of the 'primitive politico-ecclesiastical agency' — for example, surgeons from priestly medicine-men, and physicians from the surgeons; dancers and musicians from the priests, and orators and poets from the dancers and musicians.[2] Progress is inevitable because this change moves from simple homogeneity to complex heterogeneity. The Victorians believed, like Spencer, that the division of labour is natural, inevitable, and beneficial. Here is where science had its crucial impact: the scientists after mid-century propagated this view by word and example. Their message and their model could hardly be resisted.

The list of emerging 'sciences' in Victorian England is long — philology, sociology, anthropology, economics, political science and psychology, among others. By the 1880s even education, literary study and theology made claims to be sciences.[3] One of the most important and dramatic examples of the formation and professionalization of disciplines along scientific lines was history. Its path to the status of a scientific enterprise was not exactly like that of the other disciplines, for each followed its own route; but history was important because of its enormous popularity and influence among the Victorians, for whom the 'genetic' turn of mind was a fundamental intellectual characteristic, and it was dramatic because it involved an exceptionally sharp change from history as *literature* to history as *science*. In 1828, Macaulay wrote: 'History, at least in its state of ideal perfection, is a compound of poetry and philosophy. It impresses general truths on the mind by a vivid representation of particular characters and incidents.'[4] In 1902, J.B. Bury, in his inaugural address as Regius Professor of Modern History at Cambridge, declared that though history 'may supply material for literary art or philosophical speculation, she is herself simply a science, no less and no more'.[5] Between these equally remarkable statements stood an immense change in the concept of the historical enterprise, in many ways illustrative of the changing contours of Victorian intellectual life.

The transformation of Victorian historiography has often been depicted in terms of progress from error to truth, ignorance to enlightenment, or in terms of the development of historical methods from primitive to advanced.[6] To interpret the transformation in this manner, however, is to commit the same sin of present-mindedness of which the early Victorian historians were justly accused. What really lay behind the changed concept of history was a completely altered perception of the social and cultural functions of history, with significant institutional consequences. History in the world of the men of letters like Macaulay was a coherent operation with procedures and critical standards consistent with its functions and those of other forms of literature. The different social and cultural functions of academic historians like Stubbs, Maitland and Bury towards the end of the century required different procedures and standards as well as institutional settings.

In the early and mid-Victorian years (1830s through the 1860s), history, like the literature of which it formed a part, was intimately associated with the needs of the literate public. As Rosemary Jann has put it, the main features of historical writing in the time of the men of letters 'all derive from one basic contrast: the "age of history" was also an age of rapid and unprecedented change'.[7] Amidst the intense sense of change wrought by the population explosion, industrialization, urbanization and political turmoil, the reading public wanted to establish continuities with the past, to be assured that English institutions were sound, to use the past as a guide through perilous times, and to secure a basis for hope that continuing change would be beneficial. Hence the early and mid-Victorians were profoundly historically-minded: they approached their public issues in historical terms; and they constructed myths of parliamentary freedom and individual liberty which gave them a national identity.[8]

The Victorians needed a particular kind of history — one with strong continuities with imaginative literature. It is worth remembering that many of the best novels were historical — Scott's *Ivanhoe* and the Waverley novels, Thackeray's *Barry Lyndon* and *Henry Esmond,* Dickens' *Barnaby Rudge* and *Tale of Two Cities,* and George Eliot's *Middlemarch* to name only a few. Like the novelists, the historians were supposed to educate as well as entertain. Most historians responded by trying to give the public support and comfort through emphasis on the continuities between past and present, the relevance of past events to present issues, and the survival of time-honoured causes and institutions. The Whig historians — Palgrave, Hallam, Macaulay and others — provided support and political advice by celebrating the evolution of the proudest elements of nineteenth-century English life — the rule of law, the supremacy of parliament and the liberty of the individual. Not all the early and mid-Victorian historians agreed with the Whigs in their sense of finality — their sense that their own times were the climax of historical progress — but in their present-mindedness, in their conscious approach to the past through the needs and interests of the present, all the early and mid-Victorian historians were Whiggish — James Mill and Carlyle as well as Macaulay.[9]

Their primary concern with current public issues made many of the Victorian historians highly partisan. In their partisanship, the early-nineteenth century historians were carrying on a tradition begun in the seventeenth century, when legal and constitutional precedent had been used to dispute crucial constitutional issues. In the 1830s and 1840s, history was consciously written by Tories, Whigs, and Radicals alike to justify their policies. George Grote, a philosophic Radical, wrote his *History of Greece* to overturn the Tory praise of despotism offered by Mitford; Hallam wrote his *Constitutional History* to counteract Hume's conservative account. Macaulay bludgeoned Tory interpretations in his historical essays, and all of his historical works showed the effects of his training in the political brawls of the *Edinburgh Review.*[10] Yet Macaulay's *History of England from the Accession of James II* (published 1848-55), grew out of a different kind of partisanship. Macaulay's early life coincided with times of violent warfare and revolution. For England to have escaped revolution was to him a great source of satisfaction. Like most early and mid-

Victorian historians, Macaulay shared the view of eighteenth-century conjectural historians, that history should be philosophy teaching by example; and he believed that the purpose of history is to 'supply statesmen with warnings and examples'.[11] But he could not abide the common partisanship of historians, for their disputes threatened to disrupt the consensus established in 1688. He was for the 'trimmers' of 1688 — Halifax and William III — and that made him a Whig in early-Victorian England. He was a partisan for consensus and civil peace.[12]

All of the Victorian historians believed in the didactic function of history, but many of them believed that historical lessons had to do less with specific political issues than with moral law. Here again the influence of Enlightenment philosophical history was strong. The past was regarded as illustrating moral law. Indeed, as religious doubts grew in the minds of both readers and writers of history, history itself tended to become a new sacred text.[13] For Carlyle, who had abandoned orthodox Christianity and imbibed German idealism, history showed the unfolding of God's will. He held that the historian's objective was to reveal the one great truth — that there is a reality superior to the world of matter, and that this divine realm unfolds to overcome the artificial. Thus Carlyle believed that the historian should be a prophet warning of the disastrous consequences of ignoring the great truth.[14] For Thomas Arnold, who was Regius Professor of Modern History at Oxford and author of a widely read *History of Rome* (3 volumes, 1845-6) as well as headmaster of Rugby School, history supplied proof of the operation of unchanging moral laws. As he said in his lectures at Oxford, history sanctions and elaborates moral law, for if one begins the study of the past with the moral notions from the Scriptures, then he can deduce or confirm the laws of human behaviour 'with a certainty equal to that of the most undoubted truths of morals'.[15] Later in the century, J.A. Froude, a disciple of Carlyle, stated this early-Victorian assumption succinctly: history teaches one all-important lesson with distinctness, namely that 'the world is built somehow on moral foundations; that, in the long run, it is well with the good; in the long run, it is ill with the wicked'.[16]

The concept of history as politically or morally instructive led the Victorian historians to try to write long narrative works of striking dramatic power. To do its work, historical writing had to be attractive. According to Macaulay, the talent required of a historian 'bears a considerable affinity to the talent of a great dramatist'.[17]

History, it has been said, [wrote Macaulay] is philosophy teaching by examples. Unhappily, what the philosophy gains in soundness and depth, the examples generally lose in vividness. A perfect historian must possess an imagination sufficiently powerful to make his narrative affecting and picturesque. Yet he must control it so absolutely as to content himself with the materials he finds, and to refrain from supplying deficiencies by additions of his own.[18]

By contrast, an analytical style would have dampened response and dissipated conviction. Like all men of letters, the historians wanted to reach a wide audience. Consequently, they paid much attention to style and emphasized the heroism and villainy of major figures in the past. And since one of their central ideas was to assert the autonomy of the individual against the vast impersonal forces of materialism and political revolution, they made history a series of biographies of public figures.

The inclination towards dramatic narrative of political events was accentuated by the fact that many of the early Victorian historians began their careers writing for the great journals. The journalistic world of the 1830s and 1840s was extremely fast-paced as well as violently partisan. Historians like Macaulay and Froude learned to write very quickly, to make a given body of information go a long way, and to seize attention by emphasizing the controversial and the picturesque. They tended to be aggressively self-confident and dogmatic in judgement and interpretation. Macaulay, for one, was well aware of the pitfalls of journalism; periodicals, he wrote

are not expected to be highly finished. Their natural life is only six weeks. Sometimes their writer is at a distance from the books to which he wants to refer. Sometimes he is forced to hurry through his task in order to catch the post. He may blunder; he may contradict himself; he may break off in the middle of a story ... All this is readily forgiven if there be a certain spirit and vivacity in his style.[19]

Yet Macaulay deliberately adopted dramatic strategems, because he wanted to impress the emotions and the imagination as well as the reason: 'The best portraits are perhaps those in which there is a slight mixture of caricature, and we are not certain that the best histories are not those in which a little of the exaggeration of fictitious narrative is judiciously employed'.[20] Such views led many Victorian historians to paint the past in artificially brilliant colours. Their willingness to assign the imagination as well as the understanding a role in historical interpretation made some of them supply from their own minds information not available from their sources — to invent, for example, speeches or conversations to illustrate important points.[21]

These characteristics, however, do not mean that the early and mid-Victorian historians were deliberately inaccurate or unconcerned with the truth. Rather, they show that Victorian history derived from a concept of truth and an idea of the purpose of history that differed from those of later academic historians. To function as a guide or prophet for the public, the historian — even more than the novelist, who was certainly required by the Victorians to be accurate — had to report the truth. But the Victorian historians, like the other men of letters, did not value knowledge for its own sake. They would have agreed with Macaulay's dictum that 'no past event has any intrinsic importance'. What counts most are the lessons to be learned. 'Facts', Macaulay wrote, 'are the mere dross of history. It is from the abstract truth which interpenetrates them, and lies latent among them, like gold in the ore, that the mass derives its whole value . . .'[22] Given this emphasis on the lessons to be learned from accounts of past epochs, rather than on the reporting of new information, the Victorians concerned themselves more with the truthfulness of a historical account as a whole, with judging the essence of an interpretation, rather than with testing the correspondence of propositions to individual facts. Carlyle, for instance, regarded himself as a 'heroic truth-seeker', but felt that such truth as he sought was to be found by poetic or intuitive insight into the meaning of a train of historical events. Similarly, Macaulay said that no painting and no history 'can present us with the whole truth: but those are the best pictures and the best histories which exhibit such parts of the truth as most nearly produce the effect of the whole'.[23] The Victorian historians, then, simply did not think in terms of making a 'contribution' to the field of history. Their object was not to add to the stock of unassailable facts.

Because of their didactic concept of history, the Victorian historians did not set high store by research in original sources, even though they often did try to immerse themselves in the spirit and temper of the times they were writing about. All of them depended largely on published secondary materials. Carlyle and Macaulay were perhaps the outstanding exceptions to this rule: Carlyle slaved over the letters and speeches of Cromwell and Frederick the Great, and Macaulay gained an unparalleled knowledge of the popular pamphlets, broadsides, and ballads of the late-seventeenth century. Yet even these two made it clear that research and reporting of facts were not their primary aims.

Carlyle positively despised the drudgery of historical research. Macaulay in 1840 published a long article on Ranke without remarking on Ranke's achievements in accumulation and criticism of historical documents.[24] When, after mid-century the English began in the Rolls Series to follow the continental example of publishing original sources, the publications were tainted by the ineptitude of the editing.[25]

The Victorian idea of testing historical evidence (or 'authorities') for truth was not so much correspondence with facts as compatibility with preconceived principles or interpretations. Among the Victorian historians, the utilitarian Grote had the most severe sense of historical evidence, but while his critical appraisal caused him to reject ancient legends as sources of historical information, he none the less composed his twelve-volume *History of Greece* to demonstrate the truth of his cherished view that the democratic, political and social system of Athens 'acted as a stimulus to the creative impulses of genius, and left superior minds unshackled to soar above religious and political routine . . . to become the teachers of posterity'.[26]

If what is meant by 'scientific historian' is one who takes as an end in itself the discovery of new information about the past, or one who devotes himself mainly to the critical examination of original sources, then clearly none of the early and mid-Victorian historians was a scientific historian. Some of them — Kingsley and Froude, to take two Regius Professors of Modern History as examples — denied that history could be a science.[27] Yet there were among the early Victorian historians two schools which did believe that history is a science, albeit a science quite different from that being defined by Huxley and the other practising scientists of the day. One of these schools descended from the philosophic historians of the eighteenth century. Perhaps 'school' is too exalted a label for this species of historian, for in the early-Victorian period, it applied to only two major figures — James Mill and George Grote. Their rationalist predecessors such as David Hume, James Robertson, and Adam Ferguson, were more primitive social scientists than historians. They had studied the past in order to discover and elucidate the universal laws of human behaviour. They believed that human nature is everywhere and at all times the same; thus the historian's task is to show the operation of the abstract principles of human behaviour in different circumstances and stages of progress.[28] Mill and Grote, both Philosophical Radicals, propounded the enlightenment proposition that the advancement of rationalism had been the key to progress. They, too, believed that there could be a science of society, of which the basis would be historical learning. Their interest in past societies was two-fold: firstly, to assess the place of a given society on the scale of enlightenment; and secondly, to apply the lessons from their study to the issues of the present — that is, to advance the cause of democratic political institutions and rationalist education. In the case of Grote, his enthusiasm for Athenian democracy generated considerable sympathy for his subject; but in the case of Mill, his Eurocentric views prevented him from feeling any sympathy for Indian civilizations at all. In both cases, the present-mindedness, the biased use of sources, and the sense of the direct applicability of lessons from the past were much like the attitudes of conventional Whig historians.[29]

The other group of Victorian historians who thought of their history as science were, to use Duncan Forbes's term, the 'Liberal Anglicans' — Thomas Arnold, Richard Whately, J.C. Hare, Connop Thirlwall, H.H. Milman, and A.P. Stanley.[30] These Anglican scholars were part of the romantic reaction against the enlightenment and its English offspring, Utilitariansim. Unlike the Whig historians, they learned much from Vico, Herder, and the German romantic historians, especially Barthhold Niebuhr. But what they learned was not so much the 'scientific method' as the romantic idea of history — that is, each age in the past was 'immediate to God', to use Ranke's phrase. They believed that each period in every nation's history had its own spirit or frame of mind; hence, they rejected the notion that all people at all times are essentially the same.

Like the other Victorian historians, however, the Liberal Anglicans wanted above all to write 'practical' history. They wanted their histories to guide people; thus their intent was didactic and their audience general. They thought of history as a science in that it is most useful when it discovers the general laws of historical process. Yet, though they were relatively well informed about natural science, they were too much in the Idealist philosophical camp to take empirical science as their procedural model. They did not think that a historian stood outside the subject matter and objectively observed it. Rather, the historian in their view was part of the subject matter, both as a product of historical development and as an imaginative participant in the reconstruction of the past. It is, therefore, in the search for the laws that govern historical change that history claims to be a science.

The Liberal Anglicans saw historical change as the rise and development of nations, each nation going through the same cycle of infancy, transition and maturity. For them, history could be a science precisely because of its cyclical character. Science requires more than one instance of a phenomenon in order to allow general inferences. Since historical change is cyclical, it allows for verification of general laws. Universal history in their eyes was a rhythmical pattern of growth and maturity, from which the comparisons of the various nations at analogous stages of development could be made. The study of the past could fulfil its practical function because of the scientific validity of the laws of development. Hence, like the rationalist and Whig historians, the Liberal Anglicans believed in the immediate applicability of the record of the past to the present.

Even though the practitioners of Liberal Anglican history considered their work scientific, they entertained no desire to specialize or to conduct research. In their view, what the historian should try to do is discover the particular stage of development of the state under review, and then relate the circumstances of that stage to the features of other nations at the same stage, and thus to the whole of the past. As believers in the providential course of history, they were concerned as much with the whole as with the parts of the historical record. The scope of their enterprise prevented both specialized study and original research. Arnold, for instance, was powerfully influenced by Niebuhr on the history of Rome, but he thought of his own work as popularizing and moralizing Niebuhr's findings.[31] To know the present well was more important than to conduct deep research into the past. Arnold declared in his lectures at Oxford that only an antiquarian devotes himself to the mere recovery of information about the past; the difference between the antiquarian and the scientific historian is the historian's 'lively and extensive knowledge of the *present*', which stimulates him to deduce the laws of history.[32]

Early and mid-Victorian history came in several different modes — Whig, prophetic, Liberal Anglican, and rationalist — thus there was a remarkable variety of historical styles. These different types of historical writing produced not only differing interpretations of the past, but also different *kinds* of historical explanation. Indeed, history in the time of the men of letters appeared in all the principal forms distinguished by recent theoretical analysts. To use Hayden White's terminology, there were 'Formists' like Carlyle, influenced by the romantic interest in the variety and uniqueness of the phenomena of the past and inclined to make generalizations about the historical process not verifiable by empirical observation. There were 'Organicists' like Thomas Arnold, who had a strong integrative impulse and found satisfaction when the particulars of the past had been synthesized into a whole — a universal history informed by Christian morality. There were 'Mechanists' like James Mill, who wanted to reduce the mass of particulars to the demonstration of a few causal laws. And there were 'Contextualists' — perhaps the best example was Macaulay — who singled out a great event like the Norman Conquest or the Glorious Revolution in order to show its links to surrounding social features and to posterity.[33] Yet whatever the variety of the styles of history, the shared characteristics were of primary importance. All these Victorian historians saw history as a branch of literature, with strong similarities to drama; all believed in the practicality of historical study to public-minded citizens and were consciously present-minded; all concerned themselves more with the truthfulness of the whole account than with meticulous accuracy of detail; all emphasized interpretation rather than research; and all agreed that the central function of history is didactic.

That the reading public agreed with the Victorian historians on the educative function of history is shown by the remarkable popularity of historical works and the status of the historians as national sages. Macaulay's *History of England* (4 volumes, 1848-55) was a phenomenal best-seller — by 1875, 140,000 copies of the set had been sold, and even more in the United States. Lord Halifax wrote to Macaulay amidst the turmoil of 1848: 'I have finished your second volume, and I cannot tell you how grateful all lovers of truth, all lovers of liberty, all lovers of order and of civilized freedom ought to be to you for having so set before them the History of our Revolution of 1688.'[34] Carlyle's *French Revolution* was also a tremendous popular success, and his lectures *On Heroes and Hero-Worship*, delivered in 1840, were the rage in fashionable conversations. J.A. Froude's *History of England from the Fall of Wolsey to the Defeat of the Spanish Armada* (9 volumes, 1858-70) was also a great success: most volumes went through three editions before the work was completed, and then complete sets sold well through the 1890s.[35]

Even at Oxford and Cambridge, where professorial lectures were notoriously unattended, the Victorian style of history could be popular: Thomas Arnold attracted very large audiences for his statutory lectures as Regius Professor at Oxford in 1841-2, and so did Charles Kingsley at Cambridge in 1859.[36] The general agreement that historical study is a good preparation for life, especially for members of the governing elite, got history introduced as a course of study at the ancient universities — in the Law and Modern History honours school at Oxford in 1850 (fully implemented in 1853), and as part of the moral sciences tripos established at Cambridge in 1848, later in the Law and History tripos founded in 1868.[37]

The courses of study at Oxbridge, however, were not seen as preparation for entry into the historical profession, because down through the 1850s in England there *was* no independent historical profession. Other than the ability to communicate to a wide audience, a man of letters needed no set of qualifications before he could practice as historian. He certainly did not need to be affiliated with a university: Macaulay was a journalist, politician, and civil servant (he *refused* the Regius chair at Cambridge in 1849 so he could devote himself to his *History*); Carlyle was a man of letters; Grote a banker; Hallam a lawyer and man of property; Palgrave a barrister; and Lingard a Catholic priest. Men of letters who wrote history displayed no jargon, no special tools, no exclusive access to a body of materials or knowledge. Like other men of letters, the historian was a preacher, not a priest; such status as a historian might enjoy, accrued from having his works read and approved by the literate public. The natural scientists of the 1840s and 1850s, by their special knowledge and skills, had the means of establishing an autonomous profession; not so the historians. The 'science' of history envisaged by Mill, Grote, or the Liberal Anglicans did not form the basis of a historical profession because it required no special traning or exclusive access to privileged knowledge, but wide reflective reading and general moral insight.[38]

Down through the 1850s, then, two assumptions governed the enterprise of historical writing: first, history is immensely important to the understanding of the present; and secondly, it takes a good man rather than a specially trained expert to write good history. The Regius professorships at Oxford and Cambridge reflected both points. The two chairs had been established by George I to prepare young men for public and diplomatic service. The professors were supposed to give public lectures but were encumbered by no provision that the holder be an active historian, much less a distinguished research scholar. The appointees of the eighteenth century were all nonentities, some of whom even neglected to give the required lectures. In the first half of the nineteenth century, the professors generally gave serious attention to historical studies once they were appointed, but they rarely were appointed *because* they had distinguished themselves as historians. Thomas Arnold was the exception, for he already had written an impressive history of Rome before he was appointed. But his successor, J.A. Cramer, was a classical scholar with no achievements or interests in modern history. Cramer was succeeded by H.H.

Vaughan, a noted university reformer and a man devoted to learning, but not to history. Vaughan had already stood for the Readership in Logic in 1839 and White's Professorship of Moral Philosphy in 1841.[39]

At Cambridge, it is true, Macaulay was offered the chair in 1849, but when he refused, it went to Sir James Stephen, the lawyer and man of letters. The grounds for Stephen's appointment had nothing to do with historical expertise, but with the fact that he was deeply involved 'in the practical business of life'.[40] What one can detect in the course of these appointments is not an increasing inclination to professional expertise, but a general improvement of the quality of the holders, in terms both of breadth of learning and seriousness of moral purpose. Thomas Arnold, Charles Kingsley, Sir James Stephen — as well as Macaulay — were all Victorian heavyweights, who succeeded in their assignment of speaking to the public on major issues. Their appointments, which roughly coincided with the establishment of the historical courses of study, were a measure of the importance the Victorians attributed to history as a part of the general education of the ruling class.

It seems obvious that once there were historical schools and triposes at Oxford and Cambridge, and eminent men to attract students into them, then the establishment of professional history would follow: students would read history, and some of them would remain at the universities to teach their subject. But that proposition makes only the slightest beginning at describing the professionalization that occurred. What happened is that by 1900, while the bureaucracy of professional historians was being established — professors, editors, archivists — a new (for England, at least) kind of history was adopted, with new functions, standards, procedures, audience and institutional mechanisms. There are two key questions about this new historical style: (1) what were its main characteristics?; and (2) why did it replace the history as written by the men of letters? The answers must be multi-faceted, but the principal reason was the impact of natural science on the historians.

If one must look to the impact of science for the explanation of the changing style of history, then two further questions must be addressed: first, what concept of science did the historians have in mind?; and secondly, why did they adopt that particular view rather than an alternative? The answers to these questions can be detected in a lively debate which occurred at about mid-century on the issue as to whether history could ever be a science. This debate was raised partly by the accomplishments of the practicing scientists, their propagandizing for the scientific method and their claims for improved public understanding and support. But the debate was focused with special clarity by the publication in 1857 of H.T. Buckle's highly synthetic, schematic and aggressively scientific *History of Civilization in England*. Buckle's work created a sensation when its first volume appeared, and by the time the second volume was published, Darwin's *Origin of the Species* had burst like a rocket on the public consciousness, with the result that commitment among historians on the question of whether history could be a science was inescapable.

Buckle's extraordinary book was the fruit of the claims of rationalists like John Stuart Mill and Auguste Comte that there could and should be a science of society. For purposes of social and political reform Positivist thinkers sought to establish the 'laws' of human behaviour. This objective made Comte and Mill, like their predecessors of the Enlightment, essentially sociologists; but their sociology was largely historical. They assumed that the record of human achievement supplied the data from which the laws governing change over time could be inferred. Comte, for instance, wanted to discover the general principles that explained the 'fact' of human progress. These principles could be discovered by extending the methods of the physical sciences — the 'positivist spirit' — to the study of history. Comte believed that there was more than one method in the physical sciences: logic in mathematical sciences like astronomy; experiment in chemistry and physics; and the comparative method in biology. Sociology must adopt the comparative method, the data for comparisons being supplied by historical study. Comte believed that although the results of this scientific study of the past would not yield results as exact as those of physical science, they would be adequate to bear 'prevision' by which people could control the future. He believed that historical science showed human development had already gone through two phases — the theological and the metaphysical — and had entered the third phase — the positive. Thus the practical utility of his sociological method is that it 'connects the present, under all possible aspects, with the whole of the past, so as to exhibit at once the former course and the future tendency of every important phenomenon'.[41]

The Comtean view of history was secular and scientific, but it was just as present-oriented as Whig history and just as synthetic as Liberal Anglican history. Along with the rest of Comtean philosophy, it appealed in England mainly to the Utilitarians, who, as we have seen in the cases of James Mill and Grote, also wanted to discover for reformist purposes the laws of human behaviour. The Comtean ideas were given their most influential treatment by John Stuart Mill in his *System of Logic* (1843). Mill had his doubts about some of Comte's notions, but not about his historical ideas. Mill said that he took his concept of the historical method, which he called the 'Inverse Deductive Method', directly from Comte.[42] In *System of Logic*, Mill argued that there can be sciences of human nature and social behaviour. The latter science — sociology — had to proceed by generalization from observed historical facts to confirmation of the generalizations by reference to psychological laws on which all behaviour depends. Hence Mill declared that while it is not possible to deduce *a priori* the course of human development from the laws of human nature, history 'when judiciously examined, affords Empirical Laws of Society'.[43]

The Positivist view of scientific history was not at all like the scientific scholarship already highly developed by German historians, for the German school revolved around critical examination of sources, research in archives, delight in details and deliberate abstention from concern with the present. But it was the Comte-Mill approach with which Buckle challenged his readers. He posed a dual challenge, especially to other historians. First, he offered a blanket condemnation of historical thinking in England. He asserted that while other fields such as law, geology, and philology had made great strides in gathering the materials suitable for understanding the past, historians had made little use of them:

> In all the other great fields of inquiry, the necessity of generalization is universally admitted, and noble efforts are being made to rise from particular facts in order to discover the laws by which those facts are governed. So far, however, is this from being the usual course of historians, that among them the strange idea prevails, that their business is merely to relate events, which they may occasionally enliven by such moral and political reflections as seem likely to be useful. According to this scheme, any author who from indolence of thought, or from natural incapacity, is unfit to deal with the highest branches of knowledge, has only to pass some years in reading a certain number of books, and then he is qualified to be an historian; he is able to write the history of a great people, and his work becomes an authority on the subject which it professes to treat.[44]

In short, Buckle's first challenge was for historians to improve their professional competency by means of wider reading in more fields and by means of combining these fields in a search for general laws. The second challenge was for history to take the natural sciences as its model, as he considered himself to have done: 'I hope to accomplish for the history of man something equivalent, or at all events analogous, to what has been effected by other inquirers for the different branches of natural science'.[45]

In Buckle's view, human social behaviour shows the same regularity as natural phenomena, and for a simple reason: whenever we do anything, we do it because of some motive or motives, which themselves are the results of 'antecedents'. Therefore, if the historian knows all the antecedents, plus all the 'laws of their movements', he could 'with unerring certainty predict the whole of their immediate results'.[46] Even the rates of marriage, crime and suicide vary regularly with the national circumstances, which ultimately derive from the climate, food, soil and 'General Aspect of Nature' — the last being the topographical features that control the association of ideas in any given people. Such thinking enabled Buckle to make truly whopping generalizations, the main one being that in Europe natural phenomena tended to 'limit the imagination, and embolden the understanding', while outside Europe, 'all nature conspired to increase the authority of the imaginative faculties, and weaken the authority of the reasoning ones'.[47]

Buckle's book caused a furor in the English literate public. As H.J. Hanham has said, for a generation 'no one could claim to be an educated man who had not read his Buckle'.[48] Darwin himself wrote to a friend: 'Have you read Buckle's second volume? It has interested me greatly; I do not care whether his views are right or wrong, but I should think they contain much truth. There is a noble love of advancement and truth throughout, and to my taste he is the very best writer of the English language that ever lived'.[49] The book was reviewed by an impressive number of men of letters and academics — Leslie Stephen, Goldwin Smith, John Morley, Sir Henry Maine and Lord Acton, among others.[50]

The widespread attention, however, did not mean that Buckle's work was received with approval. Most of the reviewers attacked the book ferociously. Some of the critics pointed out that Buckle made mistakes in details; others contended that Buckle generalized without enough evidence.[51] Macaulay, for example, wrote in his diary that Buckle 'wants to make a system before he has got the materials; and he has not the excuse which Aristotle had, of having an eminently systematising mind'.[52] But the theme which dominated the criticism was an assertion of free will against Buckle's idea of material causation. It was this point that led many reviewers to conclude that there could be no science of history, at least in Buckle's sense.

The most influential exponents of this view were Charles Kingsley, J.A. Froude and Lord Acton. None of them was opposed to science *per se*. Kingsley had long before concluded that science provided a means of studying God's work, and that it was an instrument of material progress. In 1846, he had advised young men that in scientific study 'you are walking in the very path to which England owes her wealth; that you are training in yourself that habit of mind which God has approved as the one He has ordained for Englishmen . . .'[53] But as he declared in his inaugural lecture as Regius Professor at Cambridge, Kingsley believed that 'History is the history of men and women, and of nothing else'; therefore, exact science is limited in the study of the past. History, he said, cannot belong to the 'positive' sciences because people have free will: 'For man can break the laws of his own being, whether physical, intellectual, or moral.' Ultimately, the only certainty proved by history is a moral law: 'that as the fruit of righteousness is wealth and peace, strength and honour; the fruit of unrighteousness is poverty and anarchy, weakness and shame'.[54]

Froude, like Kingsley a strong Protestant, carried much this same message into the camp of natural science. Lecturing at the Royal Institution in 1864, Froude argued that natural causes can be set aside by free will. If there is free choice, there can be no science of man. Further, scientific procedures are of limited use in historiography, since no experimentation is possible, and since historical evidence is both incomplete and fallible. Froude was persuaded that history proved the good prospered and the wicked suffered, but, as he added, 'this is no science. . .'[55]

Acton had been trained in German scholarship as well as in Liberal Catholicism at the feet of Dr Johann Ignaz Döllinger, the eminent German historian and theologian. He and Döllinger were much influenced by Ranke's lectures in Munich in favour of original research in manuscripts and the critical methods of German scientific history. When Acton returned to England in the 1850s, he intended to put his prodigious Germanic learning at the service of English Catholicism. His view was that science is dangerous to Catholics 'only when they rejected it and permitted it to be usurped by their enemies'.[56] Yet he could not tolerate Buckle's work. He contended in *The Rambler* in 1858 that Buckle had not mastered his sources and had misapplied his scientific reasoning. Buckle, he wrote, 'looks at men not as persons, but as machines; and the result he contemplates is not the action of these machines, but their productions'. Buckle had denied the existence of free will in individuals, but in Acton's view our personal consciousness of free will is sufficient proof that it exists. Acton readily admitted that the actions of people *en masse* are subject to enumeration, but such numerical averages do not constitute laws. No individual must obey a statistical average. Buckle, therefore, had eliminated moral issues from history, and that is to eliminate what is most important in historical study.[57]

Obviously, Buckle had run afoul of a powerful need in the Victorian psyche to believe that human beings are independent agents in the historical process. He also seemed to most Victorians to deny that history demonstrates the reward of the virtuous and the punishment of the wicked. In a sense he had raised certain aspects of early and mid-Victorian history to the cosmic level — the belief in progress, the concern with making history useful to the present — but his determinism clashed with Victorian individualism. The Victorians needed history, but they did not need a history that envisioned them as cogs in a world machine. Nevertheless, the outcome of the dispute whether history was a science affirmed that in some ways it *could* be. Kingsley and Froude, for instance, both concluded that there could be no objection to learning what one can from the application of scientific methods of dealing with evidence, as long as the limits of this attempt were recognized. Froude told the Devonshire Association for the Advancement of Science and Literature that

> History itself depends on exact knowledge, on the same minute, impartial, discriminating observation and analysis of particulars which is equally the basis of science. . .[58]

Acton agreed entirely. He became one of the strongest English proponents of the idea that history was a science, which he equated with archival research, systematic criticism of documents and the division of labour.[59]

Buckle had helped to force science on the attention of English historians, and had helped them to see what they did *not* mean by science. But they could not reject science altogether as a model for history because science was succeeding in making itself the paradigm for the acquisition and function of knowledge. Its intellectual prestige was overwhelming. Alternatives to the Positivist concept of science and scientific history were readily available from two sources — the practising natural scientists themselves, and the German historical scholars. The messages about science from these two sources proved to be compatible with historians' assumptions about human behaviour and national progress; and they also proved to be compatible with each other.

It is true that many historians, like other Victorians, could find objectionable elements in the message put out by spokesmen for science like Huxley and the scientific naturalists. But those elements could be isolated from the epistemological aspects of the scientists' idea of science. Huxley *et al.* defined science as a method of inquiry, a process of discovering the truth through research into the discrete sections of the material world, such that the scientist does not have to know the whole in order to understand a part. What is required of the investigator in this idea of science is not special moral insight or universal knowledge, but hard work and impartiality. Each investigator can be confident that his own discoveries, no matter how small, are permanent contributions to the march of mind, and that his specialized research is sanctioned by the natural principle of the division of labour which had made England great. If one wished to draw metaphysical or theological conclusions from the accumulation of scientific knowledge, he could do so without endangering the permanence of the contributions themselves; sceptics could simply set them aside as unverifiable and unessential speculations.

The idea that activities outside the physical sciences could properly be called 'scientific' was encouraged by the men of science themselves. The logic of their effort to improve the economic and social position of natural science had led to a desire to make the whole society more 'scientific' and thus to an invitation to others to transform their fields of interest into sciences. Hence they gave a very broad definition to science: as Huxley put it in 1854, science is 'organised common sense'.[60] The view that any systematic, empirical investigation constitutes a science spread outwards from the scientific community. To Mark Pattison, for instance, 'science' came to mean any deep and careful learning, the pursuit of truth in any field by disinterested, specialized research. The scientific spirit, he wrote, 'can only be educed by setting the understanding to investigate for itself the laws of some one chief department of knowledge, or division of objects. It is not matters known that make science, but the mode of knowing'.[61] Matthew Arnold believed much the same. In *Schools and Universities on the*

*Continent,* he celebrated the German belief in *Wissenschaft* — 'science, knowledge systematically pursued and prized in and for itself'.[62]

This methodologically-oriented conception of science was highly compatible with German university scholarship and in particular with at least part of the 'scientific history' which flourished in the first half of the century. The foundations of this scientific history had been laid by professors of law and philology at the University of Göttingen in the eighteenth century. Historians like Niebuhr, Mommsen and Ranke combined these critical methods with a romantic affection for past ages to form the scientific school of history. These scholars were profoundly religious and believed that the will of God lay behind the course of historical events, but they actually wrote history so as to relegate God to the periphery. From their religious assumptions, they concluded that a sense of the finality or superiority of the present constituted a grave error. To them, each age was immediate to God, therefore the historian's duty was to write about the past in its own terms. No past age should have been regarded as having existed as a prelude or stepping-stone for a later age. Thus for Ranke, the notion of history for its own sake necessarily involved the rejection of writing history for practical uses. As he put it, 'To history has been assigned the office of judging the past, of instructing the present for the benefit of future ages. To such high offices this work does not aspire; it wants only to show what actually happened.'[63]

The German scholars believed that the duties of writing about the past in its own terms and of showing how things actually happened entailed complete impartiality, as well as the most rigorous critical methods. The idea was to avoid the fictitious, the exaggerated, the literary effects, and in Ranke's phrase, to 'stick severely to facts'. History was to be written solely on the basis of unimpeachable original sources, recovered after exhaustive research and meticulous examination. Of course, as many later critics have pointed out, the German scientific historians were not able to escape their own biases and preconceptions. But it remains true that in the late-nineteenth century they were taken at their own estimation as producers of objective accounts of the past, history written disinterestedly, for its own sake, on the basis of massive research in original sources.

In the 1860s and 1870s, many English historians, under the influence of the natural sciences, began to take German scholarship as their model for the historical enterprise. When they did, they ignored the admonitions of Ranke and others to strive always for the *'Zusammenhang'* (connectedness) of all events and times, which made universal history possible. Thus scientific history in England did not take the route of Buckle towards highly abstract demonstrations of universal laws. It followed instead the road to specialization — the accumulation of masses of facts, allegedly without reference to issues external to history itself.

As one might expect, the universities proved to be the natural home for the new style of history, for it could thrive only in a sheltering environment. But not all academic historians plunged immediately into scientific history in its mature form. At Cambridge, for example, the first important exponent of history as a science was John Seeley, who continued to believe that history is a practical guide to public-minded citizens. In his own undergraduate days at Cambridge (he matriculated in 1852) and in the years following, Seeley was preoccupied with the impact of science and scepticism on Christianity. His reconciliation of the conflict, which he expressed in his study of Christ's mission, *Ecce Homo,* was that the real meaning of Christ's life was neither theological nor ecclesiastical, but in the broadest sense political. The essential element in early Christianity was the establishment of a new polity bound together by brotherly love. Hence, the church had nothing to fear from science, and the main function of its universities was to prepare the clerical and secular elite to spread the idea of Christian brotherhood. Science and Christian morality, he thought, were both revelations of the same higher law.[64]

As Regius Professor of Modern History (he succeeded Kingsley in 1869), Seeley propounded to students, and to the general public, a view of history both moralistic and scientific. History, he said in his inaugural lecture, 'is the school of statesmanship . . . the school of public feeling and patriotism'. Since history is a science, it must exclude some things from its purview, but include politics and political institutions. Combined with political economy, this 'political science' (history) instructs the present by shedding light on political structures and on nations the way science illuminates physical forces. Even though the records may be incomplete, the study of the recent past has 'the interest of an experimental study'. It follows that the historian should know the present before going to the past, in order to know what questions to ask.[65]

Seeley believed that the function of the historical professor, like that of the university as a whole, was to teach the governing elite. But he also thought that the professor and fellows ought to 'extend the bounds of knowledge' by research on the German pattern. His motive was common to many dons and professors in the 1860s and 1870s: to recover the authority once exercised by religion. A liberal education for men, he thought, requires teachers who are masters of their subjects. Teachers find 'the way to influence the students most powerfully is by becoming as learned as possible'.[66] Mastery of a subject comes from 'the rigour of scientific methods', first used in his view by German scholars. Though 'conscientious and exact research' was not popular among the students, Seeley admitted, history could be made attractive to them by the generalization of facts into the principles of social action: 'If we borrow from science its rigorous method, let us borrow at the same time what science has to offer' — the example of theorizing.[67] Seeley's leadership in historical study at Cambridge eventually came to be known as the 'thoughts without facts' school. Nevertheless, his teaching effectively popularized the idea that scientific research methods, specialization and theorizing about a science of society together gave the best liberal education to future statesmen.

Meanwhile, at Oxford, John Richard Green, E.A. Freeman and William Stubbs ascribed a somewhat different meaning to historical science, a meaning that gradually came to prevail in both universities. This little band of friends, which G.P. Gooch has called 'The Oxford School', shared similar backgrounds and introductions to the study of the past. All three were undergraduates at Oxford near mid-century, and all three as young men had been caught up in the Oxford Movement. Green and Freeman later moved away from Tractarian theology and eventually became political and religious liberals, while Stubbs remained a staunch high churchman. But all three derived their initial interest in the past from a thoroughly high-church fascination with ecclesiastical architecture and history. Freeman and Green, for instance, first met at a meeting of the Somersetshire Archaeological Society, at which Green gave a paper on Dunstan. Thus, for all three, interest in the past was essentially antiquarian, in which spirit the study of the past was for its own sake. As Freeman put it:

> The High Church movement, instead of proscribing learning, fostered it. Its aesthetical and historical side, its love of antiquity, its appeal to the writing of other ages and of other tongues, completely fell in with the spirit and studies of the place [Oxford].[68]

To the antiquarian influence of the Oxford Movement, the trio added natural science. For them at least, these two intellectual themes dovetailed in promoting the idea of knowledge for its own sake. Green, for example, abandoned his Tractarian theology while a student at Oxford and took his degree in natural science. He developed a strong interest in geology and natural history, and especially in the great debate over Darwin in 1859 and 1860.[69] Neither Freeman nor Stubbs took as active an interest in science as Green, but both of them found no conflict between religious belief and scientific methodology. Stubbs's view was that science presented problems to the believer only when it over-stepped the boundaries of its legitimate investigation of the world.[70] Freeman was rather more positive. As early as 1849, Freeman had observed that interests in history and in science were distinctive features of the age. Like the sciences, he said, history was concerned with 'outward facts or phenomena; and though it assigns those facts to the working of certain laws or principles, it does not pretend to invest those laws with the character of eternal and immutable truth'.[71] Later, Freeman admitted that historians and scientists use different evidence, but he insisted that the differences were of degree, not of kind. History, he insisted, is a science in the sense of *'knowledge* and *learning'*, and no one has the right to exclude it from the ranks of sciences.[72]

Stubbs stated the nub of the matter most clearly: the study of history may be justified as a mental discipline, as an aspect of cultivation, or for its own sake. The third justification was supreme, for by it 'History assumes the dignity of a science'.[73]

A number of important conclusions followed from the proposition that history ought to be studied for its own sake. One was that it ought to be free from the desire to prove a given philosophy or partisan political position. The temperaments of the Oxford School as well as the German example weighed against abstract philosophizing. Stubbs wrote to Freeman in 1858: 'I do not believe in the Philosophy of History, and so do not believe in Buckle.'[74] He preferred to think that 'we can try to learn here and there a thing as perfectly as it can be learned, without knowing everything'.[75] As for partisanship, they all felt that it distorted the accuracy of one's account of the past, and thus was inconsistent with the scientific spirit. The first principle of real historical work, Freeman declared, was 'dare to be accurate'.[76] Hence the Oxford School rejected the deliberate writing of history as a 'political weapon', to use Stubbs's phrase, and 'not as an increase of knowledge, not as an investigation of truth, nor as a study of History for its own sake'.[77]

On this fundamental point the Oxford allies were inconsistent in both theory and practice. Freeman and Stubbs both felt that history was eminently practical in that it helped people to understand the present, and both of them stuck firmly to the history of politics or political institutions. They also believed that the study of history contributed heavily to the formation of moral characteristics. For Stubbs these good qualities were toleration and restraint in political life.[78] Like Seeley and the Whig historians, Freeman devoutly adhered to the doctrine of the practicality of political history for all citizens. He never tired of asserting that 'History is past politics and politics present history.'[79] Green tried to write broad cultural history in his *Short History of the English People,* but it, too, is essentially a political survey; and his major piece of research work stood firmly in the tradition of political history. Further, all three of them were just as Whiggish as Hallam or Macaulay in their actual interpretations of English history. They celebrated the progress of the English nation (indeed, of the 'Anglo-Saxon race') towards the constitutional liberty and parliamentary institutions that graced nineteenth-century England. In this sense they continued the tradition of liberal nationalist history.[80]

Nevertheless, all three of the Oxford School thought of themselves as writing non-partisan history; and their doctrine of non-present-minded history became more influential than their own interpretations. Freeman, it is true, was a strong Liberal in late-Victorian politics and was as violently polemical in his critical and political writing as any early Victorian. Yet he insisted that his study of history had shaped his view of contemporary politics and not the other way round. It was Stubbs who most firmly insisted on non-partisan history. Since history should be written for its own sake, it should never be studied with the present in mind. It should be done 'forwards' — from the past to the present. He wrote: 'Simply, it was not my work to make men Whigs or Tories, but to do my best, having Whigs and Tories by nature as the matter I was to work upon, to make the Whigs good, wise, sensible Whigs, and the Tories good, wise, sensible Tories. . .'[81] In fact, the central *motif* of Stubbs's majestic *Constitutional History* plays down the heroic and the villainous; for the evolution of the constitution, though clear and steady, was not what the past politicians had ever actually intended.

One of the salient attributes of the Oxford School's concept of history was the notion of the 'contribution', defined as a permanent increment to the stock of knowledge. Green wrote to a geologist friend in 1862:

Whatever comes to you never let go your *ideal.* I think it is a great thing and one that 'lifts one up forever', to have laboured with singleness of mind for knowledge. If I could advance History, if you could advance Science, by a single fact. . . I am sure we could both willingly lose all thought of ourselves, and be content to remain obscure, and it may be poor. But knowledge is great riches.[82]

In this idea, the use of writing history stands in relation, not to political or moral guidance for the present, but to the sum of historical knowledge itself. Stubbs admitted that there may be useless *learning,* the accumulation of other people's ideas; but he declared that no *knowledge* is useless, for every bit contributes to the field: 'The man who has, out of independent study, produced such results, has made a contribution, small or great as the case may be, to the great stock of sound material which constitutes real knowledge.'[83]

Another attribute of the new school of history was that it had to be a research activity done in the original sources. By constant reiteration, and by mutual reinforcement in print, Green, Freeman and Stubbs established a new critical standard for history in England — principally that it must be written from original sources. Later historians would surpass them in this regard, for all three men actually depended on chronicles, most of them printed, rather than on archival records. However, their message was unequivocal. Any historical writing, Freeman stated, 'which is good for anything must be founded on the mastery of original authorities . . .'[84] Green experienced first hand the control that the newly emerging discipline could exercise. His first book, the *Short History* (1874), gave a general account, largely from secondary sources, for a wide public. It was extremely popular, but Green felt that the historical scholars sought to condemn him to the ranks of 'picturesque compilers'; hence, he devoted himself afterwards to the longer, more detailed research work, *The Making of England* (1882).[88]

Again, it was Stubbs who did the most to consolidate the new idea of the historical enterprise. His first book, the *Registrum Sacrum Anglicanum,* was a source of pride to him as a work of original research. He provided models for other historians in the 19 volumes he edited for the Rolls Series and a new model textbook for historical students in his *Select Charters of English Constitutional History* (first published in 1870, ninth edition, 1901). The latter was to help apprentice historians to learn to deal with original documents, so that they might try to emulate works like Stubbs's own *Constitutional History,* which remained the standard work and the exemplar of institutional history until well into the twentieth century. As a model, the *Constitutional*

*History* taught that history should be rooted in original sources, balanced and temperate in judgements, highly detailed and analytical, and severe and austere in tone.

All of these attributes of historical work were related to new standards of writing and a new sense of the legitimate audience. There is no question that Green and Stubbs wrote extremely well — very clear, if not exciting, prose.[86] Freeman wrote works that were far too detailed to be popular, for he could not bear to omit a fact. But the Oxford School expressed reservations about concern with style. They contended that a desire to write popular works led to seduction by the 'sensational and picturesque', which as Stubbs said 'is very apt to corrupt and destroy the more valuable features of painstaking and conscientious truthfulness'.[87] Hence the Oxford School established a prejudice against popular historical writing, and they did their best to discredit the older historical style. Freeman's fiercely critical articles on Froude showed what treatment popular and 'unscientific' historians could expect to receive from the hands of the experts.[88] (Freeman later earned much the same treatment from J.H. Round.) Accuracy in details and mastery of documents henceforward were to be much more important in the *evaluation* of historical works than their general effects.

By the same token, the audience for historical writing which counted for critical purposes would consist only of those who had familiarity with the original sources. This principle was not easily established, for the tradition of significant popular history did not — indeed has not — surrendered all its privileges. Men of letters like Andrew Lang continued to argue that history ought to be interesting to more than experts, and that the attractiveness of a historical work was a valid and important standard of judgement.[89] Further, as Freeman rather irritably recognized, historians were thought to employ no special jargon or techniques. Consequently, the historian had to expect to be criticized 'by men who have no more claim to judge your work than I have to judge the work of the chemist or the astronomer'.[90] Nevertheless, no matter how intrusive or tempting was the appraisal by general readers, historians should attend only to the expert critics who could apply the standards of accuracy of research in original sources.

The concepts of history represented by the ideas of the Oxford School were very widely accepted by English academics in the late-Victorian years. They became the assumptions which governed professional history. Their acceptance can be measured in a wide variety of manifestations: numerous critical and historiographical articles and lectures; in the widespread acceptance of the manual by Langlois and Seignobos, *Introduction to the Study of History* (1889, English translation, 1898); in the meticulous and anti-anachronistic legal history of F.W. Maitland; and in Maitland's rejection of an offer of the Regius Professorship on grounds that he had nothing to say to the public, the 'muchdumbre'.[91] But they were best summed up and restated by J.B. Bury, who became Regius Professor at Cambridge in 1901.

Bury, who was born in 1861 and had studied for a time at Göttingen, was exceptionally well informed in both German scholarship and the natural sciences. As a historian, Bury was a superb analyst but never a good narrator. As Norman Baynes put it, Bury took an interest in research on each subject 'as a detached fragment to be subjected to microscopic analysis'.[92] Bury had a very strong sense of the evolution of history as a professional discipline, and he considered that Freeman and Stubbs had been responsible for putting historical research in England on the right track. In the 1890s, he joined the professionals' attack on the men of letters:

> Mr Jowett's view [he wrote in 1892] is the view of a man of letters, who judges history altogether from a literary standpoint, and who does not care to hear what happened for its own sake, but only when it is told with literary effect.[93]

Bury believed above all that history is a science, not literature. But he did not mean the science of Comte or Buckle.[94] The great advance from literature to science, he said in his inaugural address, came from German scholars, principally Niebuhr and Ranke. They had combined the scientific method with a passionate interest in the national past to make the new history. This great transformation was still going on, and its consequences were not yet fully understood. He admitted that all people naturally try to understand the present by understanding the past; and for that reason it is crucial to see the historical record accurately and 'in a dry light'. Hence the study of the past can only be useful if it goes forward in a frame of mind completely detached from the present. The historians must continue 'heaping up material' without knowing how future generations will use it. One can be sure that it will be useful in 'stripping the bandages of error from the eyes of men' only if it is completely objective.[95]

Bury, then, felt it imperative that history should stand as an independent profession, not serving any other discipline or purpose. In

1904 he said that it was accepted as self-evident that history should be studied for its own sake:

> It is one of the remarkable ideas which first emerged explicitly into consciousness in the last century that the unique series of phenomena of human development is worthy to be studied for itself, without any ulterior purpose, without any obligation to serve ethical or theological, or any practical ends. This principle of 'history for its own sake' might be described as the motto or watchword of this great movement of historical research which has gone on increasing in volume and power since the beginning of the last century.[96]

History for history's sake was bound to have important institutional consequences. For one thing, scholarly books of history, even in popular subjects, did not sell to the general public. S.R. Gardiner's mammoth *History of England from the Accession of James I to the Outbreak of the Civil War* found only about 100 buyers for the first two volumes in 1863, and subsequent volumes never made more than a small profit. Gardiner supported himself mainly by teaching in various schools and colleges, until Oxford fellowships rescued him after 1884.[97] The new scientific history, following the example of German scholarship and the claims of the natural scientists, gravitated naturally to the universities. At Oxbridge, one of the first tasks of the research-oriented historians was to claim the professorships for themselves. Their claims were largely won with the appointment of Stubbs and Seeley as Regius Professors in 1866 and 1869, respectively, even though Froude, who was despised by the Oxford allies, succeeded Freeman in 1892 and Seeley was outdistanced as researcher in the eyes of his younger professional colleagues by the 1890s.

At both Oxford and Cambridge, the elaboration of career structures for historians was bound up with the development of the honours courses in history. The tutors continued to control the honours courses even after the separation of history from law at Oxford in 1873 and from moral sciences at Cambridge in 1875. This caused much friction with the professors, who typically objected to the fact that the tutors spent their time preparing students for the exams instead of inculcating a love of history for its own sake. The professors played no part in the 'cramming' process, and the insistence of professors like Stubbs and Freeman on lecturing about their research reduced their undergraduate attendance to a dozen or less.[98] The tutors generally taught by commentary on a single text, while the research professors sought to turn the teaching methods towards examination of original documents. Gradually, the research orientation affected historical teaching at both universities. Stubbs deliberately set out to found a school of professional historians at Oxford, and he largely succeeded. He trained many of the leading figures in the second generation of English scientific historians — J.H. Round, C.H. Firth, R.L. Poole and T.F. Tout, the last of whom went on to develop the school of history at the University of Manchester.[99] Cambridge lagged behind; and it was not until the tenure of Mandell Creighton as Dixie Professor of Ecclesiastical History that the scholarly types were able to move the curriculum towards training in the methods of historical scholarship.[100]

Meanwhile, the careers of tutors were changing subtly. With the inspiration of Stubbs, a number of Oxford history tutors worked out a system of co-operative lectures, which allowed each one to specialize. A History Tutors Association was founded to supervise the operation. Much the same scheme was developed at Cambridge by the Board of Historical Studies. One can conclude that in general by the 1890s, the history tutors had become specialists and were producing books on their own special subjects.[101]

Other institutional changes had to do with publications. One was the founding of large projects for the publication of original documents, the most important being the Rolls Series, begun in 1857 in an attempt to catch up with the French and German governments in the publication of 'historical treasures'; the Selden Society publications, started by Maitland in 1886 to make available documents in English legal history; and the Historical Manuscripts Commission, begun in 1872 to locate and circulate information about private archives.[102] Another change was the initiation of a large co-operative project in which experts in each of the special areas of European history would contribute chapters — *The Cambridge Modern History.* Lord Acton undertook to plan and edit the work in 1898. His letter to the contributors stressed the virtues of 'the progressive division of labour' and the need to write from the original documents in order to meet the 'scientific demand for completeness and certainty'.[103]

The most important of all the new publication projects was the *English Historical Review.* The new-style historical scholars needed an outlet for their work more suited to their tastes than the great quarterly and monthly reviews. In the 1860s, relatively scholarly but still generalist journals like the *Saturday Review,* the *Academy,* and *The Reader* had attempted to meet the need, but their audiences and economic arrangements were all wrong for scholarly publication. By the 1870s, Green, Freeman, Stubbs and their fellow Germanophile James Bryce began to discuss the possibility of publishing an exclusively historical journal. They knew, as Green admitted, that their proposed review 'was to be scientific and not popular', and they were not able to find a way to finance the enterprise until Longmans agreed in 1885 to underwrite its costs.[104] The meeting which gathered to plan the enterprise included many of the leading scholarly historians of the day: Bryce, Acton, R.W. Church, Mandell Creighton, A.W. Ward, York Powell, and R.L. Poole. Their object was to serve the community of research historians, and their view of history was clearly dissociated from the Victorian style. 'The object of history', Bryce wrote in the opening statement, 'is to set forth facts' and to do so without any hint of partisanship. For this reason, some topics would be excluded altogether: 'But our main reliance will be on the scientific spirit which we shall expect from contributors...' As for shedding light on practical issues, the *Review* declared, 'we shall not hesitate to let that light be reflected from our pages, whenever we can be sure that it is dry light, free from any tinge of partisanship'.[105]

To administer the new beam of light, and to assure that it always remained dry, the founders could not have made a better choice of editor than Mandell Creighton. Green had once been considered, but he had died in 1883. Stubbs was too busy. Creighton, meanwhile, had studied at Oxford, taking a first class in classics in 1866 and a second class in law and modern history later that same year — two of his examiners being Stubbs and Bryce. He had served as a tutor in Merton College until 1874 and come under the influence of Stubbs. From 1874 to 1884 he had taken a parish living, which he gave up to accept the Dixie Professorship of Ecclesiastical History at Cambridge. While still a parish priest, he had begun his multi-volume *History of the Papacy during the Period of the Reformation*, a research work characterized by its institutional orientation and resolute avoidance of the picturesque. Creighton knew his work was dull, but his view of history exactly suited the emerging professional historians who founded the *English Historical Review.* He wrote to a friend in 1882: 'I am afraid that I regard history as a branch of science, not of novel writing. There is no reason why anyone should want to know about the past; but if he does, he can have such knowledge as exists, not fancy pictures.'[106]

Creighton should be allowed the last word on the professionalization of English history in the nineteenth century. By 1900 in England, professional history, as it was identified, had come into being. As in France and Germany, this professionalization meant application of the critical method to original sources, specialization of interests and bureaucratization of historical study and publication.[107] The tradition of 'amateur' historical writing directed at a general audience did not die out; indeed, it has remained more vital in England than elsewhere in modern Europe or America. Nevertheless, the new professional history had become more important in volume and intellectual authority than the older Victorian style. It was in this sense that history in England was transformed from literature to science. For the historians, the concept of science had been defined by the scientists themselves and exemplified by German scholars. Hence its principal ideal was 'history for its own sake', which connoted a research enterprise devoted to adding to the stock of knowledge that constituted the field. Further, the new professional historians took as the only significant audience for their work the body of masters of original sources. By their research orientation and their sense of their legitimate audience, the professional historians cut themselves off from the general reading public to a remarkable degree. This meant that the professional historians gave up the position of immense public esteem held by earlier Victorian historians. They preferred the role of scientist to that of public sage due to the immense prestige of natural science in mid and late-Victorian England.

Not all of the newly emerging disciplines in England adopted exactly parallel concepts of their work as that taken by the historians. Sociology, for instance, remained much more closely tied to the investigation of current social issues.[108] But all of them came into being as sciences, dedicated to objective research and located in the universities. J.B. Bury declared in his famous inaugural address of 1902 that 'The furtherance of research, which is the highest duty of Universities, requires ways and means.' This was a proposition all professional academics could agree with. If it required ways and means, it also required transformation of the universities.

## Notes

1. Adam Smith, *An Inquiry into the Nature and Causes of the Wealth of Nations* (Glasgow edn; Oxford, 1976), Book I, Chs. I-III.

2. Herbert Spencer, *The Principles of Sociology* (New York, 1896), II, pp. 180-226.

3. William Jolly, 'The Professional Training of Teachers', *Fortnightly Review* (September 1874), pp. 353-76; Edward Dowden, 'Hopes and Fears for Literature', *Fortnightly Review* (January 1889), pp. 166-83; Francis T. Palgrave, 'The Province and Study of Poetry', *Macmillan's Magazine* (March 1886), pp. 332-47.

4. T.B. Macaulay, 'Hallam', *Critical and Historical Essays* (London, 1883), p.51.

5. J.B. Bury, 'The Science of History' in Harold Temperley (ed.), *Selected Essays of J.B. Bury* (Cambridge, 1930), p. 22.

6. This model can be seen in G.P. Gooch, *History and Historians in the Nineteenth Century* (London, 1913; paperback edn Boston, 1959); and P.B.M. Blaas, *Continuity and Anachronism: Parliamentary and Constitutional Development in Whig Historiography and in the Anti-Whig Reaction between 1890 and 1930* (The Hague, 1978).

7. Rosemary Jann, 'The Art of History in Nineteenth Century England', unpublished PhD thesis, Northwestern University, 1975, p. 222.

8. Olive Anderson, 'The Political Uses of History in Mid-Nineteenth Century England', *Past & Present* (April 1967), pp. 87-105; Richard A.E. Brooks, 'The Development of the Historical Mind', in Joseph E. Baker (ed.), *The Reinterpretation of Victorian Literature* (New York, 1962), pp. 130-52; Blaas, *Continuity and Anachronism,* pp. xii-xiii.

9. For definitions of Whig historiography, see Blaas, *Continuity and Anachronism,* Chs. I and II; and Herbert Butterfield, *The Whig Interpretation of History* (London, 1931).

10. David Knowles, *Lord Macaulay, 1800-1859* (Cambridge, 1960); G.M. Kitson Clark, review of John Clive's *Macaulay: The Shaping of the Historian, History and Theory* (no. 2, 1974), pp. 145-64.

11. T.B. Macaulay, 'On Mitford's *History of Greece'* in *The Miscellaneous Writings of Lord Macaulay* (2 vols., London, 1860), I, p. 176.

12. Joseph Hamburger, *Macaulay and the Whig Tradition* (Chicago, 1976).

13. Jann, 'The Art of History', p. 225.

14. Ibid., Ch. II; John Holloway, *The Victorian Sage* (New York, 1965), Ch. III.

15. Thomas Arnold, *Introductory Lectures on Modern History*, 4th edn (London, 1849), p. 305.

16. J.A. Froude, 'The Science of History', *Short Studies on Great Subjects,* (vol. I London, 1867), p. 14.

17. T.B. Macaulay, 'History', *Critical and Miscellaneous Essays* (7 vols., new and revised edn, New York, 1861), I, p. 169.

18. Ibid., p. 146.

19. Quoted in G.O. Trevelyan, *The Life and Letters of Lord Macaulay* (2 vols., New York, 1875), II, pp. 101-2.

20. T.B. Macaulay, 'Machiavelli', *Critical and Historical Essays* (London, 1883), p. 50.

21. Jann, 'The Art of History', pp. 39, 178, 239-40.

22. T.B. Macaulay, 'History', p. 155.

23. Ibid., p. 153.

24. T.B. Macaulay, 'Von Ranke', *Critical and Historical Essays,* pp. 541-63; Knowles, *Macaulay,* pp. 10-11.

25. David Knowles, *Great Historical Enterprises* (London, 1962), Ch. 4, especially p. 116.

26. George Grote, *A History of Greece* (12 vols., London, 1846-56), I, p. viii; Arnaldo Momigliano, 'George Grote and the Study of Greek History', *Studies in Historiography* (London, 1966), pp. 56-74; M.L. Clarke, *George Grote: A Biography* (London, 1962), pp. 106-9.

27. Charles Kingsley, 'The Limits of Exact Science as Applied to History', *The Roman and the Teuton* (London, 1891), pp. 307-43; J.A. Froude, 'Science of History', *passim.*

152    *The Impact of Science*

28. Duncan Forbes, 'Historismus in England', *Cambridge Journal* (no. 4, 1951), p. 391; T.P. Peardon, *The Transition in English Historical Writing, 1760-1830* (New York, 1933), pp. 10-29.

29. For discussions of Mill and Grote, see Eric Stokes, *The English Utilitarians and India* (Oxford, 1959), pp. 48-69; Duncan Forbes, 'James Mill and India', *The Cambridge Journal* (October 1951), pp. 19-33; Momigliano, 'Grote and Greek History'; and Clarke, *George Grote,* Ch. V.

30. Duncan Forbes, *The Liberal Anglican Idea of History* (Cambridge, 1952).

31. A.P. Stanley, *The Life and Correspondence of Thomas Arnold,* 6th edn. (London, 1846), pp. 34, 290, 364.

32. Arnold, *Introductory Lectures on Modern History,* p. 84.

33. Hayden White, *Metahistory: The Historical Imagination in Nineteenth-Century Europe* (Baltimore, 1973), pp. 11-29.

34. Trevelyan, *Macaulay,* II, p. 205.

35. For figures on Macaulay's and Froude's sales, see ibid., pp. 216, 217, 237, 323, 327, 345; and James Westfall Thompson, *A History of Historical Writing* (2 vols., New York, 1942), II, pp. 296 and 304.

36. Sir Charles Oman, 'History of Oxford', *On the Writing of History* (New York, 1939), p. 226; and G.P. Gooch, 'The Cambridge Chair of Modern History', *Studies in Modern History* (London, 1931), p. 311.

37. On the founding of history honours courses, see W.R. Ward, *Victorian Oxford* (London, 1965), pp. 147-150; and D.A. Winstanley, *Early Victorian Cambridge* (Cambridge, 1940), Ch. X, especially pp. 198-213.

38. See, for example, Thomas Arnold's advice on the study of history in 'Lecture I' in *Introductory Lectures on Modern History.*

39. On the Regius chairs: Oman, 'History at Oxford'; Gooch, 'The Cambridge Chair of Modern History'; C.H. Firth, 'Modern History in Oxford', *The English Historical Review* (January 1917), pp. 1-21; and Sir Llewellyn Woodward, 'The Rise of the Professorial Historian in England', in K. Bourne and D.C. Watt (eds.), *Studies in International History* (London, 1967), pp. 16-34.

40. Quoted in Gooch, 'The Cambridge Chair of Modern History', p. 306.

41. Quoted in Leonard Marsak (ed.), *French Philosophers from Descartes to Sartre* (New York, 1961), p. 349.

42. J.S. Mill, *Autobiography* (Bobbs-Merrill edn, New York, 1957), p. 135.

43. J.S. Mill, A System of Logic, Ratiocinative and Inductive (Collected edn, Toronto, 1973), Vol. VIII, Book VI, Ch. X, especially p. 316.

44. H.T. Buckle, *History of Civilization in England,* 2nd edn. (2 vols., New York, 1895), I, p. 3.

45. Ibid., p. 5.

46. Ibid., p. 13.

47. Ibid., pp. 93-4.

48. H.J. Hanham, 'Editor's Introduction', to H.T. Buckle, *On Scotland and the Scotch Intellect* (Chicago, 1970), p. xxi.

49. Quoted as the epigraph to ibid.

50. See John Mackinnon Robertson, *Buckle and His Critics* (London, 1895).

51. Ibid., pp. 25, 197-202, 229-50.

52. Quoted in ibid., p. 26.

53. Charles Kingsley, 'On the Study of Natural History', *Miscellanies* (2 vols., London, 1863), II, p. 364.

54. Charles Kingsley, 'The Limits of Exact Science as Applied to History', *The Roman and the Teuton,* pp. 308, 317 and 334.

55. Froude, 'The Science of History', p. 14.

56. Gertrude Himmelfarb, *Lord Acton: A Study in Conscience and Politics* (Chicago, 1952), p. 40.

57. Lord Acton, 'Mr. Buckle's Thesis and Method', and 'Mr. Buckle's Philosophy of History' in J.N. Figgis and R.V. Laurence (eds.), *Historical Essays and Studies* (London, 1926), pp. 305-23 and 324-43.

58. J.A. Froude, 'Scientific Method Applied to History', *Short Studies on Great Subjects,* II, p. 462.

59. Himmelfarb, *Lord Acton,* Ch. VIII and p. 223; Herbert Butterfield, 'Acton: His Training, Methods and Intellectual System', in A.O. Sarkissian (ed.), *Studies in Diplomatic History in Honour of G.P. Gooch* (London, 1961), pp. 169-98; and Herbert Butterfield, *Man on His Past: The Study of the History of Historical Scholarship* (Cambridge, 1955), Ch. III.

60. T.H. Huxley, 'On the Educational Value of the Natural History Sciences', *Collected Essays,* III, p. 45.

61. Mark Pattison, *Suggestions on Academical Organisation* (Edinburgh, 1868), pp. 266-80.

62. Matthew Arnold, *Schools and Universities on the Continent* (Vol. IV of *The Complete Prose Works of Matthew Arnold,* edited by R.H. Super, Ann Arbor, 1964), p. 263.

63. From the 'Preface' to Ranke's *Histories of the Latin and Germanic Nations from 1494-1514,* translated and edited by Fritz Stern in *The Varieties of History* (Cleveland, 1956), p. 57. See also: Butterfield, *Man on His Past,* Chs. II and IV; White, *Metahistory,* Ch. 4; Gooch, *History and Historians,* Chs. II-VI; and Trygve Tholfsen, *Historical Thinking: An Introduction* (New York, 1967), Chs. 5 and 6.

64. Sheldon Rothblatt, *The Revolution of the Dons: Cambridge and Society in Victorian England* (London, 1968), pp. 155-80; R.T. Shannon, 'John Robert Seeley and the Idea of a National Church', in Robert Robson (ed.), *Ideas and Institutions of Victorian Britain* (London, 1967), pp. 236-67.

65. J.R. Seeley, 'The Teaching of Politics', *Lectures and Essays* (London, 1895), *passim.*

66. J.R. Seeley, 'Liberal Education in Universities', *Lectures and Essays,* pp. 204, 205, and 210.

67. J.R. Seeley, 'The Teaching of History', in G. Stanley Hall (ed.), *Methods of Teaching History* (Boston, 1896), p. 195.

68. Quoted in W.R.W. Stephens, *The Life and Letters of E.A. Freeman* (2 vols., London, 1895), I, p. 311.

69. Leslie Stephen (ed.), *Letters of John Richard Green* (New York, 1901), pp. 44-5.

70. W.H. Hutton (ed.), *Letters of William Stubbs* (London, 1904), p. 127.

71. Quoted in Stephens, *Life and Letters of Freeman,* I, p. 118.

72. E.A. Freeman, *The Methods of Historical Study* (London, 1886), pp. 118, 145.

73. William Stubbs, *Seventeen Lectures on the Study of Medieval and Modern History* (Oxford, 1887), p. 83.

74. Quoted in Hutton, *Letters of Stubbs,* p. 42.

75. Stubbs, *Seventeen Lectures,* p. 97.

76. E.A. Freeman, 'On the Study of History', *Fortnightly Review* (March 1881), p. 325.

77. Stubbs, *Seventeen Lectures,* p. 103.

78. Ibid., pp. 22-3.

79. Freeman, *Methods of Historical Study,* p. 44; 'On the Study of History', p. 320.

80. Blaas, *Continuity and Anachronism,* Ch. II, Part C; Norman Cantor, 'Introduction' to *William Stubbs on the English Constitution* (New York, 1966), pp. 1-13; J.W. Burrow, 'Editor's Introduction' to E.A. Freeman, *The History of the Norman Conquest in England* (Chicago, 1974).

81. Stubbs, *Seventeen Lectures,* p. 35.

82. Quoted in Stephen (ed.), *Letters of J.R. Green,* p. 107.

83. Stubbs, *Seventeen Lectures,* p. 93.

84. Freeman, *Methods of Historical Study,* p. 158.

85. See Green's letters to Freeman, quoted in Stephen (ed), *Letters of J.R. Green*, pp. 425-6 and 482.

86. Robert Brentano, 'The Sound of Stubbs', *Journal of British Studies* (May 1967), pp. 1-14.

87. Stubbs, *Seventeen Lectures,* p. 114; Freeman, *Methods of Historical Study,* p. 100.

88. Jann, 'The Art of History', pp. 163-4.

89. Andrew Lang, 'History As She Ought to Be Wrote', *Blackwood's* (August 1899), pp. 266-74; Augustine Birrell, 'The Muse of History', *Contemporary Review* (June 1885), pp. 770-80; G.M. Trevelyan, *Clio, A Muse* (London, 1913).

90. E.A. Freeman, 'Study of History', p. 325.

91. C.H.S. Fifoot (ed.), *The Letters of Frederic William Maitland* (Cambridge, Mass., 1965), pp. 272 and 274. See also David Thomson's review essay on C.V. Langlois and S. Seignobos, *Introduction to the Study of History*, translated by G.G. Barry (London, 1898) and on Allen Johnson, *The Historian and Historical Evidence*, in *History and Theory* (no. 2, 1967), pp. 236-41.

92. Norman H. Baynes, *A Bibliography of the Works of J.B. Bury* (Cambridge, 1929), p. 100.

93. Quoted in ibid., p. 107.

94. Doris S. Goldstein, 'J.B. Bury's Philosophy of History: A Reappraisal', *American Historical Review* (October 1977), pp. 896-919.

95. J.B. Bury, 'The Science of History', in Stern (ed.), *Varieties of History,* pp. 210-23.

96. J.B. Bury, 'The Place of Modern History in the Perspective of Knowledge', in Harold Temperley (ed.), *Selected Essays of J.B. Bury* (Cambridge, 1930), p. 45.

97. C.H. Firth, 'Samuel Rawson Gardiner', *Dictionary of National Biography*.

98. Oman, 'History at Oxford', pp. 235-7.

99. Hutton, *Letters of Stubbs,* p. 134; R.W. Southern, *The Shape and Substance of Academic History* (Oxford, 1961), pp. 12-17; F.M. Powicke, *Modern Historians and the Study of History* (London, 1955), Ch. II.

100. Jean O. McLachlan, 'The Origin and Early Development of the Cambridge Historical Tripos', *Cambridge Historical Journal* (no. 1, 1947), pp. 78-105; Louise Creighton, *Life and Letters of Mandell Creighton* (2 vols., London, 1905), I, pp. 227-83.

101. Oman, 'History at Oxford', p. 246.

102. Knowles, *Great Historical Enterprises,* Ch. 4; C.H.S. Fifoot, *Frederic William Maitland: A Life* (Cambridge, Mass., 1971), Ch. XI.

103. Acton's letter to the contributors is reprinted in Appendix I to Acton's *Lectures on Modern History* (London, 1960).

104. Stephen (ed.), *Letters of J.R. Green,* pp. 173, 217, 234, 238, 246, 433-7. See also Creighton, *Life of Mandell Creighton,* I, 333-44; H.A.L. Fisher, *James Bryce (Viscount Bryce of Dechmont, O.M.),* (2 vols., New York, 1927), I, pp. 194-6.

105. *English Historical Review,* 'Prefatory Note' (January 1886), pp. 1-6.

106. Quoted in Creighton, *Life of Mandell Creighton,* I, pp. 230-1.

107. The professionalization of historical studies is defined by Felix Gilbert, 'The Professionalization of History in the Nineteenth Century', John Higham, Leonard Krieger and Felix Gilbert (eds.), *History* (Englewood Cliffs, NJ, 1965), p. 329.

108. For the development of sociology, see Philip Abrams, *The Origins of British Sociology, 1834-1914* (Chicago, 1968); David J.D.Y. Peel, *Herbert Spencer: The Evolution of A Sociologist* (London, 1971). See also J.W. Burrow, *Evolution and Society: A Study of Victorian Social Theory* (Cambridge, 1970); and Reba N. Soffer, *Ethics and Society in England: The Revolution in the Social Sciences* (Berkeley, 1978).

# 6 THE REFORM OF THE UNIVERSITY SYSTEM

Natural science exerted the most powerful force affecting the topography of Victorian high culture. It had two main channels of influence: (1) the effort to improve the professional status of scientists; and (2) the transformation of other areas of intellectual activity into professional disciplines. Both channels cut directly through the universities and contributed to the university reform movement. Some observers, like Mark Pattison, believed that natural science alone had been sufficient to alter the nature of the universities. In fact, however, the English university reform movement was made up of several potent ingredients, any one of which would have worked powerful effects. These forces included a cluster of desires and ambitions: to open the universities to students of all religious denominations; to broaden the curricula in order to include 'modern' subjects; to make the universities and their education more productive and useful; and to convert them into research establishments.

Although not all of these elements of the reform movement worked harmoniously together, they were stoutly resisted by the defenders of the *status quo*. At issue was nothing less than different conceptions of the nature and purposes of universities. But the opposition to reform was gradually over-ridden by pressure from both inside and outside the universities. By the end of the century, the university system in England had undergone enormous changes — new universities founded and the old ones vastly altered. In new and old universities alike triumphed a new idea of a university — an institution that was national, secular, professional, and devoted in large measure to research. At the same time, many of the old styles and forms of Oxford and Cambridge were retained, as well as the goal of providing a liberal education to the sons of professional men and the governing elite. Yet for the most part, the substance changed while the style remained the same: the character of the university system was altered, particularly in regard to the status, function, and career patterns of tutors and professors.

The movement to reform the universities sprang from a number of different sources, some from outside the universities, some from within, and not all had exactly the same objectives. Science, of course, was one source. Another was utilitarianism. Here one can see the desire to make all institutions conform to middle-class values of work, productivity and efficiency. The utilitarians in the 1820s and 1830s wanted to make the universities more useful to the main activities of the nation — mainly to business and industry, but also to political and social progress in general. They believed that imperfections in political and social institutions resulted from ignorance and superstition, which were protected by archaic bastions of privilege, and which could be reformed by 'the march of mind'. The fortresses of privilege had to be neutralized, and the most important of these was the Church of England, with its monopoly over Oxford and Cambridge. Hence the utilitarians regarded the universities as inefficient in terms of the national interest, and worse, as perpetuators of an aristocratic social system. In the *Westminster Review,* Dr Southwood Smith, a close friend of Bentham's, argued that the universities had too little connection with the real life of England. Their education was useless, for their contention that the classics were good mental discipline for anyone regardless of vocation was 'as if the man who is to live by rope-dancing were to labour for instruction at the anvil'.[1] The utilitarians believed that more subjects ought to be taught, and that meant the universities would have to stop educating everyone as if he were going into the clergy.

The utilitarians held that the tutors would have to become more efficient. Because the clergy claimed a monopoly in education, they claimed to be competent to teach everything — politics, economics and the sciences, as well as divinity. Actually, the utilitarians argued, since the Oxbridge tutors were clergymen by profession, they failed to teach anything well, including theology and the classics. Merit selection (a system which would afford the middle class an entrée) ought to prevail: all teachers of the various subjects should be chosen from those who knew the subjects best. Even literature should be taught by people who were 'literary men by profession'.[2] Religious instruction itself was taught, according to the utilitarians, by 'drones and sluggards', instead of by 'professors, whose talents and learning would adorn the science they taught'.[3] If the clerical monopoly were broken and the universities restored to the nation as a whole, then not only better teaching but also advancement of learning would result. The utilitarians believed the march of mind required the universities to be productive in learning and scholarship. Such productivity should be encouraged by providing outlets for self-interest, that is, career structures for advancement in the separate fields. As the universities stood, the utilitarians felt that the interests of the nation were sacrificed to 'an enormous and insatiable greediness, and a crapulous self-indulgence'.[4]

Another important source of the external university reform movement was Dissent. The Nonconformists made up the central corps of the rapidly-growing business and industrial class, but they were excluded from both Oxford and Cambridge by the religious tests. This disqualification was bound to be a point of grievance with the English Dissenters, who grew less patient with second-class citizenship as their economic and social power grew and as their religious fervour was rekindled by the influence of Evangelicalism. Especially after repeal of the test and corporation acts in 1828, Catholic emancipation in 1829, and the reform act of 1832, the Dissenters expected additional steps in curtailing the privileges of the Church of England. The Nonconformists thought of Oxford and Cambridge as national, as opposed to ecclesiastical, institutions; therefore, they demanded abolition or relaxation of the university religious tests.[5]

The great Whig journal, the *Edinburgh Review,* combined elements of both the utilitarian and the Nonconformist demands in its campaign for university reform. The Scotsmen who produced the *Edinburgh Review* naturally were influenced by the example of the Scottish universities, which differed sharply from the English. Probably because of their connection *via* Calvinism with continental universities, the Scottish universities had been constructed more on the professorial model and were open to students from a wider range of economic and social standing than were Oxford and Cambridge. Further, the Scottish universities offered a much broader curriculum, including study in a number of subjects, with philosophy instead of the classics or mathematics as the centre-piece. Thus the *Edinburgh Review* put forward a concept of a university that would be a national institution, open without test to students of all denominations, offering a wide range of subjects taught in part by a strengthened professoriate, and operating more efficiently and productively for national purposes.

Easily the most influential advocate of university reform to appear in the pages of the *Edinburgh Review* was Sir William Hamilton, the Scottish philsopher and lawyer, who had been educated at Edinburgh and Glasgow. Hamilton published a series of articles in the *Edinburgh Review* in the 1830s that stated the Whig-Liberal case for the next two decades. His argument centred on a distinction between the original (and to him, proper) definition of a university and the actualities of Oxford and Cambridge. 'A university', he wrote, 'is a trust confided by the state to certain hands for the common interests of the nation . . .'[6]

The universities had been established in the middle ages by *public* authority for *public* advantage, but the colleges, which were *private* corporations for *private* advantage, had usurped the functions and privileges of the universities. According to Hamilton, the present system of collegiate domination over the universities was a breach of trust by college officials, which subverted the very functions of the universities.

The universities, Hamilton said, were supposed to give instruction in all the major subjects, but the colleges had reduced instruction to one — classics at Oxford and mathematics at Cambridge. In universities proper, teachers were chosen by merit, each teacher concentrating on a single subject. In the Oxbridge colleges, one person taught all subjects, in so far as subjects were taught at all. Actually, the tutors were not qualified to teach *any* subject. In universities, degrees signified important achievement; in the current system they did not. The results were that Oxbridge graduates were poorly trained, even in classics and theology; and that was the reason the Oxbridge instructors played such an insignificant role in the literature and science of the secular world.[7]

What had to be done, in Hamilton's view, was to recover the original, national character of the universities from the 'present corruption'. Oxford, for instance, had to be saved from the colleges. Unlike some extreme reformers, Hamilton did not mean to abolish the colleges, for he approved of collegial living and its tutorial discipline. 'A tutorial system', he wrote, 'in subordination to a professorial (which Oxford formerly enjoyed) we regard as affording *the condition of an absolutely perfect University*.'[8] But the condition in which the colleges comprehended the entire university, in which the colleges were co-terminous with the university, had to be broken. Hence, control over the university had to be taken from the Heads of Houses and restored to university officials; and the tutorial system of instruction had to be subordinated to professorial instruction again. The curriculum had to be broadened so that clergymen, lawyers, and physicians each received training appropriate to their vocations.

Lastly, the Dissenters had to be admitted to the universities. Hamilton, like most of the reformers, admitted that as private corporations the colleges could accept or exclude religious sects as they pleased. *Collegiate* religious tests could not be abolished. For this reason, it had been suggested that Nonconformists be allowed to open their own colleges within the universities. But Hamilton, like most Dissenters themselves, disliked the principle of religious tests; thus he regarded the proposal to establish Nonconformist colleges as mistaken. He thought that a better solution would be to open halls or hostels that imposed no religious tests at all. In such halls, a student could reside in the university without belonging to a college. Further, Hamilton contended that all teachers and students ought to enjoy 'academic freedom' — that is, freedom from religious tests for degrees or appointments — while those interested in entering the Anglican clergy could study orthodox divinity in a theology faculty. In short, by Hamilton's plan, the universities would again become national, rather than ecclesiastical, institutions.[9]

The utilitarian, Dissenting, and Whig reformers hoped to have Parliament act to alter the ancient universities, and offered a bill to abolish the religious tests as early as 1834. The bill was soundly defeated by the House of Lords, but it proved to be only the first in a series. Meanwhile, the reformers took up an idea of the poet Thomas Campbell to establish a university in London, free of all religious bars. Led by Joseph Hume and Lord Brougham, both of whom were connected to the philosophic Radicals, the reformers established on the Scottish (and therefore continental) model the 'University of London' — soon to become University College, London — which opened its doors in 1828. Its curriculum was much broader than those of Oxford and Cambridge, and included physical and moral sciences, history, political economy and modern languages. University College was a completely secular institution, and its professorial system of instruction brought to many orthodox minds the threat of the higher criticism and unconventional theology which flourished in German universities. Yet when Anglican churchmen founded a 'college for general education' in London, to counter the influence of 'the Godless college in Gower Street', they established it — King's College — on the Scottish pattern of a broad curriculum and professorial teaching.

Meanwhile, 'London University' applied for a charter to grant degrees, and the applicants found their request resisted by both Oxford and Cambridge. Finally, in 1836 a compromise settlement joined the two London colleges as University College and King's College of the University of London, which was empowered to grant degrees. Later in the century, the provincial civic universities were founded on the twin London principles of no religious tests and the professorial system of instruction. But the London University for many years was allowed no function other than examining students and granting degrees. This condition was confirmed in 1858, when the University received its new charter, which allowed it to examine for degrees, students from a number of colleges other than University or King's, and indeed authorized London to examine anyone who presented himself for a degree. The University of London, as opposed to its affiliated colleges, remained an examining body until the end of the century.[10]

In any case, the founding of the University of London would not have quieted the reform movement, partly because the reformers wanted to exploit the ancient universities' resources on behalf of their own sense of the national interests, and partly because the reformers objected to the Church's monopoly over the prestige-granting power of these ancient universities. Thus the mainstream of even the external university reform movement flowed towards Oxford and Cambridge. The external reformers were, after all, mainly from the English bourgeoisie; and their overriding concern was to obtain access to the privileged positions of the landed orders, not to destroy those positions altogether. They wanted the ancient universities, it is true, to reflect more bourgeois values like hard work, utility and productivity; but no one of consequence seriously considered the establishment of a wholly new system while leaving Oxbridge to die on the ecclesiastical vine. The ancient universities were too rich, too politically powerful and too socially attractive to allow extreme reconstructions of higher education.

The continuing pressure applied by the external reform movement turned a number of people inside the universities into reformers. Some devoted denizens of Oxford and Cambridge argued that the universities must reform themselves before the rough and insensitive hands of Parliament did it. But the internal university reform movement, a growing minority of professors and fellows in the 1830s and 1840s, included more people than simply those nervous about the autonomy of the institutions. The internal reformers contained some men motivated by the various goals of the utilitarians, Dissenters and Liberals, others who were concerned about the social and moral condition of the nation as a whole, and still others moved by a sense of the inadequacy of work and career patterns of the teaching force. If the external reform movement exerted a force without which significant reforms would not have occurred, the internal reform movement did most to shape the character and direction of these reforms.

One of the concerns shared by many of the internal reformers arose from the traditional idea of the function of a university as it had been expressed by Coleridge. At both universities, there were young men deeply troubled by the social dislocations, class divisions and political instability of the new industrial order. Men like John Sterling and F.D.

Maurice, who had learned much from Coleridge and Carlyle, believed that these social problems were the result of the 'cash nexus' and its underlying moral corruption and social disintegration. The solution to national problems, these broad church Anglicans thought, lay in the clerisy: the universities would send out to every corner of England a morally and religiously-sound clergy and aristocracy to serve as a cultural elite that would restore the community of England. At Cambridge, the famous elite undergraduate society, the Apostles, adopted such Coleridgean views soon after its founding in the 1820s. Its membership, including A.H. Hallam, R.C. Trench and Alfred Tennyson, recognized that the whole atmosphere of the university would have to be revitalized in order for the university to produce a genuine clerisy. In particular, they wanted to replace the routine of studying merely for honours exams with deep soul-searching, a love of truth and spiritual rebirth. Simple memorization of a few texts like Paley's *Evidences* could not produce a clerisy.[11]

At Oxford, perhaps the best example of this kind of reformer was Benjamin Jowett, an immensely influential tutor at Balliol from the 1840s. The similarity between Jowett and the Cambridge Apostles may seem odd, since his fame as a tutor rested at least in part on his successful preparation of students for the same exams that the Apostles condemned. Nor was Jowett a disciple of Coleridge, even though he had high respect for Coleridge's ideas. He was, however, like the Apostles in that he was a student of German philosophy and scholarship and a liberal churchman. Further, his whole tutorial career was a practical application of the clerisy ideal. Jowett not only trained his students for the exams, but he also took great care in guiding their first steps in their careers. He did not try to recruit young men into the clergy; indeed, he prided himself on his ability to foresee the role in which each could excel. Jowett saw a multitude of public tasks that needed doing — religious, political, social and administrative. What he preached to his students was that each should discipline himself to hard work and dutifulness, traits suitable for a ruling class. At the same time, Jowett believed that Oxford would have to be improved in order to produce the clerical and lay leaders for the future. In the 1840s, therefore, he urged that the spectrum of subjects taught be expanded to include philosophy, modern theology, history and philology; and he proposed that the restrictions on fellowships be abolished, and that the number of professors be increased to give the tutors a goal for their careers as teachers.[12]

Another concern of the internal reformers pertained to academic freedom. In the first decades of the nineteenth century, when university orthodoxy was 'high and dry', disputes about a tutor's or a professor's religious belief did not often interfere with appointments or performance of duties. But as Broad Church liberalism on one side of the theological spectrum, and Tractarianism on the other, took hold in the Church of England, doctrinal confrontations in the universities became more frequent and bitter, and men were denied posts because they were perceived as unorthodox. Jowett himself was denied the mastership of Balliol in 1854 — in part because of his liberal theology. Sometimes such disputes produced reformers — men who believed that doctrinal matters should not interfere with the teaching of non-theological subjects.

Henry Halford Vaughan was a case in point. Vaughan, a fellow of Oriel, had decided against taking orders and had turned to a career in the law. But in 1839, Vaughan stood for the readership in logic at Oxford. The Tractarians had doubts about his religious views and put up their own candidates. They also sought to have Vaughan re-subscribe to the Thirty-Nine Articles as proof of his orthodoxy. He refused on grounds that religion was irrelevant to the issue, his belief being that religious truth and truth in other areas of thought could be pursued separately. His position, however, was acceptable to neither the Newmanites nor liberal churchmen like Thomas Arnold, all of whom insisted that the university was a Christian institution for Christian education. Arnold wrote to Vaughan:

> as to a man's Christian faith I would just as soon vote for an unbeliever to be Divinity Professor as Professor of Logic because I would not put an unbeliever into any place of instruction in a Christian university if that place implied that he was a member of the university generally and not merely called in to lecture on a particular subject.[13]

Eventually, Vaughan withdrew his candidacy. He became Regius Professor of Modern History in 1848, after the collapse of the Oxford Movement had dampened theological in-fighting. But the experience helped immeasurably to make Vaughan a reformer, one who believed that clerical power over the universities would have to be broken before the universities could become centres of scholarship and learning. Where orthodoxy clashed with merit, orthodoxy would have to give way.

Probably the most widespread and powerful concern among

internal critics of the universities was to construct permanent and respectable careers within the university. Here again, reformers saw the church connection as the obstacle. The standard career pattern for Oxbridge dons led from undergraduate to fellow to orders to a parish living or the bar, and resignation of the fellowship. A career in university teaching was not thought of as a possibility, not least because a man had to resign a fellowship when he married, but also because fellowships were regarded as steps in a career structure leading out of the university. In the first half of the century, however, the desire for professional careers within the university gradually took hold. One reason had to do with the examination system itself. By the 1840s, the honours examinations had created a demand for better teaching, and more, better prepared, teachers. This demand had generated the system of private coaches, who for a fee prepared ('crammed') a student for his exams. Especially at Cambridge, this private teaching industry caused professional jealousy among the tutors, particularly those who felt a strong urge to pastoral care for their students. At both Oxford and Cambridge, the demand by serious students for good teaching in the 1830s and 1840s increasingly won favourable response from the dons.[14]

The impulse within the universities to establish teaching careers had yet more complicated origins. In the first half of the century, no doubt due to the impact of Evangelicalism and the general shift from eighteenth-century aristocratic to Victorian values, the students at Oxford and Cambridge became older, more serious and harder-working. The products of Arnold's Rugby and other reformed public schools, and their parents, expected more systematic teaching and more consistent display of the work ethic from the dons. One former student of Arnold's recalled: 'Dr. Arnold's great power as a private tutor resided in this, that he gave such an intense earnestness to life. Every pupil was made to feel that there was a work for him to do — that his happiness as well as his duty lay in doing that work well.'[15] Students such as these were not to be denied better teaching; and as they took their BAs and won fellowships, they became reforming dons. They wanted to teach better than their tutors had taught them, and to exercise greater intellectual and moral influence over their students. They agreed with Arnold that their instructional ideal required more serious learning on their own part:

Every improvement of your own powers and knowledge, [Arnold wrote to a tutor in 1839] tells immediately upon them [students]; and indeed I hold that a man is only fit to teach so long as he is himself learning daily. If the mind once becomes stagnant, it can give no fresh draught to another mind; it is drinking out of a pond, instead of from a spring.[16]

Not surprisingly, many of these dons found models of the devotion to learning in natural science and German university scholarship.

The combined pressure of the external and internal reformers persuaded the Russell government in 1850 to appoint Royal Commissions to investigate conditions in the old universities. The two Royal Commissions stimulated and focused a debate over the nature of universities that extended through the 1850s. A look at three prominent figures in the debate will set out the main positions in the discussion and help carve in relief the principles that were selected for implementation. The three figures are H.H. Vaughan, E.B. Pusey and Mark Pattison.

Vaughan had established his credentials as a university reformer by the time he became Regius Professor of Modern History in 1848. He took the extreme professorial position — that the university should be a secular institution dominated by its professors. The university should rule over the colleges and the professors over the tutors. Further, the function of the professors should be intellectual, not moral; their task should be learning, not teaching. The professors should pursue knowledge for its own sake, and not for any political or moral object. Hence the professors should look upon teaching as only a secondary task. Their principal activity should be gaining mastery over a special subject, so that they could speak authoritatively in the field of inquiry, contribute to knowledge through research and restore the scholarly reputation of the university. Teaching, in Vaughan's view, would remain in the hands of the colleges, but collegiate activities should be subordinate to the scholarly functions of the university. Above all, a class of scholars unencumbered by teaching duties or religious restrictions should be cultivated. Vaughan and other reformers wrote to Russell and Gladstone: 'It is highly desirable to encourage the residence of men at Oxford who shall devote themselves to the pursuit of special departments of knowledge, and acquire high eminence in learning.'[17] This was a theme heard frequently throughout the rest of the century.

Many reformers, while agreeing with Vaughan that the professoriate should be strengthened and more effort devoted to deep learning, found his antipathy to teaching unacceptable. They wanted to maintain, indeed to strengthen, the university's connection with the country's governing and professional elites. Jowett, for instance, called Vaughan's proposed class of learned professors an 'intellectual aristocracy'.[18] Vaughan contributed to the credibility of this criticism by his unusual performance of his duties as Regius Professor. During the 1850s, Vaughan was forced to teach undergraduates in the new School of Law and Modern History. In this role he was very uncomfortable. Vaughan insisted that since research comprised the main function of the chair, residence in Oxford was not required. Despite much opposition, including some from fellow reformers, he resided in London and commuted to Oxford to give his lectures. Meanwhile, he was isolated from the students and curriculum by the tutors who controlled the Law and Modern History School. In 1857, his chair received endowment in part by a fellowship of Oriel that required residence; consequently, Vaughan resigned. The reformed Oxford of the mid-Victorian years expected its professors to be teachers as well as scholars, while Vaughan wanted to devote himself exclusively to scholarship.[19]

The opposite ideal — Oxford as a centre for moral education — was most prominently argued by the leading university conservative, the Reverend E.B. Pusey, Canon of Christ Church and Professor of Hebrew in Oxford. Pusey was a distinguished scholar and ardent churchman. With Newman and Keble he was one of the leaders of the Tractarian movement and for many years the most influential opponent of intellectual and institutional liberalizing tendencies in the university.[20] He had opposed admission of Dissenters into Oxford and had stoutly defended the requirement of subscription to the Thirty-Nine Articles. To him, the university was a guardian of the Church, and it had to defend the idea of dogmatic truth against the destructive claims of human reason. Further, when still a newly-minted Oxford BA, Pusey had gone to Germany to study at first hand the new theology and philosophy. The rationalism of the German philosophers had shocked him. He returned to England to prepare his countrymen to resist the coming invasion of rationalism and scientific scholarship. He hoped to promote the recovery of the cathedral chapters as centres of religious learning and to resist the incursion into Oxford of the Germanic model of a university. The German system, he recognized, had advantages in the mastery over special fields that the division of labour among professors allowed. But he also felt that it had the serious moral flaw of subjecting immature students, who were without moral guidance, to the authoritative — and potentially dangerous —

theories of the professors. Hence Pusey linked intellectual conservatism to a participatory education theory: the lecture system, he argued, worked with passive students who can only imitate the ideas of the professor; while the tutorial system strengthened the moral resilience of the students.[21]

Pusey believed that the Royal Commission on Oxford had raised two key issues: in the words of his biographer, 'whether Oxford education should be collegiate or professorial, and whether it should be lay or clerical'.[22] To Pusey, it was clear that Oxford education had to be collegiate and clerical. Certainly, he hoped that the tutors would be able to expand their pastoral influence over their students; and he had no objection to providing a professional career structure for clergymen-teachers. But since the main object of education was to strengthen the moral and religious fibre of the students, collegiate teaching was best, for the 'cathechetical' mode of teaching in the colleges required students to strain their minds to understand, compare and judge various ideas. For the same reason, a clerical teaching body was preferable to lay professors. To reformers like Vaughan, who supposed that universities were places for learning, Pusey responded with an older view based on scepticism about the human intellect:

> The object of a University is not simply or mainly to cultivate the intellect. Intellect, by itself, heightened, sharpened, refined, cool, piercing, subtle, would be after the likeness, not of God, but of His enemy, who is acuter and subtler far, than the acutest and subtlest. The object of Universities is, with and through the disciplines of the intellect, as far as may be, to discipline and train the whole moral and intelligent being . . . The type of the best English intellectual character is sound, solid, steady, thoughtful, patient, well-disciplined judgement. It would be a perversion of our institutions to turn the University into a forcing-house for intellect.[23]

For conservatives like Pusey, the link between a professorial university, German scholarship, and religious decay was clear. Henry Mansell put it this way:

Professors we,
From over the sea
From the land where Professors in plenty be;
And we thrive and flourish, as well we may

In the land that produced one Kant, with a K,
And many Cants with a C.

Nevertheless, most of the college tutors in the 1850s, a crucial element in the internal reform forces, took the position of neither Vaughan nor Pusey. Their view was that elaborated forcefully by Mark Pattison, at the time fellow and tutor of Lincoln College, Oxford. From the day he had gone up to Oxford in 1832, Pattison had devoted his life to study — not so much to publishing, but to broad and deep learning in all the ways of understanding human experience. He began his career with an exalted idea of the college fellow, but was soon disillusioned by the reality. As a conscientious tutor at Lincoln, he found that he did not have the time to master all the subjects he was required to teach; that cramming students for exams was not a satisfying profession; and that the arguments of natural science about the narrowness of the curriculum were unanswerable. Hence Pattison, like Jowett and other reforming dons, coupled his hankering for specialization in teaching with the desire for a broader curriculum, and for a harder-working, more decent and dedicated body of tutors. The key to their reforms, he thought, was to open the fellowships to merit by examination.[24]

Pattison gladly co-operated with the Oxford Royal Commission of 1850, sending a long and closely-reasoned case for reform. He still thought of the university's main function as one of teaching, and he strongly supported the collegiate-tutorial system, provided the close fellowships were opened to competition. 'My imagination', he later recalled, 'was wholly preoccupied with the beneficial relation which the college system establishes between tutor and pupil.'[25] He told the Royal Commission that the professorial system aimed at an inferior type of mental cultivation, a smattering of knowledge at best. The lecture system was appropriate only for a preliminary stage of education or for 'popularisation'. But in England, a 'cultivated clerisy' needed 'liberal education', which he defined as rigorous training and disciplining of the faculties. For this purpose, the tutorial system was best, because it actively engaged the student in a profound consideration of the subject matter and encouraged a genuine love for learning. For Pattison, then, the university's goal was intellectual (as opposed to moral) development among students and teachers, for which the proper mode of instruction was the collegiate system.[26]

As the views of Vaughan and Pattison show, the university reformers were divided on the issue of a professorial versus tutorial,

German versus English, model of the university. But most of the Oxbridge reformers could agree on some essential points: that the professoriate ought to be revived and enlarged; that the professors ought to devote themselves largely to learning; and above all that the tutors ought to have professional careers as teachers. As C.A. Swainson, fellow of Christ's College, told the Cambridge Royal Commission:

> The difficulty of retaining men of ability in the University, in my opinion lies in this, that the Lecturers and Tutors are underpaid; their offices lead to nothing; when they cease to hold their Fellowships their employment is gone; they must begin life afresh... The duty of lecturing is not the business of life; no one hopes that it will be so, and therefore cannot enter into it with such energy and devotion as is desirable.[27]

To establish careers in teaching, the fellowships had to be opened to competition by merit, the requirements for orders and celibacy abandoned, and professorships marked out as the top rungs on a career ladder.[28]

In connection with such careers, the reformers hoped, the tutors would be allowed to specialize in their teaching and win respect as masters of their subjects. Further, the curriculum ought to be broadened, though Oxford and Cambridge should continue to give a liberal education and not training for specific vocations, and especially not training for business and industry. There was some sentiment among the reformers for reducing the expenses of an Oxbridge education, but few reformers seriously considered a major expansion of the social stratum which the universities served.[29] The reformers assumed that a liberal education would be a good preparation for all vocations by not providing specific training for any. It would offer mental discipline suitable for application in a wide variety of occupations important to the upper classes, not least the church, law, medicine and civil service.[30]

When the two Royal Commissions reported (on Oxford in 1852; on Cambridge in 1852-3), both sets of commissioners emphasized two items: (1) the curricula of both universities should be broadened to include a wide variety of modern subjects, especially natural science; and (2) professional careers in teaching and learning had to be constructed for the tutors. Both Commissions approved of the recent additions of courses of study in natural science, law and modern history and moral science; and they expressed hope that such studies would become important in the university scene. Neither Commission opted to choose between teaching and scholarship, for both agreed with long-standing arguments that the universities ought to be improved as seats of education *and* learning. The Oxford commissioners put their hope for a revived university in the professoriate. Enlarged and better endowed, the professoriate could take its place at the top of the university's career structure. This 'body of learned men, devoting their lives to the cultivation of Science, and to the direction of Academical education', would open up careers that might attract the ablest men away from ecclesiastical life into academic life.[31]

One of the reasons that the Oxford Commission opted for a system in which the professors would dominate both learning and teaching is that they wanted to encourage the deep scholarship associated with professoriates; but they also chose this system because they foresaw enormous difficulties in opening the college fellowships to merit.[32] It would be easier to suppress some fellowships and apply their stipends to new chairs. The Cambridge commissioners saw fewer obstacles to improvement of the body of fellows. Their main problem was to circumvent the system of private coaching. To accomplish this they suggested two remedies: '(1) that there shall be a definite and permanent career provided for teachers, and (2) that a reasonable latitude of choice be allowed to the pupils as to what teachers they will select for their guidance.'[33] These two remedies required a number of actions. The fellowships should be opened to merit: this was the crucial step. In addition, there would be established a staff of lecturers or sub-professors, which, unlike the fellowships, would be unencumbered by requirements of holy orders or celibacy. These sub-professors, like the professors, would be paid from college funds. They would be organized in boards of studies, which would encourage and co-ordinate the specialized, co-operative teaching of tutors, sub-professors and professors. In this way, rewarding careers in a structure of promotion within the university would retain men, experts in their teaching fields, who at the moment went outside into the church or the law.[34]

The two Royal Commissions came fairly close to what the internal reformers wanted, and especially to what the tutors wanted. Parliament acted in 1854 and 1856 to institute the new dispensation. Both universities were opened to Dissenters, in that subscription to the Thirty-Nine Articles was not to be required for the BA at either university. Advanced degrees and fellowships, however, still required subscription — a requirement not relaxed until 1871. The governing bodies of the universities were reconstituted to give more power to the resident MAs, as opposed to the total body of graduates. The new courses of study set up in 1848 and 1850 were endorsed. From the point of view of the tutors, the most important change was that all fellowships were opened to merit, to be determined by competitive examination. (All concerned seem to have assumed, however, that all competitors for a fellowship at either university would come from that particular university.) The number of fellowships devoted to teaching grew, but a large number of so-called 'prize' or 'idle' fellowships continued to exist, mainly for the benefit of young men preparing for the clergy or the bar. On the whole, the university reform acts contributed decisively to the creation of a vital teaching force. As John Sparrow has put it, 'This was the vital change; over the next couple of decades it restocked the Common Rooms of Oxford [and Cambridge] with a new breed of don' who did most of the teaching, rather than the private coaches.[35]

In the late 1850s and 1860s, Oxford and Cambridge became much more conscientious and 'professional' institutions. The importance of being earnest, as preached by Thomas Arnold and shared by men like the Cambridge Apostles and Benjamin Jowett, created a much more busy and hard-working atmosphere. Classics at Oxford and mathematics at Cambridge still dominated undergraduate studies; but they were more thoroughly taught. The reformers of the 1840s and 1850s, particularly those inside the universities, had wanted to preserve the traditional links between the universities and the learned professions — namely the clergy and the law — and the new tutors of the 1850s and 1860s still thought of Oxbridge as giving a training partly intellectual and partly moral to England's social and political elite.[36] They wanted, as Arnold at Rugby had wanted, to instill in their students a particular ethic of Christian morality and public service. For this purpose, it was wonderfully convenient that they (especially Jowett) were able to shape the new civil service exams so that they required the traditional classical education.[37] Further, the tutors went to great lengths to 'reach' their students through athletics and collegial comradeship. A more or less orthodox muscular Christianity became the style of the most active dons. The towpaths along the Isis and Cam fairly teemed with well-conditioned, perspiring tutors leading their crews to victory — dons like Henry Sidgwick, Henry Jackson and Leslie Stephen at Cambridge; and Charles S. Parker and T.H. Green at Oxford.[38]

The figure of John Hardy in Thomas Hughes's *Tom Brown at Oxford* (first published in 1858) beautifully caught the image of the new don. By hard work and self-denial, the perfectly virtuous Hardy had risen from servitor to college fellow — thereby displaying the earnest values cherished by the mid-Victorian upper classes and also perpetrating the myth that any sturdy chap, no matter how poor, could make it at Oxbridge. Hardy became a reforming don, making great improvements in the undergraduate life of his college by administrative reforms to protect innocent students from indebtedness, by encouraging serious reading for the honours schools and by taking a very active role in rowing. Hardy wanted Oxford and Cambridge to play an important national role, for they and the public schools 'are the heart of dear old England'. Hardy thus thought of the universities as the training grounds for a national clerisy: 'A low standard up here for ten years may corrupt half the parishes in the kingdom.'[39] And Hardy succeeds in attracting the students to his views by taking an interest in all they do; he is able to get them to 'meet me nearly half-way in reading, and three-quarters in everything else'.[40] Hardy is portrayed as a scholar, learned in his subject, unlike the older, despised, dons; but above all he is a conscientious teacher, training future professional leaders for their due places in the elite.

The Oxford and Cambridge moulded by the reforms of the 1850s and 1860s were seen by many Victorians to have entered a golden age. The combination of earnest students and enthusiastic dons in institutions devoted mainly to teaching seems to have caught the fancy of a large part of the late-Victorian middle and landed classes. The university novel, for instance, took a new form in reflecting the changed attitudes towards the universities. The comic and rowdy novels of the early decades of the century *(Pendennis,* for instance) gave way in the 1840s and 1850s to sincere reformist novels like *Tom Brown at Oxford.* These in turn were replaced by novels that romanticized the universities: novels that then, and until the Great War, portrayed both dons and students as virtuous and mutually respectful.[41] Such portrayals reflected the satisfaction that the upper classes felt with the fact that Oxford *and* Cambridge had become more 'useful', serious institutions — universities that taught a wide variety of subjects, including some regarded as modern, but that still prepared the male offspring of the elite for posts in the government and the professions, as well as academia. Few people that counted other than the utilitarians and some scientists had wanted the old universities to train young men for industrial, technical, or commercial careers. Most upper-class mid-

Victorians felt that a liberal education taught by dons who themselves displayed the earnest values of the middle class was exactly the right formula.

The formula, however, depicted a compound that included some elements capable of changing themselves and the whole mixture. The real 'golden age' did not last as long as the fictional genre that commemorated it. Even before 1914, the English university system had changed again. For one thing, new universities — the red bricks — grew up on a pattern and with functions that differed from those at Oxbridge. For another, within the ancient universities the logic of some of the mid-century reforms continued to operate; and by the end of the century that logic had made Oxbridge a distinctly different place from the earnest higher public schools of the 1850s and 1860s. By 1900 Oxford and Cambridge had become places where research and specialized study by a secular as well as a professional body of scholars and scientists dominated the terrain.

The reforms of the 1850s at Oxford and Cambridge had done little to appease the desire of people like the utilitarians to open higher education to a wider public and to connect the universities to business and industry. In particular, the industrial north of England felt the need for universities closely related to the tasks of the lower-middle and middle classes of the great provincial cities. In 1832, churchmen had tried to meet this need by establishing a university at Durham; but it had been founded on the Oxbridge model largely to train clergymen, and had not thrived. Gradually, the provincial towns began to provide for themselves. In 1851, by a bequest of the Manchester merchant John Owens, Owens College, Manchester was founded. It was constituted on a professorial system, with strong emphasis on instruction in the natural sciences. It was there that Henry Enfield Roscoe, who was appointed in 1857, led the school of chemistry to national eminence. Other cities followed the Manchester example: Mason's College in Birmingham, and university colleges in Sheffield, Leeds, Bradford, Liverpool and elsewhere. In 1881, the university colleges of Manchester, Birmingham, Liverpool and Leeds joined to form the Victoria University. In the years before 1900, Birmingham, Liverpool and Leeds each won independent university status. At each of these, research by a professorial staff, with relatively heavy emphasis on science, was a primary function.[42]

The red bricks represented the direct result of the application of industrial wealth to higher education. Perhaps for that very reason they were not able (and are still not able) to bestow the status carried by

Oxford and Cambridge. Yet in the late-Victorian period, the ancient universities themselves evolved in the same general direction as the red bricks. More and more, research came to be seen as an essential requirement for university teachers — for tutors and fellows as well as for professors. This evolution was a puzzling and complicated phenomenon, the reasons for which were numerous, obscurely inter-related and often subterranean. One obvious reason was the continuing example of the German universities, which had long been potent in English thinking and became more so in the 1860s and early 1870s, as Germany achieved national unification with an impressive, even frightening, display of national efficiency.[43] Another clear cause was the influence of natural science and its models of research and university organization. As we have seen, the more science won a place in the universities, and the more the scientific paradigm of knowledge and its acquisition affected other disciplines, the more the universities had to be altered towards the research and professorial system. This process had scarcely begun to have its effect at the time of the reforms of the 1850s.

In addition to the influence of Germany and natural science, which by themselves would have been necessary if not sufficient for the changes to come, certain tendencies inherent in the reform movement of the 1840s and 1850s helped destabilize the very conditions the movement created. For one thing, the desire on the part of tutors to exercise greater authority over their students led to specialized teaching. Co-operative teaching arrangements among the colleges at both Oxford and Cambridge began to be built in the 1860s, and were regularized thereafter. A tutor at one college could direct his teaching to one segment of a field, while colleagues in other colleges devoted themselves to different subjects. The specialization of teaching, and therefore of knowledge and study, was encouraged by the reformers' desire to improve the teaching of the old universities at a time when the traditional source of authority — dogmatic religion — was losing its hold.

A second source of change was the superior status awarded to learning over teaching in the reforms of the 1850s. Change flowing from this point was quite unintended by most of the internal reformers, who clearly thought of teaching as the primary function of a university. The situation arose from the problem of what to do with the professoriate. While many external reformers had wanted the professors to dominate both the teaching and the research of the universities, the tutors were determined to retain control over the curriculum. They had wanted to set the professorships up as the top rung on a ladder of promotion, but to keep the teaching control of the professors to a minimum; hence the tutors readily identified the professoriate with learning rather than teaching, and thereby unwittingly gave scholarship higher status than teaching. After the 1850s, the liberal reforming tutors, who were the most active and influential of all the fellows, increasingly thought of their posts as requiring both learning and teaching, with the former a qualification for the latter.[44] Indeed, learning and research, which the reforming dons of mid-century had seen as the means to the end of better teaching, tended to become ends in themselves.

This process can be traced in the evolution of relations between Jowett, who became master of Balliol in 1870, and one of his star pupils, T.H. Green, who had come up to Oxford in 1855 and had in the 1860s earned the dominant position among Balliol tutors. Green had been introduced to Hegelian philosophy by Jowett, but he soon carried German Idealist philosophy to lengths that Jowett never intended. Jowett had studied German philosophy in order to strengthen Christianity by application of modern thought. Green became a rigorous and systematic Idealist philosopher in order to reconstruct on a purely rational basis a system of thought which retained the essence of Christianity while abandoning all the traditional, mythical elements of orthodoxy. In so doing, Green made himself into an expert in a highly technical and difficult philosphic system, a critic of the sloppiness of 'amateur' philosophers like Spencer and Lewes, and the first professional academic philosopher in England.[45]

Green soon became uncomfortable with his tutorial task of teaching the same texts in classical philosophy year after year and sought to give instruction in German Idealism. He encouraged students to try to advance the system by their own efforts. This instruction was suitable for advanced students in philosophy but not for the average undergraduate seeking to win high honours in the Greats exam. Jowett, who admired Green's sincerity and seriousness, disapproved of his teaching, partly on grounds that Green was attempting to sell a system of thought to immature students, and perhaps partly on grounds that Green's offbeat teaching hurt Balliol's success in the honours rankings.[46] But at the basis, the two men clashed over different university ideals. Jowett continued to think of the university as a place where future statesmen, civil servants and professional men were cultivated on a nourishing intellectual diet. He had done a great deal of scholarly work himself, but he did not value research for its own sake.

Green, however, thought of the university as a place for research as well as teaching, and he wanted the universities, not least by construction of a graduated professoriate, to encourage advanced study.[47]

Jowett won the battle and forced Green to withdraw from teaching his advanced Hegelian philosophy to the Balliol undergraduates. Yet men like Green eventually won the war, partly because they took support from a tendency towards research and specialization within the old tradition of liberal education itself. As Sheldon Rothblatt has pointed out, the ideal of liberal education at Oxbridge in the late-Victorian years tended to become a research ideal.[48] This was something of a paradox, since 'liberal' in the concept of liberal education had meant 'broadening', in the sense of breaking out of the narrow confines of vocational training and achieving independence from self-interest and prejudice. Certainly, for anti-traditionalists like Mill, liberal education called for a staggering number of subjects — the classics, literature, modern languages, philosophy, mathematics and history, for a start.[49] Yet it is important to remember that both the reality and the idea of liberal education in England had included sanctions for specialized study. After all, mathematics and classics at Cambridge, and the classics alone at the public schools and Oxford, actually constituted liberal education. This narrowly defined liberal education was defended in part on grounds that it offered deep learning in original texts, as opposed to the smattering of knowledge that a student got from dipping into many subjects.[50] Further, while most of the early advocates of liberal education were sceptical of research as an important activity of a university, they had long claimed in connection with the liberalizing effects of education that knowledge is good in itself. Newman, for instance, in his defence of liberal education in his *On the Scope and Nature of University Education* said that the object of a university is 'the diffusion and extension of knowledge rather than the advancement'. A liberal education should train a gentleman in right habits of thought — reasonableness, steadiness, consistency, versatility — and not give either vocational preparation or a smattering of information about everything. The knowledge gained in a liberal education in this sense is 'its own end': it is good in itself.[51]

By the late 1860s, a second phase of the university reform movement was coalescing. This phase aimed at converting the universities into research institutions and the newly professionalized careers of fellows and tutors, as well as of professors, into specialized research. Of the many advocates of this view, probably the most important was Mark Pattison, who had done an about-face on the relative merits of colleges and universities, tutors and professors. The main reason for his dramatic change of view was his profound personal disappointment in losing the election in 1851 for the Rectorship of Lincoln College. Bitterly resentful, Pattison turned away from his life as an active tutor to one as a reclusive student of books.[52] Further, from the beginning of his career at Oxford, Pattison had objected to the dominant part played in teaching by the examinations themselves. Even after the reforms of the 1850s, Pattison felt that university teaching amounted to little more than cramming students for honours; thus for the tutors to supplant the private coaches had been no great advance. In such a system, the real value of learning for its own sake was nil. As he himself turned more and more to learning, he objected to the reformed university structure, which he thought had been erected simply to please the public. In Pattison's thought, then, advancement of the cause of learning was linked to rejection of the claims of the public.[53]

In 1868, Pattison published his extremely influential book, *Suggestions on Academical Organisation*, to assert his new view of the ideal university and contrast it with Oxford and Cambridge. His argument rested on the assumption that both the ancient universities *and* their colleges were national institutions and ought to serve the public interest. He believed they were not servicing that interest, as he defined it, because the main reform of the 1850s — abolition of the close fellowships — had not resulted in learning and teaching by men who were masters of their subjects. Many fellowships were still devoted to the support of young men preparing for professions other than teaching or scholarship: they were prizes for undergraduate achievement and therefore *idle*. The fellowships ought to be transformed into endowments for learning, available only to those with 'scientific and literary qualifications'. Further, the limitation of fellowships to clergymen that still existed in some colleges should be removed. Only when the endowments of the colleges were restored to what Pattison regarded as their original purpose — subsidy of learning — could a 'national university' be useful to the whole nation.[54]

It is crucial to understand that by making the universities properly useful to the nation Pattison did not mean that they should undertake any directly utilitarian research work or even that they should prepare students to earn a living. 'The classes now approaching us', he wrote, 'are not insensible to culture, but they esteem it for its bearing on social prosperity, not for its own sake.'[55] The 'middle and lower classes' would like the universities to help open socially-prestigious positions to meritorious students, to help a young man rise in the world. But Pattison had no patience with the idea of a university as an instrument of social mobility. Properly, he said, 'the highest form of education is culture for culture's sake.' A university should be a centre of science and learning, a 'home where the cultivation of knowledge for its own sake shall be a profession, a life business'.[56] Hence a university should be organized so that the people composing it were appointed for intellectual merit alone. It followed that the ideal pattern for a university devoted to learning for its own sake — 'an establishment for science' — was the 'graduated professoriate of the German type'.[57] Pattison found the German universities far superior to all others as 'establishments for the cultivation and encouragement of the highest learning'. Even though a university still should have education as a major purpose, the German model was best, because at the advanced levels of education the inquiring intellect and the appreciation of knowledge for its own sake could only be taught by one who was himself an original investigator.

Pattison's plan envisaged the rise of a new class in the universities. The essential characteristic of this new class, he said, was each member's self-identification 'as primarily a learner, and a teacher only secondarily'. Disinterested research would be the essential qualification for class membership: 'It is requisite then, that the university teacher should be first himself a man of science; that science should be his own pursuit, and the object of his own life, with its ends and rewards, and that it should not be merely taken up that he may teach it again to others.'[58] This 'professional class of learned scientific men' was essential to teaching at the really important levels; therefore, mere educational reform at the universities would not do. The funds of the colleges had to be used to endow a new class of professors, lecturers, tutors, and 'professor fellows'. This class alone could teach the essential 'scientific' habit of mind — the independent inquiry into 'the laws of some one chief department of knowledge, or division of objects'.[59]

The *use* of such a university, in Pattison's view, had meaning only in the context of knowledge itself. A university did not exist to give practical information to society (although such information would be a by-product), or to socialize the governing class, or to offer lessons 'for life' to its students. Pattison, and an increasing number of allies, tended to assume that civilization or culture consisted of a storehouse of refined learning, the tending of which unquestionably was in the national interest. He wrote:

The object of these 'suggestions', has been to insist that the university be no longer a class-school, nor mainly a school for youth at all. It is a national institute for the preservation and tradition of useful knowledge. It is the common interest of the whole community that such knowledge should exist, should be guarded, treasured, cultivated, disseminated, expounded.[60]

Since 'useful' in this context by a curious inversion meant 'for its own sake', Pattison realized that the endowment of a class of people in a research institute devoted to producing knowledge for the sake of a cultural stockpile would not go down easily with the practical-minded middle class. A campaign would be required to move public opinion and to persuade Parliament to seize the college endowments. Scientists like Huxley and Lockyer stood ready as allies; thus the university reformers merged with the advocates of pure science to wage a campaign for the endowment of research.

The main organizer of the campaign to endow research was the young Oxford scholar, Dr Charles Appleton. He was a fellow of St John's, who had taken his BA in 1863. Like many young men of his generation in the educated classes, Appleton found that his studies in liberal philosophy and theology turned him against his early intent to enter the clergy. In 1865 he went to Germany for further studies in philosophy and became an ardent Hegelian. He also became an energetic advocate of German universities and German scholarship. Back in England, Appleton in 1869 founded a new journal called the *Academy*, which he intended to be an outlet for the emerging 'scientific' knowledge — that is, academic research. In retrospect, the *Academy* appears to have been a transitional phase in the development of specialized academic journals. At the time, it was the organ of all those interested in promoting specialized research and an academic culture. It also promoted the cause of university reform as espoused by Pattison.[61] Then, in 1872, Appleton founded an association named the Society for the Organisation of Academical Study, which he hoped would be the means of both endowing research and disendowing teaching at Oxford and Cambridge.

The Society was a short-lived but interesting organization. When it met first in November 1872, it included among others Appleton, Pattison, Dr Rolleston, Dr Carpenter, Sir Benjamin Brodie and John Seeley. It was supported by Norman Lockyer and *Nature*. At its first meeting, the speakers were full of praise for German universities and German learning, and they expressed determination to encourage, as their prospectus put it, 'mature study and scientific research'. All of them argued that under the reforms of the 1850s, Oxford and Cambridge were caught in the web of preparing students for examinations. The universities should be, Professor Rolleston said, 'places of original research', rather than utilitarian machines of teaching and examining. As Brodie declared, the real welfare of the nation is promoted 'by the growth of science and knowledge'. Pattison himself argued that 'there can be no healthy intellectual training unless the man who conducts it is a person who is himself capable of, and had the opportunity of engaging in, original research'. All agreed that the resources of the universities ought to be given to research in the physical sciences; and all agreed that 'to have a class of men devoted to research is a national object'. A new class of men in the universities ought to be supported by diversion of the fellowships of the colleges to university research posts.[62]

The Organisation for Academical Study soon broke up on two rocks: one was the concern of people like J.S. Mill that divorcing teaching from the endowments would only establish in English life a new privileged group not far different from the old close fellowship. The other was the objection by Roscoe that the organization would permanently assign Oxford and Cambridge positions superior to the new civic universities.[63] But Appleton continued his efforts and the campaign made good headway during the 1870s. For instance, with the co-operation of Norman Lockyer, Appleton published six leading articles in *Nature* on 'The Endowment of Research'. In his pieces, Appleton merged the movement to advance natural science with that of university reform by using 'science' in two ways: (1) physical science; and (2) any subject capable of being investigated by research. This conflation of meaning reflected the whole tendency of the advocates of research and deep scholarship. Further, while Appleton blurred the meaning of 'science', he made his general message crystal clear: England made totally inadequate provision for research; college endowments ought to be used to support research; careers for researchers ought to be established in the universities; the research function of the university should take priority over instruction; and the professoriate, freed from the burden of teaching, should be expanded and more liberally endowed.[64]

Appleton also joined a number of other scholars in issuing in 1876 a volume entitled *Essays on the Endowment of Research,* which became, next to Pattison's *Suggestions on Academical Organisation,* the major statement by the academics. The authors of the *Essays* made all the points stated by Appleton in *Nature* — and more. Research at Oxbridge ought to be endowed by the annexation of college fellowships: that was the main point. Hence, throughout the *Essays* there ran the theme of the disendowment of teaching. On this point the arguments were two: first, the founders of the colleges had intended to endow research anyway; and secondly, research was a higher endeavour than teaching. Pattison wrote that England was beginning to see

> that universities have other functions than that of educating youth. That liberal and scientific culture, intelligence, and the whole domain of mind, is a national interest, as much as agriculture, commerce, banking, or water-supply.[65]

Further, the authors of the *Essays* recognized that the principle of endowment represented a break with the market-place. Research should be endowed precisely because the market-place failed to provide for it; but teaching should be thrown upon some kind of fee system, because the market-place reflected a demand for it.[66] Moreover, the essayists expressed a conscious rejection of the perceived desires of the middle-class public, which they regarded as being satisfied with having the universities prepare students for careers in the professions.[67] The *Essays,* then, unmistakably showed hostility to bourgeois utility. Finally, the authors of the *Essays* conveyed a sense that the proper criterion for measuring the progress of national civilization was the development of academic culture, for which a separate class of people was required. Education, A.H. Sayce declared, was not the 'chief function of a university', the main object of which

> is the collection, the combination, and the enlargement of all existing knowledge and learning, and the production and encouragement of scholars who shall give up their lives to study and research. The work thus performed constitutes the true essence of national civilisation. The civilisation of a period is gauged by its knowledge, and above all by the will and wish to organise and increase this knowledge.[68]

The campaign for the endowment of research spread very widely among scientists and university people. It was waged by appeals to national pride. Supporters for the endowment of research pointed out deficiencies in English culture, as Bulwer Lytton had done forty years before. England had, they argued, enough people of general learning but not a learned class. Sidney Colvin wrote:

> Our society being what it is, we do not need more intellectual talk at dinner-tables, or classical allusions in leading articles; we need more science and 'special learning'; and of science and special learning the universities should be the centres.[69]

According to this view, culture is a particular circle of studious activities, which can be indexed as advanced or backward. Compared to Germany, English culture was deficient because of its lack of research. The creation of a separate class of researchers in the universities, the argument paradoxically went, would bring the universities into closer touch with the nation as a whole, for the nation would be richer by its research even though that research was not marketable. As Appleton said, research itself was national wealth.[70]

Despite some resistance, the campaign for the endowment of research, in conjunction with advancing the claims of natural science in the universities, had great success. Resistance came from men like George Brodrick, fellow of Merton College, Oxford, who retained the mid-century view of the universities and liberal education. Brodrick argued that it was good for England that the universities retain links with society as a whole, and that the non-resident (or prize) fellowships, which supported men while in training for the professions, constituted just such links.[71] In a sense, such arguments represented a revival of Coleridgean ideas — the production by the universities of a cultivated clerisy for the cohesion of the whole society. But it was a much watered-down version, and one sent out into a secularized world. The feeling that subsidy of research careers was in the national interest proved to be too strong. The Devonshire Commission, appointed to investigate the provisions for scientific advancement, denied in their third report (1873) that there was any conflict between research on the one hand and literary and scientific education on the other. In fact, the report stated, neither could be neglected without 'grave detriment to the other'. Thus the Royal Commissioners decided that the ancient universities should be centres of research as well as centres of education. In this view they agreed with the overwhelming majority of university people themselves:

> On no point are the witnesses whom we have examined more united than they are in the expression of the feeling that it is a Primary Duty

of the Universities to assist in the Advancement of Learning and Science, and not to be content with the position of merely educational bodies.[72]

In addition to various recommendations to advance physical science, the Devonshire Commission adopted as its main proposal the awarding of fellowships so as to encourage 'original research'. That required, everyone thought, a major shift in control over college funds from the colleges to the universities. In 1873, another Royal Commission (the Cleveland Commission) submitted its report on the finances of Oxford, Cambridge and their colleges, revealing the amazing disparity between the wealth of the colleges and the poverty of the universities.[73] The obvious inference was that the colleges could afford to turn over money to the university governments in order to support physical science and original research. In 1877, Disraeli's government — Lord Salisbury was the responsible minister — appointed commissioners to undertake the redistribution of college funds by revising the college statutes. By 1882, the commissioners had largely completed their revolutionary work. Prize (or 'idle') fellowships were abolished and replaced by fellowships free of restrictions about marriage and holy orders, but requiring demonstrated proficiency in learning and research. The general pattern for most colleges was that fellowships would be granted on the basis of a thesis for a period of seven years, after which they might be renewed for life. Further, the colleges at both universities were to contribute to central funds to support a graduated professoriate — lecturers, readers and professors — as well as to proceed with arrangements for co-operative teaching controlled by boards of study.[74]

The work of the Oxford and Cambridge commissioners established the patterns for the organization and functions of the ancient universities to the end of the century. Between the rise of the civic universities and the reforms of Oxford and Cambridge, the English university system had been re-oriented towards the German professorial model, even though the two old universities retained their colleges and much of their tradition of educating students in the liberal arts for public service. In both old and new universities, teachers had won for themselves secular careers as both educators and specialized researchers.

These developments in the professionalization of the academic staff of the universities were more important than the other alterations in the social functions of the universities. The university system of England had grown, but not rapidly enough to keep up with the population explosion. The number of freshman admissions at Oxbridge together went up from about 800 in the 1830s, to almost 1,000 in the 1860s, and to far more than 1,700 in the 1890s. Yet this increase in matriculants, if anything, represented a slight decrease in the proportion of the total population attending a university.[75] Thus the student bodies of Oxford and Cambridge remained an elite, and their smallness relative to the population as a whole was not made up by enrolments in the provincial universities, which remained small until the twentieth century.

Nor did the social composition of the student bodies change radically. The civic universities, it is true, recruited largely from the middle and lower-middle classes (and from artisan occupations in their evening divisions); but Oxford and Cambridge continued to draw from the upper strata: the landed orders, the clergy and the professions. What did change at Oxford and Cambridge were two things: (1) the mixture of the upper-class backgrounds of the students; and (2) the graduates' choices of occupations. Both factors reflected the secularization and professionalization of the universities — and of English society generally. In the first half of the century, the vast majority of students at Oxbridge came from land-owning or clerical backgrounds, and a large proportion of them were channelled by the universities into clerical careers: more than 60 per cent of all Oxford students and 50 per cent of Cambridge graduates went into the clergy. But at Oxford, for example, the proportion of students coming from clerical homes had declined to 28 per cent in 1870, and further declined to 17 per cent in 1910.[76] The proportion of graduates going into orders fell precipitously: at Balliol, nearly half of all BAs in 1845 were ordained, but in the years from 1845-55, only one of three took orders; only one of ten did so in the years of Jowett's mastership (1870-1893); and one in 25 in the 1890s.[77] Hence it can be said of both ancient universities in the late-Victorian period that the proportion of students from landed and clerical families went down, the proportion from professional and rich business families increased; and the graduates increasingly chose careers in the secular professions — including academic life.

Certainly, the professionalization of academic life was the change most often noted by observers at the time, and highbrow circles generally favoured the changes. As one observer remarked as early as 1869, the universities had become 'centre[s] of intellectual life'.[78] Most commentators thought it an improvement that the universities had broadened their curricula and no longer were arenas of theological party strife. Likewise, most observers felt that it was good for the national culture that the universities had become research institutions. It is true that some late-nineteenth century observers thought that the reforms had not gone far enough. Paul Vinogradoff, the eminent Russian medieval historian, wrote in 1885 that compared to German universities Oxford and Cambridge still did not encourage original research.[79] E.A. Freeman, who returned to Oxford in 1886 as Regius Professor of Modern History after an absence of almost 40 years, found the universities enormously changed, but not in entirely beneficial ways. The fellows by then tended to be married and to think of themselves as members of a 'profession', but that profession was one of teaching and not scholarship. The culprit was, Freeman believed, the examination system, which continued to turn the student into a highly specialized exam writer and the tutor into a crammer. He wrote: 'Divide, divide, is the cry; specialize, specialize; let there be no time for general culture, for common study of any kind. . .' The pressure to prepare students for exams had made research 'well nigh penal'.[80]

No doubt Freeman's observations were coloured by his relegation (perhaps the newer view was *elevation*) as a professor to the periphery of the curriculum. Yet the nostalgia he felt for the homogeneous curriculum of the past could be seen among many old hands. The new professionalized and specialized dons vastly changed the tone and flavour of university life; and some people, older sons of the universities, plainly hankered after the times before reform. P.A. Wright-Henderson, for example, found the new Oxford dons less attractive than the picturesque eccentrics of the years before 1850. The new fellows, he said, are 'hard-worked professional men, with the professional characteristics which hide, if not destroy, individuality: they are too busy, too open-minded, too cosmopolitan to be as quaint and interesting as the simple scholars, or fiery partisans, or eccentric hermits who enlivened and diversified the common-rooms of fifty or sixty years ago.'[81] This nostalgia was sometimes attached to the more serious issue as to whether the universities had lost their ability to give a shared general education to the national elite. Frederic Harrison, a Liberal and a positivist, remarked in 1911 that the reforms had broken up 'the organized torpor of Oxford in the eighteenth century', but he felt that the changes had not brought any 'real gain to learning and thought'. To him, the universities should be training grounds for future governors, whose educational needs were still met best by the classics. Such students 'should be turned out sensible men, with minds braced up to face the problems of life'. Instead, they were now being led into an effete and unmanly specialization: 'Nothing is too minutely specialised, too remote from a robust mentality, to be excluded.'[82]

Another aspect of the newly reformed universities that attracted criticism was they had not been integrated with society at large. James Bryce, for instance, believed that the university reforms had not accomplished the right goals. A Liberal, a Scotsman and a scholar of international repute, Bryce had stood with the university reformers in the 1860s and 1870s; but he came to believe that the university commissioners appointed in 1877 had failed to attack the biggest problem: 'how to make the universities . . . serviceable to the whole nation, instead of only to the upper classes — how to enable them to give in abundance the highest teaching through the ablest teachers on all subjects'.[83] Bryce did not oppose research and specialization for university staff, but he retained the assumption of the tutors' movement in the 1840s and 1850s, that research and specialization were means to the end of good teaching. Research, he said, was a legitimate function of a university; yet for the most part it did not need to be endowed, because research would be the inevitable result of first-rate teaching. In an ideal university, the best people would be employed to teach their various fields, and such people would never be content with teaching the findings of others.[84]

Bryce observed correctly that the campaign for the endowment of research had been so zealously promoted 'as to have provoked a reaction on the part of those who fear that the endowment of research may degenerate into the research of endowment'.[85] His concern was that the permanent appointment of people to research positions would amount to the creation of a new class of sinecured men. This was the point on which other Liberals like Mill and Huxley had pulled back from the movement to endow research. J.A. Hobson, an economist who was unable to obtain a university post because of his critique of capitalism, thought that by the 1890s, this academic class had been created. The vested interests in the universities *had* won for themselves a privileged position inside a 'social ring-fence', which allowed them to enjoy an 'artificially protected and specialised form of intellectual life'. One of the luxuries enjoyed by this class was its sense of having access to mysteries hidden from the public; another was freedom from commitment to the issues of real life. 'Prig, pendant, and specialist', Hobson wrote, 'have erected an orthodox system of education based on a false and untested scale of values.'[86]

In all these varying reactions to the Oxford and Cambridge that had come to exist in the middle of the 1880s, there lay several common themes. One was that the pace and tone of university life, especially for the professors and tutors, had become more busy and hard-working. Another was that the dons and professors belonged to a profession, in the sense that their careers were internal to the universities and would depend on high standards of performance imposed by the members of the profession themselves. A third theme was that the work of these professionals was highly specialized, both in teaching and research. Fourth, research had been accepted as a primary function of a university and had become a central occupation of fellows as well as professors; but it was still thought to be impeded by teaching demands generated by the examination system. Fifth, everyone noted that the universities had become secularized in at least three senses: the governance of the universities was no longer clerical; the fellows were no longer required to take orders or subscribe to the Articles; and the curriculum was no longer religious. The universities had been made more 'modern', everyone recognized. As Lewis Campbell put it, they had been nationalized.

It is easy to say that this nationalization was inevitable, for it is hard to imagine that an advanced industrial nation, increasingly shaped by middle-class mores, would tolerate antiquated clerical institutions. Yet that nationalization was of a curious kind. Oxford and Cambridge, which remained in 1900 overwhelmingly the most important universities in England, had not been tied closely to the economic and social problems of the nation. They had been made to conform more tightly than before to the bourgeois ideal of productivity, but they had not become utilitarian. They continued to give a higher education to the social and political elite, and that education was still 'liberal', though in broader terms than before 1850. But teaching had become only one of the functions of the universities, for research had become primary, at least in theory. Further, research had its uses, as Pattison thought, but not in regard to specific economic or social issues. Research was conceived of as useful to something called the 'national culture', which denoted a realm of sophisticated mental activity and a sum of specialized knowledge, which was accessible only to professional researchers. This was a new and important aspect of intellectual life in England — indeed it was a key feature of the emergence of the very concept of a national intellectual life — and it increasingly took precedence over the older, generalist world of the men of letters. The university reformers of the nineteenth century had moved the universities from the context of religion into the context of secular intellectual work. But they had by accident contributed to the creation of a new priesthood.

## Notes

1. [Southwood Smith], 'Present System of Education', *Westminster Review* (July 1825), p. 153.

2. Ibid., p. 172.

3. [T.J. Hogg], 'The Universities of Oxford and Cambridge', *Westminster Review* (July 1831), p. 58.

4. Ibid., p. 59. See also [Alexander Bain], 'Review of William Whewell's *Of A Liberal Education in General*', *Westminster and Foreign Quarterly Review* (July 1848), pp. 441-63.

5. The best account of the religious tests and their abolition is in Lewis Campbell, *The Nationalization of the Old English Universities* (London, 1901), especially Chs. I-VIII.

6. Sir William Hamilton, 'On the Right of Dissenters to Admission into the English Universities' (Supplemental), in *Discussions on Philosophy and Literature* (New York, 1855), p. 504.

7. Sir William Hamilton, 'On the State of the English Universities, with more Especial Reference to Oxford', in *Discussions on Philosophy and Literature*, pp. 383-429.

8. Ibid., p. 398.

9. Sir William Hamilton, 'On the Right of Dissenters to Admission into the English Universities', in *Discussions on Philosophy and Literature*, pp. 458-99.

10. H.H. Bellot, *University College, London, 1826-1926* (London, 1929).

11. Peter Allen, *The Cambridge Apostles: The Early Years* (Cambridge, 1978).

12. Evelyn Abbott and Lewis Campbell, *The Life and Letters of Benjamin Jowett* (2 vols., London, 1897), I, Ch. VI.

13. Quoted in E.G.W. Bill, *University Reform in Nineteenth-Century Oxford: A Study of Henry Halford Vaughan, 1811-1825* (Oxford, 1973), p. 49.

14. Sheldon Rothblatt, *The Revolution of the Dons: Cambridge and Society in Victorian England* (London, 1968); Arthur Engel, 'Emerging Concepts of the Academic Profession at Oxford', in Lawrence Stone (ed.), *The University in Society* (2 vols., Princeton, 1974), I, pp. 320-1.

15. Quoted in Stanley, *Arnold*, p. 31.

16. Quoted in ibid., p. 473.

17. Quoted in Bill, *H.H. Vaughan*, p. 163. For his testimony to the Royal Commission, see *Royal Commission on Oxford University* (1852, *c.* 1482, vol. XXII), 'Appendix and Evidence', pp. 82-92, 268-78.

18. Bill, *H.H. Vaughan*, p. 123.

19. Ibid., pp. 177-218.

20. H.P. Liddon, *Life of Edward Bouverie Pusey*, 2nd edn, (4 vols., London, 1894).

21. Ibid., I, pp. 229-30.

22. Ibid., III, p. 381.

23. Quoted in ibid., III, pp. 389-90.

24. Mark Pattison, *Memoirs* (London, 1885), pp. 109, 215-18, 237-41, and 255-8. See also John Sparrow, *Mark Pattison and the Idea of a University* (Cambridge, 1967).

25. Pattison, *Memoirs*, p. 256.

26. *Royal Commission on Oxford* (1852), 'Appendix and Evidence', pp. 44-6.

27. *Royal Commission – Cambridge University* (1852-3, c. 1559, vol. XLIV), 'Correspondence and Evidence', p. 195.

28. *Royal Commission on Oxford* (1852), pp. 93-9, and 'Appendix and Evidence', especially pp. 129-32; and *Royal Commission – Cambridge* (1852-3), pp. 79-88, 201-2, and 'Correspondence and Evidence', pp. 141-215.

29. *Royal Commission on Oxford* (1852), 'Appendix and Evidence', pp. 126, 156, 175, 205; *Royal Commission – Cambridge* (1852-3), 'Correspondence and Evidence', pp. 153, 181, 212; Abbott and Campbell, *Jowett*, I, pp. 180-1, 212-13.

30. Engel, 'Emerging Concepts of the Academic Profession', pp. 335-8; Rothblatt, *Revolution of the Dons*, pp. 90-3; Sanderson, *Universities in the Nineteenth Century*, pp. 1-9.

31. *Royal Commission on Oxford* (1852), p. 94.

32. Ibid., pp. 153-71.

33. *Royal Commission – Cambridge* (1852-3), pp. 80-1.

34. Ibid., pp. 81-5, 156, 201-2.

35. Sparrow, *Pattison*, p. 115.

36. Pattison, *Memoirs*, p. 218; Rothblatt, *Revolution of the Dons*, especially pp. 227-50; Christopher Kent, *Brains and Numbers: Elitism, Comtism, and Democracy in Mid-Victorian England* (Toronto, 1978), p. 18.

37. Abbott and Campbell, *Jowett*, I, pp. 185-6; Kent, *Brains and Numbers*, pp. 15-18.

38. For example, see F.W. Maitland, *The Life and Letters of Leslie Stephen* (New York, 1906), Ch. V.

39. Thomas Hughes, *Tom Brown at Oxford*, I, p. 105.

40. Ibid., II, p. 357.

41. Mortimer R. Proctor, *The English University Novel* (Berkeley, 1957).

42. W.H.G. Armytage, *Civic Universities: Aspects of A British Tradition* (London, 1955), Chs. 8-10; Michael Sanderson, *The Universities and British Industry, 1850-1970*, (London, 1972), Chs. 3 and 4.

43. For a brief account of German influence, see George V. Haines, *Essays on German Influence upon English Education and Science, 1850-1919* (Hamden, Conn., 1969).

44. Engel, 'Emerging Concepts of the Academic Profession', pp. 336-9; Rothblatt, *Revolution of the Dons*, pp. 175, 210-11, 215-21.

45. Melvin Richter, *The Politics of Conscience: T.H. Green and His Age* (Cambridge, Mass., 1964), Ch. 5.

46. Ibid., p. 153.

47. Ibid., pp. 149-53.

48. Sheldon Rothblatt, *Tradition and Change in English Liberal Education* (London, 1976), pp. 164-73.

49. J.S. Mill, 'Inaugural Address Delivered to the University of St. Andrews', *Dissertations and Discussions* (New York, 1874), vol. IV, pp. 332-407.

50. Sanderson, *Universities in the Nineteenth Century*, pp. 7-8.

51. J.H. Newman, *On the Scope and Nature of University Education* (London, 1915; first published in 1852), pp. xxix and 83.

52. The story of the election for the Rectorship is told in Pattison, *Memoirs*, pp. 258-95.

53. Pattison's turn towards learning is discussed in ibid., pp. 309-12 and 331; and in Sparrow, *Pattison*, pp. 117-20.

54. Pattison, *Suggestions on Academical Organisation*, Sections 1-5.

55. Ibid., p. 137.

56. Ibid., p. 146.

57. Ibid., p. 161.

58. Ibid., pp. 164 and 168.

59. Ibid., p. 266.

60. Ibid., p. 327.

61. For Appleton's career, see John H. Appleton and A.H. Sayce, *Dr. Appleton: His Life and Literary Relics* (London, 1881). For the *Academy*, see: J.C. Johnson, 'The *Academy*, 1859-1896; Center of Informed Critical Opinion', unpublished PhD thesis,

Northwestern University, Evanston, 1958; and Diderik Roll-Hansen, *The Academy, 1869-1879: Victorian Intellectuals in Revolt* (Copenhagen, 1957). See also: C.E. Appleton, 'Our First Year', *The Academy* (October 22, 1870), p. 1.

62. *Nature* (November 28, 1872), pp. 72-5.

63. Sir Henry Enfield Roscoe, *Life and Experiences of Sir Henry Enfield Roscoe* (London, 1906), p. 43; Johnson, 'The *Academy*', pp. 30-1; Roll-Hansen, *The Academy*, pp. 78-9.

64. C.E. Appleton, 'The Endowment of Research', *Nature* (June 26, 1873; July 10, 1873; July 24, 1873; July 31, 1873; August 14, 1873; and September 11, 1873).

65. C.E. Appleton, *et al., Essays on the Endowment of Research* (London, 1876), pp. 22-3.

66. Ibid., Essays III and IV.

67. Ibid., pp. 10-11.

68. Ibid., p. 204.

69. Sidney Colvin, 'Fellowships and National Culture', *Macmillan's Magazine* (June 1876), p. 142.

70. C.E. Appleton, 'Economic Aspect of the Endowment of Research', *Fortnightly Review* (October 1874), pp. 533-4. See also: George Gore, 'The Promotion of Scientific Research', *Fortnightly Review* (October, 1873), pp. 505-24; [Robert Lytton], 'Essays on A Liberal Education', *Edinburgh Review* (January 1868), pp. 67-84; and [Anonymous], 'Can Colleges Reform Themselves', *Macmillan's Magazine* (April 1872), pp. 461-71; Mandell Creighton, 'The Endowment of Research', *Macmillan's Magazine* (June 1876), pp. 186-92.

71. George Brodrick, Letter to *The Times* (May 18, 1876); and George Charles Brodrick, *Memories and Impressions, 1831-1900* (London, 1900), pp. 169-71, 181-2 and 353-60.

72. *Royal Commission on Scientific Instruction and the Advancement of Science* (Third Report, 1873), *c.* 868, Vol. XXVIII, pp. vii and lvi.

73. *Report of the Commissioners Appointed to Inquire into the Property and Income of the Universities of Oxford and Cambridge* (Parts I-III, 1873, vol. xxxviii).

74. W.R. Ward, *Victorian Oxford* (London, 1965), Ch. XII; Sanderson, *Universities in the Nineteenth Century*, pp. 151-2.

75. Lawrence Stone, 'The Size and Composition of the Oxford Student Body, 1580-1909', in Lawrence Stone (ed.), *The University in Society*, Vol. I (Princeton, 1974), Table 12, p. 103.

76. Ibid., Table 11, p. 103.

77. Richter, *Politics of Conscience*, p. 69.

78. [Charles Alan Fyffe], 'Study and Opinion at Oxford', *Macmillan's Magazine* (December 1869), p. 184.

79. Paul Vinogradoff, 'Oxford and Cambridge through Foreign Spectacles', *Fortnightly Review* (June 1885), pp. 862-8.

80. E.A. Freeman, 'Oxford after Forty Years — I' and 'Oxford after Forty Years — II', *Contemporary Review* (May and June 1887), pp. 609-23 and 814-30, especially pp. 611 and 826.

81. P.A. Wright-Henderson, 'An Old Oxford Common Room', *Blackwood's* (May 1896), p. 669.

82. Frederic Harrison, *Autobiographic Memoirs* (2 vols., London, 1911), I, pp. 133-4.

83. James Bryce, 'The Future of the English Universities', *Fortnightly Review* (March 1883), p. 385.

84. James Bryce, 'An Ideal University', *Contemporary Review* (June 1884), pp. 842-3.

85. Bryce, 'The Future of the English Universities', p. 387.

86. J.A. Hobson, 'The Academic Spirit in Education', *Contemporary Review* (February 1893), pp. 237, 241.

# 7 THE TRADITION OF CULTURAL CRITICISM AND ALIENATION IN LITERARY LIFE

The growth in university circles of the concepts of culture as a rarified activity and of university faculties as its keepers had close analogues in literary life. To the extent that the very nature of literature allowed, literary life in the late-Victorian period became professionalized. Literary people were not able to establish institutions which sheltered them from the marketplace and isolated them from the public, but they did develop certain ideas whose intended function was essentially the same. In a defensive mood, many leading literary figures in the late-Victorian period turned away from the public issues of their society and the needs of the reading public towards concepts of art and intellectual activity that emphasized the primacy and disinterestedness of art, its superiority to ordinary life, and the need for authoritative institutions for directing thought.

These developments in literary life were significant changes in a tradition of cultural criticism inherited from the Romantics and the early and mid-Victorians. Hence the great theme in the history of the tradition of cultural criticism is how that tradition led to alienation of imaginative writers. Literary alienation in England took two forms: (1) aestheticism; and (2) a movement to establish academies, or centres of intellectual authority. In both forms, the concept of the role of the thinking person altered from cultural leadership to one of isolated practice of art — from a concept of a cultured minority integrated with the whole of society to one of a minority culture. In the process, the bonds of sympathy that had prevailed in the Victorian period between writers and their public were broken.

Perhaps the strongest theme in nineteenth-century English literature was criticism of industrial society and the utilitarian and *laissez-faire* philosphies that went with it. From the Romantic poets at the beginning of the century to the aesthetes of the end, literary artists expressed a revulsion from industrial society, its urban blight, its entrepreneurial class and its entrepreneurial values. The particular formulations of this reaction varied, of course, but the underlying themes in the tradition were that the new society left little space for art and imagination, that it fragmented both the cohesiveness of the national community and the human integrity of its members, and finally that these two processes were inter-related. Raymond Williams has convincingly demonstrated that the imaginative reaction to industrial society and thought in England generated a concept of 'culture' itself, which wove together the responses to the processes of narrowing the terrain of art and fragmenting the society: 'culture' came to mean

> first, the recognition of the practical separation of certain moral and intellectual activities from the driven impetus of a new kind of society; second, the emphasis of these activities as a court of human appeal, to be set over the processes of practical social judgement and yet to offer itself as a mitigating and rallying alternative.[1]

It would be a mistake, however, to conclude from the origins of the tradition of cultural criticism — the tradition of regarding culture as going against the grain of industrial life and thought — that alienation of serious literary people in any meaningful sense had occurred. The artist, or serious writer, or 'genius' was seen as a special kind of person, and often as one who opposed central features of the new society; but down through mid-century, this corps of special people was regarded as essential to, and fully integrated with, the larger society. Their role — agreed to by both the writers and their public — was not one of isolation from the great moral, social and political issues of the day, but rather one of active engagement with them. This role was what defined the function of all men of letters at its highest level. They were to be the preachers, prophets and teachers to the reading public, and their task was to save society from the social sins, the political catastrophes and the moral degradation that industrial life and values carried in their wake. Art, according to Victorian thought, was to be used to redeem society.

This concept of the ideal utility of art, it should be emphasized, was shared even by the Romantic poets. Literary artists of the years from the 1780s to the 1830s were the first to witness at close hand the violent alterations of the social and political landscape wrought by the industrial and French revolutions. They were also among the first to experience the emergence of the new market relationship between writer and readers. As Williams has observed, the English Romantics resisted the judgement and influence of the reading public; and partly for this reason, they elaborated the idea of the creative writer as a genius possessing the special faculty of the imagination.[2] The poet, they liked to say, was properly subject only to ideal and timeless standards of judgement. But their view of poetic genius was closely related to their perception of more general flaws in modern civilization, and this thought turned them towards active engagement with public issues. The Romantics, with few exceptions, asserted that the empiricist style of thought, prominently displayed by people like Adam Smith and Jeremy Bentham, took a narrow view of human nature in emphasizing the cognitive and calculating faculties at the expense of the creative and imaginative. The rising commercial and industrial class claimed the empiricist philosophy as their own, and the Romantic poets reacted against both the world the entrepreneurs were making and the philosophy which justified it. Hence they placed, as Williams says, 'an emphasis on the embodiment in art of certain human values, capacities, energies, which the development of society towards an industrial civilization was felt to be threatening or even destroying'.[3]

One can see this active concern with vital social issues and an assertion of cultural leadership by thinkers and artists in the work of Romantics as different as the Tory Coleridge and the radical Shelley. Both felt that their world was hostile to art. Coleridge remarked in 1831:

> In this country there is no general reverence for the fine arts; and the sordid spirit of a money-amassing philosophy would meet any proposition for the fostering of art, in a genial and extended sense, with the commercial maxim — *Laissez-faire*.[4]

Coleridge's counter ideal, however, was not one of alienation, but of integration: the clerisy, as we have seen, would spread through the population to re-weave the fabric of community. The clerisy would operate through a network of the universities and the parishes to restore the wholeness of individuals and the society.[5]

Like Coleridge, Shelley felt that the early-nineteenth century was hostile to poetry, because the 'reasoners and mechanists' were seizing 'the civic crown' from the poets. Hence, Shelley, in his *Defence of Poetry* sought not only to give an exalted definition to poetry and the imaginative faculty, but also to reclaim the poets' role as legislators or prophets. Poets alone, he said, could participate in the eternal and awaken and enlarge the mind and moral sympathies of the public. Shelley's cultural ideal was Periclean Athens, where, in his view, philosopher-poets spoke to a sympathetic and responsive public. In his own times, Shelley thought, poets went unacknowledged as legislators of the world, and the result was social disaster — an aggravation of the extremes of wealth and poverty:

The rich have become richer, and the poor have become poorer; and the vessel of the state is driven between the Scylla and Carybdis of anarchy and despotism. Such are the effects which must ever flow from an unmitigated exercise of the calculating faculty.

But for Shelley, bad as the situation was, it was not hopeless. He remained confident that poetry could save society, for its supernatural powers could never be annihilated. Nowhere, he wrote, had social corruption so 'destroyed the fabric of human society' that poetry had ceased. Poetry always had the resources to restore social health: 'It is the faculty which contains within itself the seeds at once of its own and of social renovation.'[6]

In the Victorian years, the ideas of Coleridge and Shelley continued to shape criticism of English culture and to inform the conceptions of the proper functions of the men of letters. But the concepts inherited from the Romantics — the endowed clerisy and the heroic poet — were themselves altered by the market power of the reading public and by emerging Victorian morality and values. Shelley's ideal of the poet as 'a nightingale, who sits in darkness and sings to cheer his own solitude with sweet sounds' was diluted by Evangelical earnestness and the gospel of work into the ideal of the prophetic man of letters, who like Carlyle preached and warned in broad sunlight directly to the middle class. And the poetic ideal was transformed by artists like Tennyson, who consciously rejected isolation in a Palace of Art, in order to help the public make their way through times of doubt, disruption and despair. Coleridge's idea of the clerisy was adapted by orthodox clergymen as a rationale for the principle of establishment, by others as a plan for clerical revitalization, and by still others as an inspiration for more useful university careers. In all the Victorian variations, the original romantic ideas retained their orientation towards social engagement, while being grafted on to a greater degree of acceptance of the market relationship with the reading public, and a profound sympathy with the best values and concerns of the middle class.

Even in its most elitist formulation, the Victorian concept of the function of the most highly cultivated minority retained its element of active social commitment and cultural leadership. Here the prime example was J.S. Mill, who ranks with Carlyle as one of the greatest men of letters. Mill was carefully tutored by his father and Jeremy Bentham to be the perfect example of utilitarian philosophy, because James Mill and Bentham believed that public enlightenment — their cherished 'march of mind' — required staff planning officers as well as field commanders. J.S. Mill's training provided him with knowledge, skills, and above all, an identity as a leader of high culture. Utilitarianism became his religion, he recalled, 'the inculcation and diffusion of which could be made the principal outward purpose of a life'.[7] Thus from early manhood to the end of his life, Mill meant to be 'a reformer of the world', not so much by political agitation, as by intellectual proselytizing. He intended to write books 'destined to form future thinkers', to be 'a theoretical reformer of the opinions and institutions of my time'.[8]

It is undeniable that Mill's self-assigned role was embedded in a belief in intellectual elitism — an elitism of merit, as Michael St John Packe has observed, but an elitism none the less.[9] Mill's elitism in certain ways became more pronounced over the years. After his mental breakdown in 1826, Mill rehabilitated himself by reading, among others, Wordsworth, Carlyle and Coleridge. In his article on 'Genius', Mill contended that the trends of mass democracy and education were to destroy the conditions which produced geniuses.[10] In 'The Spirit of the Age', he argued that his own times (the 1830s) were an age of transition, in which there had been '*diffusion* of *superficial* knowledge', but a loss of deference to intellectual superiority. The masses of any age, he wrote, surpass the previous age in knowledge 'only in so far as they are guided and influenced by the authority of the wisest among them'; and in the new age of transition, the masses had lost faith in the authority of the wisest and most learned.[11]

Mill found ample support for his notion of how a civilization would progress in Coleridge's idea of the clerisy. In his famous essay on Coleridge (1840), Mill honoured Coleridge 'for having vindicated against Bentham and Adam Smith and the whole eighteenth century the principle of an endowed class for the cultivation of learning and for diffusing its results among the community'. He regarded Coleridge's ideal as the 'sweetest satire' on the actual state of the Church of England; nevertheless, he entirely accepted the principle of state endowment of a learned class — provided it would be in close communication with the whole people.[12] Hence Mill's sense of the ideal function and setting for learned teachers closely resembled that of the reforming tutors of the 1840s and 1850s.

Mill's primary concern, then, was for the progress of enlightenment: people of refined and deepened intellect, in a role of cultural leadership, would have to be cultivated if civilization were to advance. One aspect of the role of cultural leadership can be seen in Mill's reformulation of Benthamite philosophy. In *Utilitarianism* (1863),

Mill accepted what Bentham had not — the qualitative superiority of intellectual or spiritual pleasures over physical — and for proof he referred his readers to the testimony of the relatively few people who had experience of both.[13] Further, *On Liberty* should be read as a defence of minorities — not least the intellectually superior minority — against the mediocrity of democratic majorities. Yet Mill justified the protection of the special minority entirely in terms of social utility. It is good for the mental enlightenment of a society, he argued, to have free competition of ideas.[14] As he once observed, England and America both needed

> I do not say a class, but a great number of persons of the highest degree of cultivation which the accumulated acquisitions of the human race make it possible to give them. From such persons, in a community that knows no distinction of ranks, civilization would rain down its influence on the remainder of society . . .[15]

It was the necessity for integration of these persons of eminent cultivation with the rest of society that led Mill to break from Comte's influence. He had been influenced by Comte's ideas that the progress of a society depended on intellect, and that theirs was an age in which the masses did not look to the wisest for leadership.[16] But Mill recognized that Comte envisioned an organized and authoritative priesthood of geniuses, and he knew this was inconsistent with both his idea of the diffusion of knowledge and ideas and his sense that the progress of a society required competition among ideas. Thus he wrote to Alexander Bain, who feared, as others had done, that Mill advocated an intellectual aristocracy:

> The 'Liberty' has produced an effect on you which it was never intended to produce if it has made you think that we ought not to attempt to convert the world. I meant nothing of the kind, & hold that we ought to convert all we can. We *must* be satisfied with keeping alive the sacred fire in a few minds when we are unable to do more — but the notion of an intellectual aristocracy of *lumières* while the rest of the world remains in darkness fulfils none of my aspirations — & the effect I aim at by the book is, on the contrary, to make the many more accessible to all truth by making them more open-minded.[17]

This letter expressed a view that would have been ratified by all of the purely literary artists among the Victorian men of letters. And it expressed a sense of the function of intellect and imagination that was in fact attached to acceptance of essentially bourgeois literary conventions, of the dictation of standards and forms by publishers and circulating libraries, and of basically didactic or utilitarian aesthetic theories. But after mid-century, there began to appear in literary circles some restlessness with the whole package. Beginning with the Pre-Raphaelites, literary artists began to assert ideas of art that not only rejected middle-class values but also asserted the autonomy of art. Authors of imaginative literature in increasing numbers refused to accept the conventions of cheerfulness and moralism, and to assert the right of depicting the world in naturalistic, often pessimistic, terms. Many novelists began to rebel against the economic arrangements of publishing fiction and the three-volume novel format. And at the same time, many writers were activated by visions of intellectual isolation and, paradoxically, authoritative institutions for standards of taste and thought. The tradition of cultural criticism, in other words, began to flow in channels that led away from active involvement with the social, moral and spiritual needs of the reading public.

This process of disillusionment and alienation in literary life is well known, for it has been described by a number of perceptive literary historians.[18] What is not so clear are the reasons for the turn in the tradition of cultural criticism away from cultural leadership and the effect this turning had on the concepts of intellectual life. The reasons, I think, were a complex mixture of intellectual and material elements, which together threw literary people on the defensive. One principal intellectual element was surely the rise of science. The increasing prestige of natural science disturbed the literary world in a number of ways, none of them easily verified. Though Victorian scientists often contended that they pursued scientific knowledge 'for its own sake', and cast their institutional claims in terms compatible with liberal education, they also sought to expand the jurisdiction of the scientific method to ever wider territory. Literary people must have felt that in this sense science was pushing literature to the periphery of culture. As Matthew Arnold put it in 1882: 'The question is raised whether, to meet the needs of modern life, the predominance ought not now to pass from letters to science. . .'[19] Writers of imaginative literature like Arnold were attracted by the precision, clarity, progressiveness and alleged selflessness of science, but they also felt threatened by the scientists' desire to make England into a scientific society. Thus to the extent that science was identified with the 'calculating faculty', it came to represent a danger to the imaginative and emotional faculties. There is more to human nature, Arnold wrote, than a desire for knowledge; there are also human faculties which desire to put knowledge 'into relation with our sense of conduct, our sense for beauty, and touched with emotion by being so put'. That was the role of literature.[20]

Closely related to the advance of natural science was the decline of religion, which may be said to have produced three general effects on literary people. One was to deprive them of a 'common context' of a religious discourse and a source of values once shared with their audience. There was a lag between the abandonment of orthodox Christianity by leading literary figures and their middle-class public; hence, in the late-Victorian period, the world view of writers like George Moore, Thomas Hardy and George Gissing clashed with that of the orthodox reading public. The Bishop of Wakefield, for instance, burned Hardy's *Jude the Obscure* — presumably, Hardy said, because he could not burn Hardy himself.

A second effect of the decline of religion was to inject doubt and despair about the meaning of life into the minds of serious authors. As Arnold felt, so did other writers, that theirs was an 'iron time / Of doubts, disputes, distractions, fears', that modern people were adrift between two worlds, 'one dead, / The other powerless to be born.'[21] In so far as authors expressed truthfully their world view, they lost the ability to speak for a good part of their audience. At the same time, as writers abandoned othodoxy, they also struggled to free themselves from the old Evangelical moral code, and to substitute naturalism for Victorian literary conventions. For example, *A Mummer's Wife* by George Moore, who thought of himself as 'Zola's richochet' in England, was rejected by both Mudie's and Smith's libraries, and its readership remained tiny.[22] Hardy's pessimism and naturalism earned him frequent hysterical comments by more othodox critics, including the remark by one lecturer that Hardy 'has a curious mania for exploiting sewers; filth and defilement he faces with the calm, unshrinking countenance of a Local Board labourer'.[23]

The third general effect of the waning of orthodox faith among imaginative writers was the loss of a traditional source of inspiration. As their faith receded, literary figures lost the central objective of their Victorian predecessors — to teach the great invigorating and uplifting lessons of Victorian Evangelicalism — the need for moral regeneration and the justice of the workings of the world. As Arnold said of poetry, art should animate as well as amuse; but many late-Victorian writers found it difficult without faith to sustain the necessary confidence to produce the supportive literature the Victorian audience demanded. The role of preachers and prophets had given Victorian writers self-esteem as well as public admiration. Without the force and confidence to play that role, they tended to replace their ideal of cultural leadership with the vision of art itself as a calling. As T.S. Eliot observed with regard to Arnold and Pater, late-Victorian writers began to make a religion of art.[24]

If the rise of science and the decline of orthodox religion sapped the confidence of literary figures, so also did the failure by the tradition of cultural criticism itself to effect significant social and moral changes. In the mid-Victorian decades, the British economy emerged from its highly unstable formative years and settled into a period of prosperity. Social tensions were muted as class society reached a kind of maturity.[25] Yet the inheritors of the tradition of cultural criticism had no reason to think that the attack on individual and social atomization had succeeded. The middle class, which continued to grow in size and power, had triumphed in the realm of social morality, and it had elevated to consensus status the ideology of economic self interest. Indeed, the depression in English cereal farming which occurred between the mid-1870s and late-1890s, eroded the power of the aristocracy and gentry, and in so doing diminished the traditional source of paternalistic values as a counterweight to middle-class ideology. The landed orders began to merge with the wealthy bourgeoisie to form a single upper class, whose conspicuous consumption of material goods dominated the tone of late-Victorian and Edwardian life. All these changes represented a rejection of the anti-materialist and anti-self-interest elements in the message of Victorian cultural critics. That rejection was a source of despair to their late-Victorian successors.

The continued expansion of the cultural power of the middle class was accompanied by another social change unsettling to literary people: the fracturing of the reading public. One sense in which the reading public was fractured was, as we have seen, the multiplication of scholarly disciplines, which created specialized journals and privileged audiences. But another kind of fracturing had to do with the tremendous expansion of the reading public from the 1860s to 1900. Paradoxically, confusion and distrust about their audience in the minds of literary people in England grew simultaneously with the explosion in the size of the reading population. Why? To resolve this question, one has to understand what kind of readership was being created.

The expansion of the English reading public was a function of both the growth of the population and the spread of literacy. The population of England and Wales had doubled between 1801 and 1851, and it more than doubled again between 1850 and 1901. It swelled from 8,872,900 in 1801 to 40,000,000 in 1901. Given this rate of growth, even if the literacy rate had remained level, the number of readers would have increased impressively. But the literacy rate also shot up, especially from the 1860s. See Table 7.1.

**Table 7.1: Literacy Rates in England and Wales[26]**

| Year | Males (%) | Females (%) |
| --- | --- | --- |
| 1841 | 67.3 | 51.1 |
| 1851 | 69.3 | 54.8 |
| 1861 | 75.4 | 65.3 |
| 1871 | 80.6 | 73.2 |
| 1881 | 86.5 | 82.3 |
| 1891 | 93.6 | 92.7 |
| 1900 | 97.2 | 96.8 |

Because of a growing concern about education and the foundation of the state school system in 1870, the proportion of readers rose dramatically. The number of readers in England and Wales, including literate and semi-literate, must have been about 11,000,000 in 1851; but in 1891, it probably reached 29,000,000.

Illiteracy was practically abolished in 40 years. Yet this reading public was not only much larger than before, it was also socially more divided. The early and mid-Victorian reading public was substantially middle class. In the late-Victorian years, the middle-class public grew, but there was created alongside it a mass of working-class readers. Further, with the electoral reforms of 1867 and 1884-5, which went far towards manhood suffrage, these were readers who counted politically. But the *quality* of their literacy remained low. It was still true in 1910 that only a tiny minority of working-class children attended school beyond the age of eleven. What had been created was a mass semi-literate, working-class, reading public, about whom the serious literary figures knew almost nothing and felt little commonality of interests and values, and yet who threatened to win the dominant position in political and economic life. This new public was to unsettle literary authors as much as any feature of modern life.

The expansion of the number of readers was accompanied by a flood of reading matter. The opportunities for profit presented by the enormous new market for publications inspired many technical innovations in printing — large web perfecting presses, electro-type presses, paper-making machines, book-binding machines, etc.[27] Cheap books, journals and newspapers gushed from the presses in unprecedented volume. These publications were cheap in more ways than one. Inexpensive editions of good books did become more readily available, but the vast bulk of new reading matter was of low intellectual quality — penny magazines, shilling horror and crime novels, and sensationalist newspapers. Professor Altick reports that in the 1880s 'penny dreadful' novels sold from 10,000 to 60,000 copies each. He suggests that the total sales for all such books may have reached 2,000,000 per week.[28] The cheap newspapers of the 1890s sold in figures beyond the dreams of earlier Victorian publishers. George Newnes's *Tit-Bits,* for instance, had a circulation of 671,000 in 1897.[29] The new flood of reading matter represented a rival world of publishing to that of the men of letters, and it came from publishers wholly devoted to profit. What Richard Hoggart observed of popular 'literature' of the twentieth century seems true as well of the mass publications of the 1890s: mass publications 'are full of corrupt brightness, of improper appeals and moral evasions. To recall instances: they tend towards a view of the world in which progress is conceived as a seeking of material possessions, equality as morally levelling and freedom as the grounds for endless irresponsible pleasure.' And, as Hoggart shows, such mass publications were, and are, aggressively anti-intellectual. In them, 'All professors are absent-minded or ineffective; all scientists are weird and bespectacled . . .'[30]

If high-brow publications had reached in the late-Victorian years the same proportion of the population and the same proportion of the total reading public as in the first half of the nineteenth century, then the outlook of serious writers would have been brighter than it was. But in the circumstances of a minimally-literate population expanding at a rate faster than that of fully literate readers, serious literature seemed to many writers to be slipping to the periphery of British culture. This slippage was evident in the case of periodicals. As Adrian Poole has suggested, the new mass magazines and periodicals of the 1880s and 1890s were aimed at all segments of the market at once; consequently, the high quality periodicals were crowded out.[31] Hence, the massive expansion of the reading public during the century caused a proliferation of reviews and magazines, each scrambling for a foothold in the market. But the rate of expansion reached a peak in the 1860s, after which a decline set in. See Table 7.2.

**Table 7.2: New Magazines Begun in London, 1800-1900**[32]

| Decade | Number of new magazines started |
|--------|--------------------------------|
| 1801-10 | 20 |
| 1811-20 | 35 |
| 1821-30 | 100 |
| 1861-70 | 170 |
| 1871-80 | 140 |
| 1881-90 | 70 |
| 1891-1900 | 30 |

These figures show what a sharply shrinking market for their products the late-Victorian men of letters, including purely literary writers, faced. Further, the expanded number of magazines in the 1850s, 1860s, and 1870s caused sharp specialization of many publications. Some devoted themselves entirely to serialized fiction; others to family fiction and guidance, religion, art, sport, trade, politics and the military services, as well as the emerging academic disciplines. In short, the late-Victorian periodicals were being squeezed by new mass-circulation publications and by their own over-production at mid-century. Many of them responded by trying to stake out a claim for a safe share of the market.[33] From the point of view of a writer like George Gissing, who knew that most writers lacked transcendent talent, the late-Victorian periodical appeared to be a declining and fragmented outlet, and one increasingly coloured by cut-throat competition. This was one of the grim conditions of *New Grub Street*.[34]

A related malfunction in the world of literary folk was the clear separation of literature from journalism. As newspaper publishing became big business (especially after the repeal of the stamp tax in 1855), and the principal object of the business was profit rather than the shaping of public opinion, reporting and writing for the newspapers tended to become a specialized trade, one not available as a means of support to aspiring literary artists. When John Morley left Oxford in the latter 1850s, 'in pursuit of a literary calling', he felt he had 'little choice but journalism'.[35] Precarious as such a beginning was, Morley made his way as a journalist, editor, biographer, historian, MP and cabinet member Leslie Stephen, another young man to whom the clergy offered no option, was able to follow much the same route. But these two were generalists and not writers of imaginative literature. Of the latter type, only a few were able to maintain the early-nineteenth century link between literature and journalism — G.B. Shaw, W.E. Henley and Lionel Johnson, among others.[36] When young George Gissing began to make his way in the literary world in the 1880s, he was befriended by Frederic Harrison, who got him started in journalism. But Gissing, who by then was influenced by doctrines of the superiority and autonomy of art, found journalism degrading and gave it up.

Gissing took up tutoring as a way of supporting himself while he wrote; many others found academic careers a preferable option. Professor Altick has shown the increase in the number of literary people who supported themselves with academic work.[37] See Table 7.3.

**Table 7.3: Non-literary Occupations of British Writers**

| Occupation | 1801-35 | 1835-70 | 1870-1900 |
|---|---|---|---|
| Clergymen | 29 | 38 | 16 |
| Lawyers | 5 | 10 | 2 |
| Government office/civil service | 17 | 27 | 17 |
| Artists, architects, musicians | 11 | 21 | 10 |
| Physicians | 5 | 10 | 2 |
| Journalists | 17 | 40 | 27 |
| Teachers, professors | 4 | 17 | 25 |

These trends have continued into the twentieth century, so that the universities have replaced both the clergy and journalism as the main means of support for literary people.[38]

Finally, prominent among the economic and social problems facing late-Victorian literary folk were certain difficulties in the book-publishing system. The difficulties mainly affected the writers of fiction. The publishing of fiction, as we have observed, had become intimately tied to the economic arrangements of the circulating libraries, especially Mudie's. In 1890, Mudie's had some 25,000 subscribers and Smith's 15,000.[39] The circulating libraries had a heavy hand not only in saying what was published, but also in determining the format of fiction and the price of books. Through the 1880s, these libraries continued to demand fiction in the form of three-volume novels, and to insist that these triple-deckers be sold at 31s 6d, a price that new technology had long since made obsolete. They continued to couple these restrictions with insistence on Victorian literary conventions, including above all, standard Evangelical morality.[40]

In the 1880s and 1890s, many novelists rebelled against every aspect of the system. They demanded, of course, the right to produce novels reflecting their own view of the world and morality, and thus to break Victorian literary conventions. They also recognized that the libraries had contributed to an over-supply of novelists and novels. The simple fact that a single purchase order by the circulating libraries could assure a profit on a novel to a publisher had created a demand for novels, and it had encouraged many people of limited talent to try for careers as writers of fiction. Gissing complained of this problem in *The Private Papers of Henry Ryecroft*.[41] The system in particular had called a great many middle-class women into the writing of fiction, for these women were able to earn an income of £150 to £200 a year in a respectable occupation without leaving their homes. For instance, at Bentley's, a publisher of fiction only, the proportion of all books published by women rose from about 20 per cent in the 1830s and 1840s to more than 40 per cent in the 1870s and 1880s.[42] Hence, the scramble by periodical publishers for a share of the market was matched by the scramble by authors for publishers for their often ephemeral novels.

Inevitably, many of the fiction writers in that highly competitive world found the three-volume novel a terrible burden. Because the libraries paid proportionately more for three-volume novels than for one-volume novels, novelists were forced to spin out a modest plot or idea into three volumes. Many of the novelists of more 'modern' ideas and temperament, like George Moore and Henry James, who adopted ideas asserting the primacy of aesthetic values in literature — the importance of form and the autonomy of art — and wanted to write novels whose length and format were determined by the internal logic of their art and not by the economics of the circulating libraries. Henry James's famous essay 'The Art of Fiction', which insisted on the equal necessity of perfection in form and content, served as a criticism of the existing publishing system.[43] Gissing and others felt that the three-volume format was suitable to the conventional mode of the omniscient narrative, but that a single volume was better for the modern 'dramatic' mode, in which the narrator does not tell all, and which requires the reader to supply connective tissue.[44] Yet for all the aesthetic theories, the impression of literary life that is indelible comes from Gissing's *New Grub Street,* where the protagonist's struggle with the triple-decker arises from the plain fact that it sucked him dry. The novelist, perhaps best viewed as one of those who should never have been trapped into fiction in the first place, is paralyzed by the awesome task of continually filling up three fat volumes from a meagre stock of ideas.[45]

In the 1890s, the three-decker system did collapse. George Moore, who had waged public combat against Mudie, and who had cried 'I'll wreck this big house of yours, Mr. Mudie', claimed credit for its demise.[46] But the system actually fell for the most mundane economic reasons. The circulating libraries had helped call into existence the fashion of reading the latest novel, and so had spawned hundreds of ephemeral novels each year. Since these novels consisted of three volumes apiece, the libraries ran into a mammoth storage difficulty. Further, technology and the demand from the swollen reading public combined to reduce the time between publication of a novel and its sale in a cheap reprint. The early sale of cheap editions deprived the libraries of their market for used books, which had been a necessary part of their profit system, as well as having been a relief for storage problems. In 1894, Mudie's and Smith's declared that they would pay publishers no more than four shillings a volume for fiction, and that they must have a year's delay before the publishers sold cheap editions. They also urged publishers to abandon the three-decker format in favour of one-volume novels. In 1894, 184 three-deckers were published; in 1895, only 52; and in 1897, four.[47]

The end of the triple-decker — and the adoption of the royalty system to give authors a fairer share of the profits from their work — did not come soon enough to prevent a strong elitist reaction among British literary figures. The flowering of ephemeral novels, the struggle over Victorian literary conventions, the continued imposition on secularized authors of middle-class moral attitudes, and the sudden birth of a semi-literate mass reading public all contributed to the idea among literary artists that public tastes were being debased. Almost all the major novelists of the late-nineteenth century — Gissing, Hardy, Moore, Meredith and James, for instance — believed that the quality of taste was declining, and that 'culture' was eroding. The idea of the debasement of taste was to be an important factor in the rise of literary modernism in England and it has remained influential as an interpretation of English high culture. G.M. Young, for example, concluded about late-Victorian thought:

But, fundamentally, what failed in the late Victorian age, and its flash Edwardian epilogue, was the Victorian public, once so alert, so masculine, and so responsible. Compared with their fathers, the men of that time were ceasing to be a ruling or a reasoning stock; the English mind sank towards that easily excited, easily satisfied state of barbarism and childhood which press and politics for their own ends fostered, and on which in turn they fed. . .[48]

The 'debasement of taste' thesis, however, is a crude and impressionistic description of what happened in late-Victorian literary life. There is no reason to believe that the number of competent and serious readers of literature declined in the last decades of the century, or that the critical standards or 'masculine' responsibility decayed. What had happened was that some leading literary people simultaneously were repelled by the continuing expansion of bourgeois *mores* and styles, and were bewildered by the fracturing of their old audience and by the rise of a new one with which they had no contact and little sympathy. Literary writers also experienced a loss of confidence because of the rise of natural science and the decline of religion. They lost their assurance that they could reach all the politically-effective members of society. For all these reasons, they sensed that literature was no longer as central to English culture as it once had been; and the idea of the debasement of taste was their rationalization of the predicament.

The sense of the debasement of taste and all that it represented was the context which reshaped and redirected the tradition of cultural criticism. The pivotal figure in the redirection of the tradition was John Ruskin, himself an eminently Victorian prophet. In Ruskin's work, of which the best was produced between 1843 (the first volume of *Modern Painters*) and 1875 (the early parts of *Fors Clavigera*), embedded in reams of criticism of painting, architecture and contemporary political economy, there is an ideal of the wholeness of human beings and the coherence of society which reached back to both Shelley and Coleridge. Ruskin added to the tradition of cultural criticism the notion that art is the product of the whole ethos of society: great art is the product of a morally sound society; bad art is the result of a morally corrupt society. Hence in Ruskin's mind, the moral poverty of *laissez-faire* capitalism, its fragmentation of society, and the ugliness of the monuments of Victorian taste were intimately connected. In these attitudes, Ruskin reflected a view of the functions of art and of the criteria by which it should be judged wholly compatible with prevailing Victorian ideas. Yet throughout his work, Ruskin gave the impression that art is the highest human function, so that his criticism of the quality of his own society seemed to advocate aestheticism.

In Ruskin's view, art was a moral activity. Reared as an Evangelical Christian and powerfully influenced by Carlyle's moralism, Ruskin believed in the divine origins of nature.[49] Indeed, from his natural theology he drew a life-long enthusiasm in natural science, especially geology and botany. To him the role of an artist was to see and to communicate God's revelation in nature, every aspect of which had been designed to help humanity understand the divine message.[50] This aesthetic of realism encompassed a theory of beauty at once idealist in metaphysics and religious in spirit. Beauty, he said, has two aspects — typical and vital. Typical beauty meant the formal qualities similar to all objects that reveal their divine design. Vital beauty meant the perfect adjustment of things to life tasks, 'the appearance of felicitous fulfilment of function in living things'.[51] Such an analysis of beauty entails more than consciousness on the part of the viewer: it requires active participation by the whole person, 'the exulting, reverent, and grateful perception' of beauty. Hence perception and communication of beauty is a *moral* act. Ruskin wrote: 'I wholly deny that the impressions of beauty are in any way sensual; they are neither sensual nor intellectual, but moral.'[52]

If the perception and communication of art is a moral act and a creation by the whole person, then the moral and social conditions of a society inform all art. Ruskin felt that the power, insight and joy of a great artist are elevated qualities utterly inconsistent 'with any viciousness of soul, with any mean anxiety'. 'Great art', he declared, 'is the expression of the mind of a great man, and mean art, that of the want of mind of a weak man.'[53] By the same reasoning, the whole man is inevitably the product of the values and thought of his time. One can, Ruskin claimed, 'read the characters of men, and of nations, in their art, as in a mirror'.[54] The Gothic architecture of Venice 'had arisen out of, and indicated in all its features, a state of pure national faith, and of domestic virtue'.[55] And the hideous ugliness of industrial England reflected the moral ugliness of its makers. Capitalist industrialism, Ruskin thought, 'delights itself in the defilement and degradation of all the best gifts of its God' by its deformed values. Among the worst of its features was the erosion of the full humanity of its workers: by the principle of the division of labour, and by the subordination of men to machines, capitalist industry turned men into machines.[56]

One response to the situation was social revolution, which Ruskin and some of his disciples considered as a possibility. Ruskin imagined a return to a highly-ordered society in which workers would be organized in guilds as in medieval Europe. J.A. Hobson, William Morris, and the later tradition of English guild socialism learned from Ruskin that the logical step from aesthetic criticism of English society was more or less extensive social rearrangement. For such people, the separation of thought and thinkers, including art and artists, was unacceptable. Morris, for instance, after a period of writing escapist poetry, took little interest in what he called 'intellectual art', and hoped that the art of the future 'will not be an esoteric mystery shared by a little band of superior beings ... [but] the gift of the people to the people'.[57]

Yet there undeniably was in Ruskin's message, as there had been in Romantic ideology, the notion that art is superior to society. As Joan Evans has observed, 'Ruskin was in the strictest sense of the word an aesthete: a man for whom the art of perception was the highest exercise of the mind and soul.'[58] Ruskin, though he was quintessentially Victorian, clearly pitted art against modern life. Readers could fairly draw the conclusion that Ruskin believed society should be revolutionized to be worthy of great art. He definitely felt that society tended on the whole to drag down the strength and quality of artists. He wrote in *Stones of Venice*:

> Society always has a destructive influence upon an artist: first, by its sympathy with his meanest powers; secondly, by its chilling want of understanding of his greatest; and, thirdly, by its vain occupation of his time and thoughts. Of course a painter of men must be *among* men: but it ought to be as a watcher, not as a companion.[59]

Thus even though Ruskin spoke successfully to the new commercial and industrial middle class — more successfully in both lectures and writing than to high-brow critics — his view of the condition of English society and culture inspired, in a second line of disciples, a strategic withdrawal from society in order to defend art. The main trends in religious and intellectual life, in the development of the class society, and in the changing conditions of publishing and audience, all served to emphasize this alienating aspect of Ruskin's message. A significant number of young artists and writers concluded that there was little hope of changing the society, and therefore that art as the superior activity should be isolated from hostile influences.

There were many manifestations of this disaffection between artists and industrial society. One of the earliest was the 'flight from actuality into archaic romance' of the Pre-Raphaelite brotherhood, who tended to transform Christianity into a purely aesthetic experience.[60] Another was the exotic and escapist poetry of Swinburne and Morris. Yet another was the importation of aestheticist theories from France by writers like George Moore and Henry James. By the 1870s, the tendency of a small but highly-visible circle of poets, painters and novelists to judge all aspects of life by the standard of their support of art had coalesced into the 'aesthetic movement', which reasserted the eighteenth-century doctrine of art-as-such: that all art is *sui generis*; that art is to be created and contemplated disinterestedly; and that a work of art is autonomous.[61] Here, in direct rejection of Victorian concepts of the function of art, was a religion of beauty, an essential motive for which, was, as Graham Hough has said, 'a continual effort by the artists to carve out an enclave of their own, emancipated as far as possible from contemporary circumstances'.[62]

The similarities between certain concepts in the aesthetic movement and in the late-Victorian university reform movement are striking — and crucial to an understanding of the terrain of late-Victorian intellectual life. In general, both movements expressed not only a rejection of Victorian ways, but also a turning away from the needs and interests of the larger society. More specifically, both had ideals of a style of life, a concept of life ideally going on in a rarified realm of the spirit and intellect. And both insisted on the superiority of that realm to ordinary life and on the repudiation of 'externalist' standards for judging intellectual work.

In the aesthetic movement, there was a strong tendency to make one's life a work of art. This tendency was illustrated in the life and writing of Henry James and Oscar Wilde, and even in Samuel Butler's *Way of All Flesh*. But the message and its relation to aestheticism was best articulated by Walter Pater, fellow of Brasenose College, Oxford, and a highly influential thinker in both artistic and academic circles. Pater, whose aesthetic sensitivity appeared early in his attraction to the Oxford Movement, read Ruskin's *Modern Painters* in the 1850s and learned from it to interest himself in the critical analysis of the impressions he received from art. The experiencing of beauty rose for him to the status of religion.[63] But Pater also learned from liberal theologians and the scientific naturalists, so that while he retained an aesthetic attachment to Christianity, his world view and religious beliefs diverged sharply from Ruskin's. Pater became a materialist and an agnostic, devoted to the cultivation of aesthetic experience. As an Oxford don, he won attention for his daring and somewhat shocking denial of immortality, for his perfection of manners and dress, and for his advocacy of a highly-intellectualized *carpe diem* philosophy.

In 1866, Pater found a model for an aesthetic hero, as well as an interest in the renaissance, in reading about J.J. Winckelmann, the great German humanist of the eighteenth century. Pater believed that Winckelmann and renaissance artists had exemplified the devotion to beauty and the rejection of moralistic judgement of art. Pater celebrated the cultural coherence of the renaissance and the completeness of its personalities in *The Renaissance: Studies in Art and Poetry* (1873). In his famous concluding chapter, Pater contended that modern scientific thought supported aestheticism. Modern science, he wrote, showed that everything is in flux: physical life is only a temporary event in the motion of elements; thought and feeling are only the consciousness of unstable and flickering sense impressions. Furthermore, one's experience is entirely private. In view of these facts, the function of 'speculative culture, towards the human spirit is to rouse, to startle it into sharp and eager observation'. Thus roused, an individual mind can locate the finest moments of experience for their own sakes:

A counted number of pulses only is given to us of a variegated, dramatic life. How may we see in them all that is to be seen in them by the finest senses? How shall we pass most swiftly from point to point, and be present always at the focus where the greatest number of vital forces unite in their purest energy?

To burn always with this hard, gemlike flame, to maintain this ecstasy, is success in life.[64]

Pater's ideal life was one devoted to aesthetic experiences in every aspect of existence, not just art. Accordingly, he believed in art-for-art's sake not in the sense that art is the only worthwhile activity or the sole purpose of life, but in the sense that art is autonomous and is to be judged by its own standards of perfection.[65] This idea of art-for-art's sake was extended by later aesthetes such as James McNeill Whistler, Oscar Wilde and the poets of the Rhymers' Club into a doctrine of the independence of art and artists from all social and moral claims of society. Whistler, for instance, learned the idea of the artist as heroic genius from Ruskin and the Pre-Raphaelites, but he turned it into a concept of the artist as a member of a separate class without any obligations to society:

Art should be independent of all clap-trap, should stand alone, and appeal to the artistic sense of eye or ear, without confounding this with emotions entirely foreign to it, as devotion, pity, love, patroiotism, and the like.[66]

The Rhymers' Club — W.B. Yeats, Lionel Johnson, Ernest Dowson and Arthur Symons — devoted themselves to the isolation of the pure essence of poetry from political, moral, or religious contaminants. As Yeats recalled, they opposed 'all ideas, all generalizations that can be explained and debated', and were even reduced to silence by Symons' generalization that 'We are concerned with nothing but impressions'.[67] Wilde added a dash of *epater les bourgeois.* He wrote in his preface to *The Picture of Dorian Gray:*

> There is no such thing as a moral or an immoral book.
>     Books are well written, or badly written, that is all . . .
> No artist has ethical sympathies. An ethical sympathy
>     in an artist is an unpardonable mannerism of style . . .
> We can forgive a man for making a useful thing as long as he does
> not admire it. The only excuse for making a useless thing is that one
> admires it intensely.
>     All art is quite useless.

The fact that the aesthetes were rejecting Victorian literary conventions and were propounding a view of art as superior to ordinary life was not lost on the literate public. Gilbert and Sullivan exploited the public reaction against aestheticism by the ridiculous figure of the poet Bunthorne in *Patience* (1881). More serious criticisms of aestheticism abounded in the journals of the 1870s and 1880s. W.J. Courthope, for instance, declared that Pater advocated 'emasculated principles of art' in the conclusion to *The Renaissance*.[68] Aestheticism was characterized in the *Contemporary Review* as an 'elegant amusement for the leisure of a cultured class, a dainty trifle, the taste for which is mostly outgrown with youth . . .'[69] Principal J.C. Shairp spoke for the heart of Victorianism when he warned aesthetic poets:

> If future poets wished to win the ear of their countrymen, and to merit the honour accorded to the highest poetry, they would be wise to cultivate manlier thought and nobler sentiment, expressed in purer and fresher diction, and to make their appeal, not to the perfumed tastes of over-educated coteries, but to the broader and healthier sympathies of universal man.[70]

The hostility to aestheticism, as Professor Oscar Maurer has shown, was not unanimous.[71] Furthermore, it can be, and was, dismissed as a comical outburst of philistinism. But the angry reactions to aestheticism and the doctrine of art-for-art's sake reflected a sense on the part of many readers that some literary figures were rejecting the accepted idea of the proper function of art and letters, that they were asserting the superiority of art to the needs and values of the general reading public, and that they were declaring the existence of a separate, elevated class of highly-cultivated people. Critics of aestheticism sensed its connections with the latest in university life. One reviewer declared that Pater's *Renaissance* was an example of works by 'a class removed from ordinary mankind by that ultra-culture and academical contemplation of the world as a place chiefly occupied by other beings equally cultured and refined, which . . . forms an inner circle of Illuminati in almost every university . . .'[72]

Indeed, the second major development out of the tradition of cultural criticism was vitally concerned with the universities. This strand of thought, beginning in the tradition of severe criticism of industrial society, led to a concept of the universities as centres of cultural authority — the idea of an academy. In this line of thought the pivotal figure was Matthew Arnold, who was not only the leading literary critic in the mid-Victorian years, but also an extremely influential social critic and architect of educational institutions. In his poetry, mostly written between 1849 and 1857, Arnold had participated in the tradition of cultural criticism by stressing the confusions, doubts and uncertainties of the times. Modern life seemed to him a disease, 'with its sick hurry, its divided aims / Its heads o'ertaxed, its palsied hearts'.[73] The unnatural disquiet of modern times he recognized as directly related to the erosion of Christianity, and he felt that without some such framework it was impossible to see life steadily and as a whole. But many other modern developments were involved:

My dearest Clough [he wrote] these are damned times — everything is against one — the height to which knowledge is come, the spread of luxury, our physical enervation, the absence of great *natures*, the unavoidable contact with millions of small ones, newspapers, cities, light profligate minds, moral desparadoes like Carlyle, our own selves, and the sickening consciousness of our own difficulties. . .'[74]

Eventually Arnold, who never felt that he had much poetical energy, decided that for him the age was so unpoetical that he could not continue writing poetry. By the mid-1850s, he had turned increasingly to literary and social criticism. Modern life, he believed, required a certain kind of inspiriting, rejoicing poetry, yet at the same time prevented its being produced. Criticism, on the other hand, was both possible and necessary. Although Arnold admitted that criticism was inferior to creative work, he believed criticism was important to it. Not all epochs make the creation of great literature possible, for literary work is 'work of synthesis and exposition', and is dependent on 'intellectual and spiritual atmosphere' and a 'certain order of ideas'.[75] In such ages criticism had a vital role, for criticism

> tends to make an intellectual situation of which the creative power can profitably avail itself. It tends to establish an order of ideas, if not absolutely true, yet true by comparison with that which it displaces; to make the best ideas prevail.[76]

His view of criticism was that it would provide a vital and healthy culture in which alone creative art could thrive. Such a view of the function of criticism could not be limited to literary subjects, and Arnold moved easily between criticism of literature to criticism of society. He believed that English values and styles of thought, like English literature, were infected by 'eccentricity and arbitrariness', which in turn were related to the basic English inclination towards the practical and the partisan. Unlike the French and the Germans, the English did not prize ideas and knowledge in themselves, but always for their applications. He believed that the Englishman's tendency to take interest in the applications of ideas caused them to deal with ideas in a partisan, unreflective way; hence, most intellectual work in England was 'polemical and controversial': often blind, narrow, unrefined and self-satisfied. Thus for Arnold, the crucial role for criticism was *disinterestedness* — allowing the free play of mind on all subjects.[77]

The principle of disinterested inquiry, Arnold thought, would lead the English to recognize what they *were* and to consider what they *ought* to be. This idea of moving towards completeness of perspective was central to Arnold's social criticism. In *Culture and Anarchy*, he said in effect that England was threatened with cultural disintegration, the first signs of which were the acts of political 'anarchy' associated with the reform agitation of 1866-7: political riots, brawls and destruction of railings in Hyde Park. The division of society in a class structure (he called the three classes Barbarians, Philistines, and Populace) lay at the root of the problem. Each pursued its own interests blindly, in accordance with the prevailing doctrine that the greatest good was the right to say and do whatever one pleased. The universal advocacy by each class of its own interests made for social anarchy, and for cultural anarchy as well — the inability of people to see things as a whole and as they really are. For a remedy Arnold proposed the habit of allowing a fresh stream of ideas to flow around stock notions, and this involved a destruction of class-bound thinking.

Arnold believed that in each class there were a few — he called them 'aliens' — who had the capacity to break out of 'class-instinct' to a disinterested view of events.[78] These aliens were the agents of culture, by which Arnold meant the pursuit of perfection, the development of our whole and 'best' selves, 'by means of getting to know, on all matters which most concern us, the best which has been thought and said in the world . . .'[79] These aliens or 'men of culture' were not to be priests tending an altar of privileged knowledge, nor to be isolated from the rest of society:

> The great men of culture are those who have a passion for diffusing, for making prevail, for carrying from one end of society to another, the best knowledge, the best ideas of their time; who have laboured to divest knowledge of all that was harsh, uncouth, difficult, abstract, professional, exclusive; to humanize it, to make it efficient outside the clique of the cultivated and the learned, yet still remaining the *best* knowledge and thought of the time, and a true source, therefore, of sweetness and light.[80]

The gist of this passage is clear: the cultured minority, as in Coleridge's idea of the clerisy, should be in close communication with the people. Their role would be in the broadest sense instructional. Yet Arnold's frequently repeated wish to make the best ideas *prevail* conveyed the germ of a different notion. Arnold desperately wanted some kind of cultural authority. He despised the cacophony of parties and journals. The practical or 'Hebraising' tendency of Englishmen had created a situation in which every party or interest group had to have 'its organ of criticism'. Moreover, the doctrine that everyone above all had the right to think and say as he pleased offered no means of sorting out the good opinion from the bad. The situation degraded criticism and undermined authority in matters of intellect.[81] Culture, according to Arnold, would not only cast fresh light on conventional ideas, but also bring 'some sound order and authority' to this cultural chaos.[82]

What could be done about this 'hideous anarchy which is modern English literature', as Arnold called it?[83] He suggested the establishment of an *academy*, the function of which he took from Renan: ' "creating a form of intellectual culture *which shall impose itself* all around" '.[84] The English, Arnold said, have intellectual 'energy and honesty', but not openness and flexibility of intelligence, nor a belief that there *is* a right and wrong in intellectual matters. Unlike the French, the Englishman did not believe 'That he is bound to honour and obey the right, that he is disgraced by cleaving to the wrong.' Consequently, the English would benefit from an academy, which would maintain high standards of form, precision, and proportion, as well as promote 'a national bent towards clearness, correctness, and propriety in thinking and speaking'. An academy would establish 'a force of educated opinion', improve the journeyman work of editing and reviewing and act as 'a recognised authority in matters of intellectual tone and taste'.[85]

Arnold believed it would be impossible to establish a fully-fledged, authoritative academy in England. But he assigned to the universities the functions of an academy. This inclination put him squarely in the university reform movement, and, strangely enough, allied him with the natural scientists. In 1868, Arnold published a highly-influential report on schools and universities on the continent, contrasting the English universities unfavourably with those in Europe, especially those in Germany.[86] Far from advocating any revulsion from science, in its general sense, Arnold made it the key to his idea of university reform:

> The want of the idea of science, of systematic knowledge, is, as I have said again and again, the capital want, at this moment, of English education and of English life; it is the university, or the superior school, which ought to foster this idea.[87]

In Germany, he wrote, the intellectual life of the nation was higher than in England. That was because the German universities had as their paramount aim 'to encourage a love of study and science for their own sakes':

> *Lehrfreiheit* and *Lernfreiheit,* liberty for the teacher and liberty for the learner; and *Wissenschaft,* science, knowledge systematically

pursued and prized in and for itself, are the fundamental ideas of that system.[88]

The English universities neglected those principles; instead, they supplied a 'cast of ideas' for the upper class, to which, he rightly observed, the professional men attached themselves. Thus, according to Arnold, the professionals attended the universities but had no science; while the businessmen, who were cut off from the universities, lacked science and therefore 'intellectual power'.[89] The results were that in the nation as a whole, 'the sense of the value and importance of human knowledge' was weak, the people were vulgarised, and 'bad intellectual habits and defective intellectual action' were typical.[90]

Arnold's view of the needs of English culture, which combined the advocacy of disinterested criticism, the principle of an authoritative centre for intellectual matters, and university reform, was a prime source of stimulation for the young academics of the 1860s and 1870s who were seeking to endow research in the universities. But what the reformers took from Arnold was not exactly what he had in mind. Just as the aesthetes had twisted Ruskin's teaching, in the troubled climate of the late-Victorian years, so the university reformers distorted Arnold's. In *Schools and Universities on the Continent,* Arnold recommended the reform of Oxford and Cambridge; but he argued that it would be more important to extend higher education to all the major commercial and industrial cities, to make them 'intellectual centres as well as mere places of business'.[91] Diffusion of correct thinking and a general pursuit of individual perfection were always his ultimate aims. But many university reformers seized on the idea of an academy to promote the establishment of an authoritative intellectual elite, one largely located in Oxford and Cambridge, and speaking to itself and to a highly-educated public through a new journal of 'scientific' knowledge.

This new journal was, of course, C.E. Appleton's *Academy.* Founded in 1869, the *Academy* had a number of closely-related purposes: (1) to provide an organ for the new knowledge being produced by university researchers; (2) to promote the idea of German-style research in the English universities; (3) to give voice to 'disinterested' criticism; (4) to serve as an authority in intellectual matters; and (5) to establish a class of learned scholars in England. Although Appleton considered Arnold old-fashioned in comparison to modern university scholars, he clearly received powerful stimulation from Arnold's 'Literary Influence of Academies' and

*Schools and Universities on the Continent.* Appleton took care to obtain Arnold's approval of his new journal, as well as the approval of Pattison and many research scientists. Hence the *Academy* spoke for the converging advocates of an academic elite. In the December 1873 issue, Appleton asserted that his journal was to satisfy the English need for an academy; it would be 'a central organ of sound information and correct taste in intellectual matters'. As Mark Pattison recalled later, the *Academy* and the movement to endow research 'were but different means towards a great public end; that, namely, of bringing the knowledge latent in the community to the top, and giving it more control of the conduct of the affairs of the community'.[92]

The elitist quality of the *Academy* doomed it to failure. It was a very scholarly publication, in general supporting the new 'scientific' history, philology, anthropology and the literary aestheticism of Pater and others, as well as research in the natural sciences. But its financing was old-fashioned, forced as it was to compete for readers in the market-place. The austerity of the journal drove down its circulation from 14,615 for the first issue to 6,042 for its fourth. It was, after all, a journal devoted to overturning many of the features of the world of the men of letters; and as such it required a new means of support, namely endowment or subsidization. Eventually, poor sales forced Appleton to make the *Academy* more popular, but he still insisted on a 'scientific portion' devoted to 'the wants of a small scientific class'.[93] After Appleton's death in 1879, the *Academy's* editors followed his policies as best they could; but in 1896, the journal was sold and became a much more conventional magazine devoted to *belles lettres.* Its original functions were assumed by the new academic specialist journals, most of which survived by means of subsidies from professional societies.

Meanwhile, the *Academy* had contributed to the awareness in the literate public of the claims to autonomy and authority by an academic elite. Martin Tupper, a well-meaning friend, wrote to the publisher (John Murray): '. . . your *Academy* is "caviare to the general"; as written for the few it cannot (without radical changes) be read by the many.'[94] J.A. Symonds wrote to Henry Sidgwick: 'I should think it might become a useful organ for writers if not readers.'[95] The *Daily News,* the big Liberal newspaper, said that the *Academy* would serve the need articulated by Arnold for an English academy, but that its purposes and format would encourage writers to assume a dictatorial stance. Several other periodicals expressed reservations about the journal's academic orientation. The high church *Guardian* criticized the aloofness of the *Academy's* promoters:

Whether they are devoted to the old Athenian culture, or carry on their investigations in the groves of the New Academy, they alike claim and exercise a freedom which would be worse than slavery to common men. They sit apart, contemplating numerous forms and schools of thought without committing themselves to any.[96]

H.R. Fox Bourne, writing in the latter 1880s on the history of English newspapers, undoubtedly spoke for many journalists and men of letters when he said Appleton was 'a genuine student and an enthusiast in the cause of learning, of refined taste and aesthetic sympathies, but inclined to scholastic pedantry and — as the name he chose for the paper implied — academic arrogance'.[97]

The *Academy*, then, contributed significantly to the propagation of a doctrine of academic superiority and aloofness. It urged — and was seen to urge — the doctrine of the establishment of a separate class of learned men, shielded from the public by means of endowment but claiming the authority of priests of true knowledge and correct thinking. Hence the long tradition of cultural criticism had given birth not only to aestheticism but also to an idea of a class of thinkers separate from the claims of the wider public. Both of these strains of thought represented a desire on the part of English literary thinkers and writers to defend their activities from a hostile environment by elevating them above ordinary life. Both expressed an ideal of culture as an exalted realm of refined intellectual activity. And both exemplified the rupture of the bonds of sympathy between writers and their public. Finally, the idea of an academy — based on the ideals of detachment and a centre for cultural authority — not only dove-tailed with the institutional claims of natural science and the university reform movement, but also linked them with the doctrine of art-for-art's sake and the spirit of *epater les bourgeois*. Professionalization by university scientists and scholars, and elaboration by artists of aestheticism, represented different forms of the same effort to rise above the middle-class public.

## Notes

1. Raymond Williams, *Culture and Society 1780-1950* (New York, 1966), p. xvi.

2. Ibid., pp. 32-5.

3. Ibid., p. 36.

4. Samuel Taylor Coleridge, 'Table Talk' in Professor Shedd (ed.), *The Complete Works of Samuel Taylor Coleridge* (New York, 1853), VI, pp. 857-8.

5. For a recent discussion of Coleridge's idea of the clerisy, see Ben Knights, *The Idea of the Clerisy in the Nineteenth Century* (Cambridge, 1978), Ch. 2.

6. Percy B. Shelley, 'A Defence of Poetry', in Carlos Baker (ed.), *The Selected Poetry and Prose of Percy Bysshe Shelley* (New York, 1951), *passim.*

7. J.S. Mill, *Autobiography,* Library of Liberty edn (New York, 1957), p. 44.

8. Ibid., pp. 54-5.

9. Michael St John Packe, *The Life of John Stuart Mill* (New York, 1970), p. 98.

10. J.S. Mill, 'Genius', *The Monthly Repository* (October 1832), pp. 649-59.

11. J.S. Mill, 'The Spirit of the Age', originally published in the *Examiner* (January 6 — May 29, 1831). The edition referred to here is in Gertrude Himmelfarb (ed.), *John Stuart Mill: Essays on Politics and Culture* (New York, 1962), pp. 8-9, 11-16, 19-21.

12. J.S. Mill, 'Coleridge' in Maurice Cowling (ed.), *Selected Writings of John Stuart Mill* (New York, 1968), pp. 90-1.

13. J.S. Mill, 'Utilitarianism', in ibid., p. 250.

14. J.S. Mill, *On Liberty* (The World's Classics, Oxford, 1966), Ch. II.

15. Quoted in Packe, *Life of John Stuart Mill,* p. 482.

16. Knights, *Idea of the Clerisy in the Nineteenth Century,* pp. 145-6, 151-2.

17. *The Later Letters of John Stuart Mill, 1849-1873,* edited by Francis E. Mineka and Dwight N. Lindley (4 vols., Toronto, 1972), II, p. 631.

18. See, for example, Walter Houghton, *The Victorian Frame of Mind, 1830-1870* (New Haven, 1957), *passim;* Jereome Buckley, *The Victorian Temper: A Study in Literary Culture* (New York, 1951), Chs. X-XII; Graham Hough, *The Last Romantics* (New York, 1961); and John Lester, *Journey Through Despair, 1880-1914* (Princeton, 1968), *passim.*

19. Matthew Arnold, 'Literature and Science', in *Complete Prose Works of Matthew Arnold,* ed. by R.H. Super (Ann Arbor, 1974), vol. X, p. 55.

20. Ibid., p. 65. See also David DeLaura, 'The Future of Poetry: A Context for Carlyle and Arnold' in John Chubbe (ed.), *Carlyle and His Contempoaries: Essays in Honour of C.R. Sanders* (Durham, North Carolina, 1976), pp. 148-80.

21. Matthew Arnold, 'Memorial Verses' (1850), lines 43-4; and 'Stanzas from the Grande Chartreuse' (1855), lines 85-6.

22. Malcolm Brown, *George Moore: A Reconsideration* (Seattle, 1955), Ch. 4.

23. Quoted in Carl J. Weber, *Hardy of Wessex: His Life and Literary Career* (New York, 1940), p. 149.

24. T.S. Eliot, 'Arnold and Pater', *Selected Essays,* 1917-1932 (New York, 1932), pp. 346-57.

25. Harold Perkin, *The Origins of Modern English Society, 1780-1880* (London, 1969), Ch. IX.

26. Richard Altick, *English Common Reader* (Chicago, 1957), Ch. IX.

27. Louis Dudek, *Literature and the Press: A History of Printing, Printed Media, and Their Relation to Literature* (Toronto, 1960), *passim.*

28. Altick, *English Common Reader,* p. 308.

29. Ibid., p. 396.

30. Richard Hoggart, *The Uses of Literacy* (New York, 1970), pp. 154 and 277.

31. Adrian Poole, *Gissing in Context* (London, 1975), p. 141.

32. G.F. Barwick, 'The Magazines of the Nineteenth Century', *Transactions of the Bibliographical Society* (vol. XI, 1912), pp. 237-49.

33. Dudek, *Literature and the Press,* pp. 109-10.

34. See for instance, Gissing's comments in *New Grub Street* (2 vols., Leipzig, 1891), I, pp. 19, 48.

35. John, Viscount Morley, *Recollections* (2 vols., New York, 1917), I, p. 31.

36. Dudek, *Literature and the Press,* pp. 80, 133.

37. Richard Altick, 'The Sociology of British Authorship: The Social Origins, Education and Occupations of 1,100 British Writers, 1800-1935', *Bulletin of the New York Public Library* (June 1962), p. 401.

38. A.H. Halsey, 'British Universities and Intellectual Life', in A.H. Halsey, Jean Floud and C. Arnold (eds.), *Education, Economy and Society* (Glencoe, Ill., 1961), p. 502.

39. Griest, *Mudie's Circulating Library,* p. 79.

40. Ibid., pp. 32-3, 83. Also: Royal Gettmann, *A Victorian Publisher: A Study of the Bentley Papers* (Cambridge, 1960), pp. 214-20.

41. Poole, *Gissing in Context,* p. 133; Gettmann, *A Victorian Publisher,* p. 249.

42. Gettmann, *A Victorian Publisher,* p. 249.

43. Henry James, 'The Art of Fiction', in Walter Besant and Henry James, *The Art of Fiction* (Boston, nd), pp. 51-85. Also see Leon Edel, *Henry James: The Middle Years, 1882-1895* (Avon Books edn, New York, 1978), pp. 121-4.

44. Griest, *Mudie's Circulating Library,* pp. 100-2.

45. Gissing, *New Grub Street,* I, pp. 100-2, 154-60.

46. Quoted in Brown, *Moore: A Reconsideration,* p. 90.

47. Griest, *Mudie's Circulating Library,* Chs. 7 and 8.

48. G.M. Young, *Victorian England: Portrait of An Age* (Oxford, 1960), p. 187.

49. The best discussion of Ruskin's early life and ideas is in Joan Evans, *John Ruskin* (London, 1954).

50. Kenneth Clark (ed.), *Ruskin Today* (London, 1964), pp. 71, 85-6. See also Ruskin's own recollections in *Praeterita,* in *The Complete Works of John Ruskin,* ed. by E.T. Cook and Alexander Wedderburn, vol. XXXV, pp. 220, 314-15, 413, 475. Also see *Stories of Venice* in *Complete Works,* vol. XI, p. 49.

51. Ruskin, *Modern Painters,* vol. II, in *Complete Works,* IV, p. 64.

52. Ibid., p. 42.

53. Quoted in Clark (ed.), *Ruskin Today,* p. 168.

54. Ibid., p. 168.

55. Ruskin, *The Crown of Wild Olive* in *Complete Works,* vol. XVIII, p. 443.

56. Ruskin, *Stones of Venice* in *Complete Works,* vol. X, pp. 191-2.

57. Quoted in Hough, *The Last Romantics,* p. 100.

58. Evans, *Ruskin,* p. 412.

59. Ruskin, *Stones of Venice* in *Complete Works,* vol. XI, p. 53.

60. Hough, *The Last Romantics,* p. 40.

61. This definition of aestheticism or 'art as such' is from a lecture by M.H. Abrams, 'Art as Such: Origins of the Modern Aesthetic', Northwestern University, 1978.

62. Hough, *The Last Romantics,* p. xix.

63. Pater's early development is discussed very well in Gerald Monsman, *Walter Pater* (Boston, 1977), pp. 21-4.

64. Walter Pater, *The Renaissance: Studies in Art and Poetry* (Library edn, London, 1910), p. 236.

65. Hough, *The Last Romantics,* p. 161.

66. James McNeil Whistler, *The Gentle Art of Making Enemies* (New York, 1924. Originally published in 1890), pp. 127-8.

67. William Butler Yeats, *Autobiographies* (London, 1961), p. 167.

68. W.J. Courthope, 'Wordsworth and Gray', *Quarterly Review* (January 1876), pp. 132 and 136.

69. Roden Noel, 'Robert Browning', *Contemporary Review* (November 1883), p. 701.

70. J.S. Shairp, 'Aesthetic Poetry: Dante Gabriel Rossetti', *Contemporary Review* (July 1882), p. 32.

71. Oscar Maurer, 'William Morris and the Poetry of Escape', in Herbert Davis, W.C. DeVane and R.C. Bald (eds.), *Nineteenth-Century Studies* (Ithaca, 1940), pp. 247-76.

72. [Anonymous], 'New Books', *Blackwood's* (November 1873), p. 604.

73. Matthew Arnold, 'The Scholar Gypsy' (1853), lines 204-5.

74. September 23, 1849; quoted in H.F. Lowry (ed.), *The Letters of Matthew Arnold to Arthur Hugh Clough* (London, 1932), p. 111.

75. Matthew Arnold, 'The Function of Criticism at the Present Time', *Complete Prose Works,* vol. 3, p. 261.

76. Ibid., p. 261.

77. Ibid., pp. 269-70.

78. Matthew Arnold, *Culture and Anarchy* (Cambridge, 1955), pp. 109-10.

79. Ibid., p. 6.

80. Ibid., p. 70.

81. Arnold, 'The Function of Criticism at the Present Time', *Complete Prose Works*, vol. 3, p. 110.

82. Arnold, *Culture and Anarchy*, p. 144.

83. Matthew Arnold, 'Tractatus Theologico-Politicus', (1862), *Complete Prose Works*, vol. 3, p. 64.

84. Matthew Arnold, 'The Literary Influence of Academies', *Complete Prose Works*, vol. 3, p. 235.

85. Ibid., pp. 241, 243-5, 257.

86. Matthew Arnold, 'Schools and Universities on the Continent', *Complete Prose Works*, vol. IV.

87. Ibid., p. 318.

88. Ibid., p. 263.

89. Ibid., pp. 308-309.

90. Ibid., p. 321.

91. Ibid., p. 322.

92. *The Academy* (February 19, 1881), p. 127.

93. Quoted in Johnson, 'The Academy', p. 83. The circulation figures are also from Johnson's thesis, pp. 64-5.

94. Quoted in ibid., p. 71.

95. Quoted in Roll-Hansen, *The Academy*, p. 121.

96. Quoted in ibid., p. 126.

97. H.R. Fox Bourne, *English Newspapers: Chapters in the History of Journalism* (2 vols., New York, 1966. First published in 1887), II, p. 315.

# 8 CONCLUSION: THE WORLD OF THE INTELLECTUALS, 1870-1900

By the 1870s and 1880s, the three forces of natural science, the university reform movement and the tradition of cultural criticism had worked major changes in the economic, social and conceptual conditions of English intellectual life. They had altered the topography of high culture by reducing some features of the landscape in size and moving them to the periphery, while raising others to mountainous proportions and moving them to the centre. Not only had individual features of the scenery changed, but also their relations to each other and to the map of English society as a whole. New concepts came into existence to give order and meaning to the new topography, and a new vocabulary of 'the intellectuals' came into use to refer to the new concepts.

The growth of natural science had worked the greatest changes in the institutions and aspirations controlling intellectual activity. The efforts of the Victorian scientists to create a scientific culture in England and to win satisfying professional careers for themselves had been directed in large part at the university system, and especially at Oxford and Cambridge. Because the ancient universities enjoyed power to bestow high social status on their students and faculties, and because their endowments had the capacity to support scientific teaching and research, many Victorian scientists sought to inject the universities with science, to transform them into secular research institutes and to move them to the centre of secular high culture. To a remarkable degree the scientists had succeeded, for the claims of natural science were too compelling to be resisted even by these ancient pillars of the landed and clerical establishment. Yet as English scientists had claimed posts within the universities, they had shaped their idea of science and its functions according to the concepts of liberal education and 'useless' knowledge entrenched at Oxbridge. The Victorian scientific advocates believed that industrially-useful, practical research would always be rewarded by the natural operation of the economy; therefore, they concentrated on winning endowments for 'pure' scientific research by altering Oxford and Cambridge towards the German model. For these reasons, the scientists' campaign on behalf of science and professionalization led to their assertion of the necessity of endowing in the universities a separate class of researchers whose work — science for its own sake — was held to be good in itself.

The prestige and influence of natural science also had significant effects on people working in other areas of knowledge and ideas. In the mid-Victorian decades and after, a number of academic disciplines separated out of the generalized work of the men of letters. They crystallized into specialities according to, and largely because of, the example of natural science. History was a prime example of a discipline which became distinct from general literature in a process of becoming scientific and professional. Disciplines like history were encouraged on their route to the academic style by the widely accepted definition of science as systematic, disinterested study of any subject whatsoever. Thus these disciplines imitated the specialized research procedures as well as the political and theological neutrality of natural science. The new discipline of history stressed the accumulation of knowledge for its own sake. Its practitioners, like scientists, assigned themselves the task of making 'contributions', defined as pieces of knowledge added to the stock-pile in the field. As had long been the case in the natural sciences, the new professional disciplines regarded only qualified experts as privileged to judge work in the field. Thus in the late-Victorian period, a number of special audiences were carved out of the old general public. Furthermore, the practitioners in newly professionalized fields like history rejected the objectives, procedures, and standards held by their predecessors among the men of letters. They also established new outlets for publication (the specialist journals) and joined the movement to change the universities into research institutions. They, too, argued for the establishment of a separate class of people, isolated from the market-place of the general reading public by endowment in the universities.

Natural science, then, in two different but related ways contributed to the transformation of the universities into preserves for learned researchers. The general university reform movement tended to work in the same direction. The desire of the Whigs, Liberals, utilitarians, and Dissenters was to make the English university system more useful to a modern industrial nation, and especially to its middle class. They wanted to open the universities to a broader range of students; to widen the curricula by adding subjects like natural sciences, history and modern languages; and to impose bourgeois standards of hard work and merit selection on the university teachers. Many of the external reformers also wanted the universities to become more productive in research as well as teaching. Internal reformers — dons and professors of Oxford and Cambridge — in the 1840s and 1850s sought to erect career structures for themselves as university teachers, while loosening none of the prestigious connections between the universities and the professions. The dons wanted the status of professionals; thus they shaped their teaching careers on the model of the professions rather than that of commerce and industry. Moreover, one effect of the reforms of the 1850s was to set up learning (i.e., research) as a higher enterprise than teaching. By the late-Victorian decades, research had become the means of advancement in a university career. The university reform movement thereby interacted with the institutional advancement of natural science and with the emergence of academic disciplines to move the old universities out of the orbit of the Church of England and into the atmosphere of secular society, while, paradoxically, making them centres of pure research as well as liberal education and the natural home of the new specialists.

The processes whereby the old universities were nationalized and modernized included, in their devotion to disinterested research, a tendency towards a peculiar kind of alienation — the alienation of self-isolation and of assertions of superiority to ordinary life. Alienation of a similar but not identical kind developed out of the tradition of cultural criticism in literature. As English literary figures from the Romantic period on, criticized industrial capitalist society, they created a new tradition — that of the inevitable hostility of society to art. The intellectual, psychological and emotional effects of the rise of natural science and the decline of orthodox Christianity, the failure of the tradition of cultural criticism to renovate industrial values and the fracturing of the old, relatively compact reading public together caused many late-Victorian artists to lose sympathy with bourgeois readers and to despair of redeeming society. This complex intellectual development had two effects on literary life. One was to generate the aesthetic movement, in which some literary people articulated the doctrine of art for art's sake as a defence against what they saw as a hostile environment. In so doing, literary aesthetes rejected 'external' standards for their work, especially the utilitarian and moralistic standards of the Victorians; and they created in their own minds a privileged public of fellow writers. The second effect was to make popular among some literary people the idea of an academy. According to this notion, the universities would become authoritative centres of correct thought and writing. Both of these developments in the tradition of cultural criticism struck many middle-class Englishmen as arrogant and elitist, and both represented erosion of the remarkably close community between writers and public of early-Victorian England. Further, the explicit connection between the turn in cultural criticism and the movement to endow research in the universities broadened and made more obvious the claims being made by thinkers and writers for a class of people isolated from the controls of the market-place and the needs of the public.

Several themes penetrated all three of these major developments in intellectual life and bound them together in a strong web. One theme was alienation. The condition of alienation was, of course, not deliberately pursued by any of the agents of change in intellectual life. Nor did legal and political conditions drive the main body of English thinkers into radical alienation from the political and social system. Alienation, however, can mean many things; and by the end of the century, many scholars and writers were in a sense alienated from main features of their society, though not from the political system. Indeed, until the First World War and its aftermath, very few social and political thinkers in Britain were politically alienated. The extension of the franchise to working-class males and the economic troubles of the late-Victorian years combined to turn the attention of social thinkers and politicians to the conditions of the working class. This new focus had the effect of spreading progressive ('New Liberal') and socialist ideas. But the participants in the 'peculiarities of the English' dispute are right to regard these social reformers as only very mildly alienated, if at all. Socialists like the Fabians were social democrats — critics of industrial capitalism but reformers committed to gradualist parliamentary reform and to communication with a wide public. Such social thinkers — people like J.A. Hobson, J.L. and Barbara Hammond, R.H. Tawney, William Beveridge and the Webbs — functioned in the late-nineteenth and twentieth centuries much as did their predecessors among the Victorian men of letters.

The theme of alienation was more important in the guise of aloofness and self-isolation of scholars and aesthetes. In the case of the academic scientists and scholars, alienation had meaning in that they sought to rise above middle-class status by positing the existence of a higher plane of existence, the circle of high culture, which they took as their duty to tend for its own sake. As for the aesthetes, this vanguard of literary activists vigorously rejected the conventional expectations of literature in the minds of the middle-class reading public, and they were repelled by the new reading public with whom they had nothing in common. The links between these brands of alienation were revealed once and for all by Matthew Arnold, who was a founder of both the academic and aesthetic temperaments, and who urged upper-class Englishmen to make 'aliens' of themselves by abandoning class-bound thinking in favour of self-culture. This may have been a peculiar style of alienation, but it has contributed significantly to the characteristic English inclination to denigrate business values and to regard the best in literary culture as that which goes against the grain of ordinary concerns.

A second theme weaving through the forces of change in intellectual life was specialization. The specialization that by 1900 characterized intellectual activities seems to have been a cause rather than the result of the knowledge explosion of the mid and late-nineteenth century. Of course, once the knowledge explosion began, further specialization in the twentieth century has been necessary to get a grip on it — but only because additions to knowledge have continued to be valued more highly than synthesis and general communication. In the early-Victorian years, at least in the terrain of the men of letters, synthesis and general dissemination of knowledge and ideas were of more importance than accumulation of knowledge. Why the change in the relative valuation of general communication and specialized additions to knowledge? One reason was the example of natural science, which though it valued Newtonian-level generalizations, also valued the incremental accumulation of evidence and promoted the concept of the contribution. Yet the scientific strategy of specialization would have had tough sledding had it not enjoyed the sanction of some basic idea in English culture. This idea was the great principle of the division of labour, first articulated by Adam Smith and elevated to universal opinion by political economists by mid-century. As civilization progressed by the division of labour, so knowledge was elaborated by specialization. Further, the principle of specialization was sanctioned by evolutionary sociology, wherein progress was identified with the increasing complexity of societies from their alleged primitive and homogeneous state. Specialization must even have been impressed on the Victorian unconscious by Darwinian biology, in which the successful adaptation of species could be seen as a universal law of specialization in life. The Christian religion might have acted as a bulwark against specialization, because of its insistence on a single frame of reference for all intellectual activity; but of course steadily through the century Christianity lost the power to resist.

The third major theme in the transformation of Victorian intellectual life was professionalization. As we have seen, scientists and university dons deliberately sought and won for themselves status as professional people in universities and colleges. 'Professional' to them meant a number of things at once. At the simplest level, to be a professional meant that one earned his living from full-time occupation in an activity — natural science, history, philology, philsophy and the like. Yet professional clearly meant more than this. Many of the men of letters had earned their keep by writing, but by a curious twist of mind, writers in some areas — Macaulay, for instance — by the end of the century had been relegated to the status of 'amateurs'. In fact, to the academic scholars and scientists of the late-Victorian period, a professional in their fields was one who did *not* earn a living by sale of the products of thought — though, of course, university endowments provided professional scholars with handsome salaries and substantial suburban villas. To them, to be a professional required acceptance of certain standards and procedures in intellectual work: concentration on original research; care in the use of evidence; non-partisanship with regard to current politics and theology; valuation of work according to the idea of a 'contribution', seen as relevant to the field itself; and acceptance of the circle of fellow researchers in a field as the significant audience. The new academic professionals looked upon acceptance of these principles as morally elevating; indeed, they felt that their respective disciplines, and professional academic work in general, were a calling. Even though they had sought remunerative careers in science and scholarship, they pictured these careers to themselves as selfless devotion to a high ideal rather than as labour for personal gain. The much-used term 'disinterested' meant to them 'not-for-self-interest' as well as non-partisan. In this way, the professional academics imitated the old professions — the clergy, the bar and medicine — in adopting an ideology as close as possible to that of the landed orders. In their own way, the scientists and scholars of late-Victorian England sought to make themselves part of the 'new gentry'.

The new-style academics, then, sought to raise themselves above the commercial and industrial class at the same time as leading literary figures separated themselves, at least in attitudes and theory, from the general reading public. This conclusion points to a fourth theme penetrating the various developments in intellectual life — namely, the intricate inter-play of bourgeois and anti-bourgeois attitudes. In some ways, the transformation of Victorian intellectual life was deeply influenced by fundamental middle-class ideas and values. In university reform and the evolution of academic disciplines, for instance, the impulse towards productivity and efficiency reflected certain deeply-ingrained bourgeois values. So did the sense that the universities ought to be a part of secular rather than ecclesiastical culture, and the belief that the universities ought in many ways to be more 'modern' and especially ought to contribute to the march of mind. Furthermore, professionalization of natural sciences and scholarly disciplines adopted the principle of promotion by merit: competition rather than patronage would be the operative idea, and every junior don might carry a professor's baton in his book bag. Of course, this principle has been tempered in practice by the 'old boy' network, a product of the smallness and exclusiveness of Oxbridge; nevertheless, competition has become an important fact of university life. Finally, the powerful idea of the division of labour — a central element in the middle-class ideology of political economy — helped to define and sanctify specialization.

Yet for all the influence of these middle-class traits, English intellectual life was transformed in large part by anti-bourgeois attitudes. One of the primary impulses behind professionalization was the desire of natural scientists and university scholars to enjoy a status above the middle class. In literary life, the great tradition of criticism of industrial society often let loose its arrows on middle-class ideology, which seemed to atomize the social order and the humanity of its members. The aura of a calling which beckoned to academics, scientists and artists alike was attractive to them because it offered a life's work higher than that of the businessman. The new concept of 'culture' took its place beside the older one of 'liberal education' as explicitly contrary to the ordinary activities of getting and spending. Above all, the three forces of change in intellectual life shared a rejection of market institutions and their controls. These anti-bourgeois attitudes help explain that pervasive hostility to industry and economic growth in English high culture since the nineteenth century, a hostility which has been brilliantly analyzed by Martin Wiener in his *English Culture and the Decline of the Industrial Spirit* (Cambridge, 1981).

However they may have been pulled by tensions arising from the opposition between bourgeois and gentry ideals, the triple forces of natural science, university reform and cultural criticism worked great changes in the terrain of intellectual life. These changes were apparent to all late-Victorian observers. In his *English Literature and Society in the Eighteenth Century* (1904), for instance, Leslie Stephen noted that the intellectual world of Augustan England was very much smaller and more homogeneous than his own.[1] Literary people — the term

'literary' for the eighteenth century included writers on all subjects —
shared values and interests with a small, educated elite. But in the
nineteenth century, Stephen recognized, a writer could speak only to a
particular segment of the public. *Blackwood's* spoke for many in that
general public when it regretted the barrier 'between the erudite
oligarchy who think and write, and the plebian public who only read
and talk', a barrier that was especially high around the physical
scientists.[2] Frederic Harrison, in comparing the literature of mid-
century with that of the 1880s and 1890s, regretted the preciosity and
morbidity of modern poetry and the 'incoherent specialisation' of
science and academic scholarship. He associated a loss of robustness
and originality in thought with the specialization that had resulted
from the reform of the universities.[3] J.A. Hobson felt that the great
change had been the growth of the 'academic spirit' in intellectual life,
by which he meant the formation of a 'corporation, a clique, or a
coterie for purely intellectual purposes', an academic set who divorced
knowledge from life in the belief that scholarly knowledge was an end
in itself.[4]

The point of view of Stephen, Harrison and Hobson was that of the
men of letters. It should not be surprising that their view of changes in
intellectual life was so negative, since those changes had eroded and
narrowed the territory of the men of letters. Of course, men of letters
did not disappear from English life. Stephen, Harrison, Hobson, John
Morley, Herbert Paul, Walter Besant and many others showed that it
was still possible to have careers as men of letters. In the twentieth
century, men of letters like G.K. Chesterton, Hilaire Belloc, H.W.
Massingham, C.F.G. Masterman, J.L. Hammond, Lytton Strachey
and Desmond MacCarthy are only a few of those who have won fame
and influence. Yet John Gross is right to say that the men of letters
have fallen.[5] The question is, in what sense have they declined?

For one thing, the development of the universities as centres of
specialized research diminished the claim to authority of the men of
letters. During most of the nineteenth century, the men of letters had
enjoyed a position of cultural leadership which rested on their
inclination and capacity to provide moral as well as intellectual
guidance to a general public. In the late-nineteenth century, however,
professional scientists and scholars came forward as both critics of,
and rival claimants to, the authority of the men of letters. Attacks on
the shallowness, the partisanship and the moral pretensions of the men
of letters were common in the work of the new academics. In his
lectures on university education, Newman had criticized the

contributions of the men of letters to the crudity, flippancy and insubstantial quality of English thought:

> As the great man's guest must produce his good stories or songs at the evening banquet, as the platform orator exhibits his telling facts at midday, so the journalist lies under the stern obligation of extemporizing his lucid views, leading ideas, and nutshell truths for the breakfast table. The very nature of periodical literature, broken into small wholes, and demanded punctually to an hour, involves this extempore philosophy.[6]

The same theme ran throughout Arnold's criticism of English culture, and throughout the polemics of the university reformers and professionalizing scholars. Sidney Colvin put it succinctly:

> There comes a time when you must choose between the dispersion and fragmentariness, which is the habit of journalism and life in a hurry, and the concentration and completeness which is the habit of serious literature and life at leisure.[7]

This kind of criticism of the men of letters was devastating, especially when it was backed up by reviews of their work that were based on the research expertise of professional scholars. Expertise seemed to show that the cultural leadership exercised by the men of letters was grounded in sloppy thinking and inaccurate and insufficient information. In addition, the growth of new scientific disciplines created new audiences in which the writ of the men of letters did not, and had never, run. Audiences for professional scholarship were interested in contributions, not moral edification. From the point of view of the men of letters, the splitting of the general audience was not compensated for by the rise of the new mass audience. The mass of semi-literate readers were not interested in the work of the men of letters, and it must be admitted that only socialists involved in the intellectual and political enlightenment of the working class have continued the tradition of the Victorian men of letters with much success. Usually the experience of the late-Victorian man of letters was to face not only hostile reactions from specialists but also a vast new audience not interested in Victorian-style high-brow moral instruction.

For all these reasons, the English men of letters from the late-Victorian period on faced a crisis of confidence as well as credibility.

Each generation no doubt, regrets the passing of the great figures of the past generation, and forecasts that their like will never be seen again. But it is striking how often in the last decades of the nineteenth century it was observed, upon the death of some Victorian literary giant, that the *type* known as the prophet or sage would not be replaced. Leslie Stephen wrote to Charles Eliot Norton in 1880 that while no one at the time seemed capable of doing for the new generation what Mill and Carlyle had done for the old, still he was hopeful that some new name would emerge.[8] But most observers thought that the grand scale men of letters would never be seen again. What could not be recovered, so it was thought, was the ability of a 'George Eliot' to address a wide variety of groups in society without giving any hint of 'intellectual aristocracy'; or the capacity of a 'Tennyson' to speak to the deepest needs and concerns of a whole generation; or the power of a 'Carlyle' to affect for the better the whole of an individual's human nature. Natural science, expertise, religious unbelief and the fracturing of the general audience made these things impossible.[9]

By the end of the nineteenth century it must have been clear to most highly-educated Englishmen that the men of letters would operate on a smaller scale and provide functions less central to the national high culture. One of the signs of this decline was a change in the idea or meaning of 'men of letters'. During the late-Victorian period, men of letters came to be associated by the literate public with *belles lettres* — literature in the strict sense — and with second-rate literary work at that. In the 1870s and 1880s, confusion arose about what sorts of writers should be included under the rubric of 'men of letters'. For instance, when John Morley was corresponding with Macmillan's about the *English Men of Letters* series which he would edit, Morley said that it would not do to call Bunyan, Burns, Shakespeare or Bacon 'men of letters'.[10] No such doubts would have entered an editor's mind 30 or 40 years earlier. Later, in his *Recollections,* Morley made a distinction between men of letters and artists — the artist being superior to the man of letters or literary journalist, who lacked creativity and original vision.[11] This notion seems to have come from aestheticism as well as from the general erosion of the confidence of the men of letters. Yeats and his friends in the 1890s felt sure that men of letters were inferior to real literary artists, for artists dealt with the *essence* of their medium, be it poetry or fiction, while men of letters confused the issues by their interest in non-formal (i.e., peripheral) matters. Yeats recalled that when he tried to talk 'ideas' among the

Rhymers' Club, he was told: 'You do not talk like a poet, you talk like a man of letters.'[12]

The same forces that had restricted the men of letters to *belles lettres* and had begun to give them an image of somewhat quaint dabblers also put serious literature in a new and insecure position. What had happened was that the profound *sympathy* between literary author and public so characteristic of the early and mid-Victorian years had been broken. In his remarkably perceptive study of Charles Dickens, George Gissing wrote tellingly on this point. As Adrian Poole has noted, Gissing felt 'admiration, nostalgia, distaste' for the 'image of authorship' held by both Dickens and his public.[13] Gissing had an acute sense of the distance between his own times (the 1880s and 1890s) and that of Dickens in terms of the conditions of literary life. Gissing saw that Dickens, for all his social criticism, had no notion of outraging public sentiment or presenting a new moral system. As a self-made man, Dickens had successfully pulled himself up from the lower-middle class during the era of the formation of the commercial and industrial middle class. Hence it had never occurred to Dickens that the values of the artist should differ from those of his society: Dickens's values were those of his middle-class readers.[14] 'Sympathy with his readers', Gissing wrote, 'was to him the very breath of life; the more complete that sympathy, the better did he esteem his work.'[15]

Dickens might distort reality in order to avoid the disagreeable or to dispense justice to his characters, but he did not feel that there was anything dishonest in so doing; it was simply the obligation which arose from Dickens's idea of the writer's function. In his own times, Gissing observed with both pride and regret, that artists had rejected Dickens's moral purpose in favour of presenting absolute truth to reality, or exploring their own emotions, or asserting the superiority of the values of art, regardless of the feelings of the public.[16] The modern writer, Gissing knew, may have gained in fidelity to artistry, but he lost Dickens's instinctive sympathy with a general public.

Gissing's perceptive study of Dickens, published first in 1898, reflected a calm self-awareness that was missing in his earlier work, much of which was concerned with the difficulties faced by sensitive and thoughtful artistic people. He seems to have become aware that his own career represented a dialogue between the economic and social conditions of literary life and his own concepts of literature — a dialogue that was representative of a whole generation of writers and illustrative of dislocations in the literary world. Like Dickens, Gissing came from the lower-middle class. He attended Owens College,

Manchester, and hoped to ascend to the University of London. His academic career was cut off, however, when he was discovered to have stolen some items in order to support a prostitute with whom he had fallen in love. With no obvious career marked out for him, Gissing resorted to literature to make a living. He suffered for some years from extreme poverty and lived among the urban poor, whose life he came to know as well as anyone since Dickens himself.[17] Indeed, in his early novels, his sympathy for the poor made him a social reformer — a Radical, he put it. Gradually, however, his pessimism about the chances for reform, in combination with the stark realization that poverty degraded the poor into less than admirable creatures, killed his Radicalism. Gissing came to think that a life of art was not possible in surroundings of poverty and misery, and therefore that one had to choose between art and social reform. Strongly influenced by Ruskin and other late-Victorian devotees of beauty, Gissing adopted an aesthetic ideal for himself and his work. 'I am growing to feel', he wrote, 'that the only thing known to us of absolute value is artistic perfection. The ravings of fanaticism — justifiable or not — pass away; but the works of an artist, work in what material he will, remain, sources of health to the world.'[18] Soon he had adopted the slogan of art-for-art's sake, and had put realism to the service of aestheticism:

> My attitude henceforth is that of the artist pure and simple. The world is for me a collection of phenomena, which are to be studied and reproduced artistically.[19]

For Gissing, as for other writers who adopted the ideal of art-for-art's sake, aestheticism involved a rejection of the demands made on an artist by the general public and by the publishing market-place. In his view, artistic integrity would inevitably bring failure in the commercial publishing world. This was the main theme of his unrelievedly bleak portrait of literary life, *New Grub Street*. In that grim book all of the frustrations of the aspiring serious writers are mixed up with the dislocations and difficulties of the publishing world as the mass reading public emerged. The protagonist, a struggling novelist named Edwin Reardon, refuses to try to make his work popular or to write sleazy articles for the new 'quarter-educated'. But the pressure applied by the three-volume format for novels is unbearable. Reardon knows that a mediocre three-decker brings £150, and that he might survive on the bottom edge of the middle class by producing one a year. But three volumes a year are more than his particular gifts can sustain; and his career becomes a spiral of failure, loss of confidence, more failure and artistic dessication. He rages: 'What an insane thing it is to make literature one's only means of support . . . To make a trade of art! I am rightly served for attempting such a brutal folly.'[20]

Ultimately, Gissing's highly autobiographical attack on literary life was a protest against the basic assumptions of the Victorian men of letters. Gissing believed that the market for popular writing had called into being and maintained in sweatshop conditions a class of writers who had nothing to say. The trade was over-populated, one result being cut-throat competition among writers — hacks sabreing one another in their respective magazines in order to advance themselves.[21] Further, the market for publications had stimulated an over-production of goods, so that a good book or article was swamped by the flood of ephemeral literature. Consequently, Gissing in *New Grub Street* rebelled against a system that provided support for writers by a market economy. He assaulted the proposition that economic arrangements for writers should reflect the organization and values of capitalist society. Reardon — and here he spoke for Gissing — says: 'The world has no pity on a man who can't do or produce something it thinks worth money. You may be a divine poet, and if some good fellow doesn't take pity on you you will starve by the roadside.'[22] Reardon believes it good in itself that learned and artistic people flourish; but modern society values only producers of practical goods. It is remarkable how closely these complaints resembled those of the Victorian natural scientists, and it is remarkable also that Gissing leaned towards the principle of endowment as the remedy. He observes of Reardon and a fellow starving novelist:

> But try to imagine a personality wholly unfitted for the rough and tumble of the world's labour-market. From the familiar point of view these men were worthless; view them in possible relation to a humane order of society, and they are admirable citizens . . . These two were richly endowed with the kindly and the imaginative virtues; if fate threw them amid incongruous circumstances, is their endowment of less value?[23]

There is not much comradeship among the characters in the literary life portrayed in *New Grub Street*. The serious novelists, the literary hacks, the vengeful editors and the panderers to the mass market share no sense of community. The one aspiration that binds them together is symptomatic of a crucial conceptual development in late-Victorian society: all of the literary characters in *New Grub Street* desire what they call an 'intellectual life'. All of them regard an intellectual life as bearing special status, even though the monetary returns may be low. One of the reasons Reardon's wife stoutly opposes his acceptance of a clerical post is that she senses it would amount to a decline from the relative high status of their intellectual existence. Gissing's assumption in *New Grub Street* is that an 'intellectual life' is a way of earning a living offering high status and, at its best, a spiritually elevated existence. Further, throughout *New Grub Street,* 'intellectual' is used as an adjective to modify nouns like 'man' and 'people' to denote those who have opted for full-time devotion to books, learning and writing. Consciousness of the existence of 'intellectual lives' and 'intellectual people' is reflected in the terminology of the characters as well as in the motives and attitudes of Gissing himself. As one character says to an aspiring female writer: 'We are both intellectual people and we talk in an intellectual way.'[24]

The idea of an 'intellectual life' in this sense seems to have become widely used in England for the first time in the 1870s.[25] The most prominent example of the emergence of this concept was P.G. Hamerton's book, *The Intellectual Life,* first published in 1873. Hamerton, who was a painter, art critic, essayist and friend of C.E. Appleton, sought in his book to extol the virtues of an intellectual life and to urge young men (he did not think women were suitable for an intellectual life) to take it up. He also provided a handy guide to practical success in leading an intellectual life — methodical work habits, tolerance, a prudent marriage and so on. What distinguishes an intellectual person? Not intelligence or knowledge, or even source of income, according to Hamerton: 'It is not erudition that makes the intellectual man, but a sort of virtue which delights in vigorous and beautiful thinking . . .'[26] The essential characteristic of this style of thought is 'disinterestedness', or non-partisanship, and a disinclination to accept authority in intellectual matters.[27] Further, the intellectual man is one who devotes himself to serious study regardless of subject — a scholarly ideal for the intellectual life:

> To have one favourite study and live in it with happy familiarity, and cultivate every portion of it diligently and lovingly, as a small yeoman proprietor cultivates his own land, this, as to study, at least, is the most enviable intellectual life.[28]

Hamerton's book, then, reflected the emergence of the concepts of 'an intellectual life' and 'intellectual people' and also showed that the related idea of 'the intellectual life of the nation' had come into being. The intellectual life of England, Hamerton said, 'is the sum of the lives of all intellectual people belonging to it.'[29] This elitist concept of what constitutes a nation's intellectual life closely resembled key ideas and attitudes of the university reformers. The desire of many leading university research scholars to separate themselves from the needs and tastes of the general public in order to pursue a self-validating scholarly activity carried with it the idea of the national culture of 'intellectual life' as a minority activity. Instead of older Victorian ideas of cultural leadership, the research scholars argued that a society ought to have an 'intellectual life', a culture, a civilization (the terms were inter-changeable), and that this culture consisted of the activities of a few people who advanced the various disciplines for their own sakes. In *The Renaissance,* for example, Walter Pater defined 'the culture of an age' as its 'various forms of intellectual acitivity', meaning its poetry, art, philosophy and religious thought.[30] The university reformers in the late-Victorian years identified such activities with the scholarship of the universities. They tended to identify the 'national culture' or 'intellectual life' with scholarly research. 'A university', Mark Pattison wrote, 'is the organ of the intellectual life of the nation; it is the school of learning, the nursery of the liberal arts, the academy of the sciences, the home of letters, the retreat of the studious and the contemplative.'[31] As A.H. Sayce declared, the maintenance and expansion of knowledge by the universities 'constitutes the true essence of national civilisation'.[32]

In connection with the new terminology of 'an intellectual life' which an individual might lead, and 'the intellectual life of the nation' to refer to the circle of high culture, there came into use in the late-Victorian period a vocabulary of words like 'the intellectuals' to denote a particular kind or set of people. Although this vocabulary was more and more frequently used as the years passed, and although late-Victorian usage was not encumbered with the accretion of connotations that were added in the twentieth century, 'intellectuals' was always a more ambiguous term than 'men of letters'. Hamerton thought of intellectuals as people who were distinguished by their style and quality of thought. The noun 'intellectual' also carried connotations of 'educated' or 'cultured'; and by the end of the nineteenth century, it was sometimes used to denote members of any learned profession — academics, physicians, lawyers and serious writers.[33] The late-Victorians do seem to have agreed that all those who were involved in research, whether in the natural sciences or any other scholarly discipline, were intellectuals, and that they were bound together in 'the active pursuit of truth' by 'a common aim, a common method, a common inspiration'.[34] And most usages seem to have connoted something of the assertions of superiority that were part of the self-images of the new professional scholars and literary elite. Hamerton modestly explained to the middle class: 'In saying in this plain way that we are intellectually superior to you and your class, I am guilty of no more pride and vanity than you when you affirm or display your wealth.'[35] John Ogilvie's *Imperial Dictionary of the English Language* (new edition, 1885), which was the first English dictionary to include 'intellectual' as an adjective designating a particular kind of person, said an 'intellectual being' was a person 'having intellect, or the power of understanding; characterized by intellect, or the capacity for the higher forms of knowledge'. James Murray's *Oxford English Dictionary* (1888) recognized once and for all that 'intellectual' as a noun referring to a particular kind of person had entered the language; it meant 'a person possessing or supposed to possess superior powers of intellect'.

The most frequent uses of 'intellectual' came in connection with the concept of class: 'intellectual class', 'intellectual artistocracy', 'aristocracy of intellect' and 'intellectual ruling class'.[36] Hamerton plainly thought of intellectuals as forming a class, in his mind a class necessary to England in clarifying the lessons of experience, giving directions to men of action, and perfecting 'the national mind'.[37] In general, the late-Victorians seem to have thought that an intellectual class was forming; that it mainly was based in the universities; that it was detached from, and felt itself superior to, the rest of society; and that it was distinguished by scholarly research. Even in *New Grub Street,* which has nothing to do with universities, Gissing caught something of the scholarly associations of the word. At one point Reardon does some scholarly articles, which fail to sell; and Reardon is said to 'put aside his purely intellectual work and [begin] once more to search for a "plot" '.[38] At the very end of the century, the word 'intellectuals' was given a *political* connotation in connection with the Dreyfusards and Pro-Boers, and this usage has become more habitual in the twentieth century; yet even in those first cases, the usage actually emphasized the detached thinking of university people.[39]

The term 'the intellectuals', therefore, came back into use in the late-nineteenth century, and from its first continuous usage it had to do with the perceived formation of a separate and learned class. This essential element in its meaning has remained prominent to the present day. The question remains, was it actually a new class? One may argue from a nominalist point of view that no social class can exist in the way that a table or chair does, and therefore that if a social class is real, it is so only in the minds of people at a given time and place. Assuming this point of view is valid, then 'the intellectuals' in late-Victorian England *had* emerged as a social class, for the late-Victorians clearly thought of them as such. But if one looks at the issue from another point of view, that a social class manifests itself in organizations, ideology, formal and informal social links and political action, all rising from common relations to the means of production, then the answer is not so clear. The late-Victorian intellectuals did, I think, articulate a number of ideas about their cultural functions and their relationship to the market economy that amounted to an ideology. However, this ideology in England did not generate a political movement of its own; and English intellectuals have generally continued to ally themselves with one of the three major political parties. Certainly, the late-Victorian intellectuals had many formal and informal social links among themselves, mainly as a result of their common association with universities. But given the relative exclusiveness of the English universities, especially Oxbridge, and the relatively small segment of the population from which their students (and therefore their faculties) were drawn, the late-Victorian intellectuals had almost as close social connections with the ruling class — the landowners, the upper-middle class and the professions — as with each other. Thus it seems most reasonable to think of them much as one thinks of the professions — separate from the ruling class in some ways, but very much a part of it in others.

Despite this ambiguity, the fact that a new set of terms related to writing and thinking — 'intellectual life of the nation', 'an intellectual life' and 'the intellectuals' — came into use in the last decades of the century shows clearly that important changes had occurred in the realities and the concepts governing serious intellectual work. The language of 'the men of letters' had been appropriate to a particular landscape of economic and conceptual conditions for writers early in the century. The most important features of that topography were the market relationship between authors and the reading public and the general agreement among authors and their audience on a role of cultural leadership for the men of letters. These two features of the world of the men of letters had been transformed by the end of the century. Science and scholarship had succeeded in establishing endowed positions for themselves which put them beyond the controls of the market-place of the general public. They had no intention of providing moral leadership for a general audience; nor did the literary artists who accepted the doctrine of art-for-art's sake. The situation of the men of letters was vastly altered by these changes, for they found that their range had become limited, that there were new rivals to their cultural authority, and that the old, compact audience had fragmented. The result was a confused condition in late-Victorian high culture, one characterized by the separation of scholars and natural scientists from the general public, the fracturing of that public into separate audiences, the rise of a mass semi-literate audience, and the slippage of literature, now narrowly defined, towards the periphery of intellectual life. Hence the emergence of the vocabulary and concepts of 'the intellectuals' in England pointed to a transformation of intellectual life and the fragmentation of high culture.

## Notes

1.  Leslie Stephen, *English Literature and Society in the Eighteenth Century* (London, 1907), pp. 33-6, 50, 136-40, 176-81; John Gross, *Rise and Fall of the Man of Letters* (London, 1969), pp. 87-8.

2.  [Robert B. Lytton], 'Quinet's Creation', *Blackwood's* (February 1872), pp. 207 and 216.

3.  Frederic Harrison, *Autobiographic Memoirs,* vol. I (2 vols., London, 1911), pp. 22-4, 133-7.

4.  J.A. Hobson, 'The Academic Spirit in Education', *Contemporary Review* (February 1893), pp. 236-7.

5.  Gross, *Rise and Fall of the Man of Letters, passim.*

6.  J.H. Newman, *On the Scope and Nature of University Education* (Everyman's edn, London, 1915), p. xxxix.

7.  Sidney Colvin, 'Fellowships and National Culture', *Macmillan's Magazine* (June 1876), p. 141.

8.  F.W. Maitland, *The Life and Letters of Leslie Stephen* (New York, 1906), p. 341.

9.  [Julia Wedgwood], 'The Moral Influence of George Eliot', *Contemporary Review* (February 1881), pp. 173-85; [Julia Wedgwood], 'A Study of Carlyle', *Contemporary Review* (April 1881), pp. 584-609; Roden Noel, 'The Poetry of Tennyson', *Contemporary Review* (February 1885), pp. 202-24; R. Warwick Bond, 'Ruskin: Man Prophet', *Contemporary Review* (July 1900), pp. 118-33.

10.  Simon Nowell-Smith (ed.), *Letters to Macmillan* (New York, 1967), pp. 164-5. See also Gross, *Rise and Fall of the Man of Letters*, p. xiii.

11.  To express fully his definition of a 'man of letters', Morley quoted Doudan's *Republic of Letters,* the gist of the passage being that a man of letters is not an original artist but one who reads widely and absorbs the viewpoints of others, through whose eyes he sees the world. See John Morley, *Recollections* (2 vols., New York, 1917), I, pp. 1 and 94.

12. W.B. Yeats, *Autobiographies* (London, 1961), p. 166.

13. Adrian Poole, *Gissing in Context* (London, 1975), pp. 108-9.

14. George Gissing, *Charles Dickens* (Port Washington, New York, 1966; first published in 1898), pp. 1-2, 80.

15. Ibid., p. 75.

16. Ibid., pp. 82-3; 89-91; 94-5; 245-6; 259.

17. The best biography of Gissing is Jacob Korg, *George Gissing: A Critical Biography* (Seattle, 1963).

18. Quoted in Korg, *Gissing*, p. 57.

19. Quoted in ibid., p. 71.

20. George Gissing, *New Grub Street* (2 vols., Leipzig, 1891), I, p. 66.

21. The prime example of the cut-throat competitor is the character of Alfred Yule. See *New Grub Street*, I, p. 228 and II, p. 82.

22. Ibid., I, p. 253.

23. Ibid., II, pp. 218-19.

24. Ibid., II, p. 54.

25. In her *Autobiography*, which she wrote between 1855 and the early 1870s, Harriet Martineau spoke of having entered at an early age her 'intellectual life', by which she meant a career of study and reflection. This is the earliest usage of 'intellectual life' in this sense that I know of. Harriet Martineau, *Autobiography*, 2nd edn by Maria Weston Chapman, (2 vols., Boston, 1877), I, pp. 50 and 53.

26. P.G. Hamerton, *The Intellectual Life* (New York, 1885; first published in London, 1873), p. viii.

27. Ibid., p. 91.

28. Ibid., p. 116.

29. Ibid., p. 433.

30. Walter Pater, *The Renaissance: Studies in Art and Poetry* (London, 1910), p. xiii.

31. Mark Pattison, 'A Chapter of University History', *Macmillan's Magazine* (August 1875), p. 308.

32. A.H. Sayce, 'The Needs of the Historical Sciences', in C.E. Appleton *et al* (eds.), *Essays on the Endowment of Research* (London, 1876), p. 204.

33. For uses of 'intellectual' as 'educated', see J.R. Seeley, 'Liberal Education in Universities', in J.R. Seeley, *Lectures and Essays* (London, 1895), p. 232; William Archer, 'A Plea for An Endowed Theatre', *Fortnightly Review* (May 1889), p. 610; and Hobson, 'The Academic Spirit in Education', pp. 245-6. For 'intellectual' designating mental workers, including professional people, see Walter Besant, 'Is It the Voice of the Hooligan?', *Contemporary Review* (January 1900), pp. 27-8.

34. Henry Nettleship, 'On the Present Relations between Classical Research and Classical Education in England', in *Essays on the Endowment of Research*, p. 244. See also Hamerton, *The Intellectual Life, passim,* especially pp. 68, 521-2.

35. Hamerton, *The Intellectual Life*, p. 518.

36. Colvin, 'Fellowships and National Culture', p. 141; [Julia Wedgwood], 'Moral Influence of George Eliot', p. 177; Edward Dowden, 'Hopes and Fears for Literature', *Fortnightly Review* (January 1889), pp. 166, 177; [J.H. Millar], 'Mr. Jowett and Oxford Liberalism', *Blackwood's* (May 1897), p. 726.

37. Hamerton, *The Intellectual Life*, pp. 519-22.

38. Gissing, *New Grub Street*, I, p. 205.

39. K.V.T., 'The Dreyfus Case: A Study of French Opinion', *Contemporary Review* (October 1898), p. 603; F. Edmund Garrett, 'Sir Alfred Milner and His Work', *Contemporary Review* (August 1900), p. 153.

# SELECT BIBLIOGRAPHY

The purposes of this brief bibliographical essay are to point out the main sources for each of the chapters and to suggest readings for anyone who might want to study the subjects of the chapters more fully.

## Chapter 1: 'Introduction'

Anyone wishing to investigate intellectuals should begin with the works of Edward Shils, especially his article on 'Intellectuals' in the *International Encyclopedia of the Social Sciences,* vol. 7 (New York, 1968), and the essays in *The Intellectuals and the Powers* (Chicago, 1972), of which the title article is the most important. Shils stresses the 'propensities' of intellectuals in any society; thus his work tends to be abstract as well as comprehensive. However, for this reason, his ideas serve well as a body of hypotheses about intellectuals to be tested by historians of any particular culture. Robert Michels's somewhat older 'Intellectuals', in *Encyclopaedia of the Social Sciences,* vol. 8 (New York, 1932) is concerned mainly with the political and social activities of intellectuals, especially in revolutionary, socialist and nationalist movements. A classic on the subject that still rewards reading is Julien Benda, *The Treason of the Intellectuals* (translated by Richard Aldington, New York, 1928), which argues that in adopting the political passions and material concerns of laymen, modern intellectuals have betrayed their tradition of attending to transcendental matters. In *Men of Ideas: A Sociologist's View* (New York, 1965), Lewis Coser stresses detachment as the defining characteristic of intellectuals. Florian Znaniecki's *The Social Role of the Man of Knowledge* (New York, 1940) is a theoretical study of the social functions of academics from the point of view of the sociology of knowledge. George B. Huszar (ed.), *The Intellectuals: A Controversial Portrait* (Glencoe, Ill., 1960) offers an interesting selection of readings by and about intellectuals. Philip Rieff (ed.), *On Intellectuals* (Garden City, New York, 1960) is a worthwhile collection of theoretical and case studies of intellectuals.

For nineteenth-century England, the classic study of the cohesion and inter-connections of 'the academic and intellectual class', is Noel G. Annan, 'The Intellectual Aristocracy', in J.H. Plumb (ed.), *Studies in Social History* (London, 1955, pp. 241-87). This is a glittering essay which seems to show that nearly every Victorian of any intellectual importance was related to all the others. It makes no distinction between 'men of letters' and 'intellectuals'.

For the history of ideas in Victorian Britain, the best books are mainly studies of literary figures: Raymond Williams, *Culture and Society, 1780-1950* (New York, 1966); Basil Willey, *Nineteenth Century Studies* (London, 1949); Basil Willey, *More Nineteenth Century Studies: A Group of Honest Doubters* (London, 1956); Walter Houghton, *The Victorian Frame of Mind, 1830-1870* (New Haven, 1957); Jerome H. Buckley, *The Victorian Temper: A Study in Literary Culture* (New York, 1951), and Richard Altick, *Victorian People and Ideas* (New York, 1973).

For the social context in which Victorian thinkers worked, one should begin with Harold Perkin, *The Origins of Modern English Society, 1780-1880* (London, 1969), a rigorous synthesis of oceans of social history. It is especially useful for its emphasis on professionals as 'the forgotten middle class'. G. Kitson Clark, *The Making of Victorian England* (New York, 1967), is a brilliant re-interpretation of Victorian history, with valuable remarks on professionals as the new gentry. For a straightforward, readable history of Victorian professionals, see W.J. Reader, *Professional Men: The Rise of the Professional Classes in Nineteenth-Century England* (London, 1966).

**Chapter 2: 'The World of the Men of Letters, 1830s-1860s'**
The starting point for any study of the men of letters must be John Gross, *The Rise and Fall of the Man of Letters* (London, 1969), a fascinating impressionistic survey of nineteenth-century editor-writers. J.W. Saunders, *The Profession of English Letters* (London, 1964) is all too brief on the nineteenth century, but it gives a useful account of the writing trade from the renaissance to the present. Richard D. Altick, 'The Sociology of Authorship: The Social Origins, Education and Occupations of 1,100 British writers, 1800-1935', *Bulletin of the New York Public Library* (June 1962, pp. 389-404) is an indispensable, pioneering sociological analysis. The social and intellectual conditions of eighteenth-century men of letters are brilliantly analyzed in Ian Watt, *The Rise of the Novel: Studies in Defoe, Richardson and Fielding* (Berkeley, 1962). For all its exemplary combination of literary analysis and cultural history, however, Watt's book has not completely replaced the older works by A.S. Collins: *Authorship in the Days of Johnson* (London, 1927) and *The Profession of Letters* (London, 1928).

There are a number of useful studies of the ideas that governed the work of Victorian men of letters. In *The Victorian Sage* (New York, 1965), John Holloway brilliantly analyzes the rhetoric of leading thinkers to illustrate the fulfilment of the 'sage's' function. Ben Knights, *The Idea of the Clerisy in the Nineteenth Century* (Cambridge, 1978) provides good descriptions of the variations on the clerisy ideal, but it is marred by an animus against the very idea of an intellectual elite. Richard Stang, *The Theory of the Novel in England, 1850-1870* (New York, 1959) is a clear account of Victorian ideas about the novel. For a similar study of poetry, one should begin with Walter Houghton and G. Robert Stange (eds.), *Victorian Poetry and Poetics* (Boston, 1959), a marvellous anthology with equally good introductions.

The standard study of Victorian publications and readers is Richard D. Altick, *The English Common Reader* (Chicago, 1957). This product of prodigious research provides a mass of information on literacy, book sales, and the circulation of journals. George H. Ford's *Dickens and His Readers: Aspects of Novel-Criticism Since 1836* (New York, 1965) is an excellent example of the study of the intimate relationship between writers and their readers. R.K. Webb, *The British Working-class Reader, 1790-1848* (London, 1955) is a good introduction to the literature produced by the upper classes for the working class. Other useful surveys of literature for the working class are: Margaret Dalziel, *Popular Fiction 100 Years Ago* (London, 1957) and Louis James, *Fiction for the Working Man, 1830-1850* (London, 1963). The upper-class reading public is analyzed in Alvar Ellegard, 'The Readership of the Periodical Press in Mid-Victorian Britain', *Götesborgs Universitets Arsskrift* (vol. LXIII, 1957); and surveyed impressionistically in Amy Cruse, *The Victorians and Their Books* (London, 1935).

The organizational and technical side of the publishing world is surveyed in F.A. Mumby and Ian Norrie, *Publishing and Bookselling*, 5th edn (London, 1974). This massive history, while indispensable, is not as interesting as the bolder and more erratic account of technological changes in printing and their effects on literature by Louis Dudek: *Literature and the Press: A History of Printing, Printed Media and Their Relation to Literature* (Toronto, 1960). Two good examples of the history of nineteenth-century highbrow periodicals are: John Clive, *Scotch Reviewers: The Edinburgh Review, 1802-1815* (London, 1957); and G.L. Nesbitt, *Benthamite Reviewing: The First Twelve Years of the Westminster Review, 1824-1836* (New York, 1934). Charles Morgan, *The House of Macmillan, 1843-1943* (London, 1944), is a solid, old-fashioned narrative history of a great publishing firm. Royal Gettmann, *A Victorian Publisher: A Study of the Bentley Papers* (Cambridge, 1960) is an illuminating study of the mediation by publishers between authors and the public. The most fascinating account of an institution with which Victorian writers coped is Guinevere Griest, *Mudie's Circulating Library and the Victorian Novel* (Bloomington, Indiana, 1970).

The life and work of the men of letters can perhaps most easily be studied through biography. Excellent biographies of some literary giants are: Edgar Johnson, *Charles Dickens: His Tragedy and Triumph* (2 vols., New York, 1952); Gordon N. Ray, *Thackeray: The Uses of Adversity, 1811-1846* (New York, 1955) and *Thackeray: The Age of Wisdom, 1847-1863* (New York, 1958); Gordon S. Haight, *George Eliot: A Biography* (Oxford, 1968); G.O. Trevelyan, *Life and Letters of Lord Macaulay* (2 vols., London, 1961); Michael St John Packe, *Life of John Stuart Mill* (New York, 1970); and Emery Neff, *Carlyle* (New York, 1932).

Contemporary statements on the position and functions of writers are innumerable, and only a few can be listed here. Edward Lytton Bulwer, *England and the English*, 3rd edn (2 vols., London 1834) gives a brilliant opinionated survey of high culture at the beginning of the Victorian period. Thomas Carlyle made a classic statement of his ideal of the Victorian men of letters in *On Heroes, Hero-Worship, and the Heroic in History* (Everyman's Library edn, London, 1965). Two novels which offer marvellous portraits of literary life are Charles Dickens, *David Copperfield;* and W.M. Thackeray, *Pendennis.* Anthony Trollope's *An Autobiography* (London, 1950) is wonderfully revealing as to the work habits, financial arrangements, critical ideals and cultural functions of the most methodical of the great Victorian novelists. A word of caution: some later critics do not take Trollope's seemingly straightforward remarks seriously.

### Chapter 3: 'The Worlds of Science and the Universities'

The history of science in early Victorian England is the subject of a rapidly-growing number of books and articles, but there is as yet no standard, comprehensive study of science in its social and cultural context. The most important single work is Susan Faye Cannon's *Science in Culture: The Early Victorian Period* (New York, 1978). This is a fascinating and enlightening, but often irritating and provoking, study of the cultural functions of natural science. George A. Foote, 'Science and Its Function in Early Nineteenth Century England',

*Osiris* (vol. XI, 1954, pp. 438-54) is a good introduction to the subject. The history of scientific organizations has received much attention. G.W. Roderick, *The Emergence of A Scientific Society* (New York, 1967) is a brief, clear, elementary narrative of the growth of scientific institutions in England from about 1800 to the present day. D.S.L. Cardwell, *The Organisation of Science in England* (London, 1957) provides the basic history of scientific organizations, full of details but weak on interpretations. Dorothy Stimson has presented a concise readable history of the oldest scientific organization in *Scientists and Amateurs: A History of the Royal Society* (London, 1949). The Royal Institution has received a number of treatments, of which a recent, rather contentious one is Morris Berman, *Social Change and Scientific Organization: The Royal Institution, 1799-1844* (Ithaca, New York, 1978). The BAAS has attracted even more attention. On this vital Victorian institution, the standard history is O.J.R. Howarth, *The British Association for the Advancement of Science: A Retrospect* (London, 1922). Of the numerous articles on its founding, one of the best is A.D. Orange, 'The Origins of the British Association for the Advancement of Science', *The British Journal for the History of Science* (December 1972, pp. 152-76). A.E. Musson and Eric Robinson have provided much organizational as well as economic and technological history in their massive *Science and Technology in the Industrial Revolution* (Manchester, 1969).

For biographies of leading scientists in early-nineteenth century England, one should consult: Sir Harold Hartley, *Humphrey Davy* (London, 1966), which has particularly good chapters on Davy as a romantic scientist: Arnold Thackray, *John Dalton: Critical Assessments of His Life and Science* (Cambridge, Massachusetts, 1972), which is especially valuable on the changing images of Dalton within the scientific community; and L. Pearce Williams, *Michael Faraday* (London, 1965), which is a magisterial biography, equally good on technical and general subjects.

On the crucial subject of the relations between science and religion, one should consult Cannon's *Science in Culture,* plus Owen Chadwick's *The Victorian Church* (parts I and II, London, 1966 and 1970), a big and brilliant history of the various sects, and C.C. Gillispie's *Genesis and Geology* (New York, 1962), a wonderfully readable study of the relations between scientific thought and natural theology in the late-eighteenth and early-nineteenth centuries.

Primary sources giving contemporary statements of the concepts of science are especially useful. A good selection can be found in George

Basalla, William Coleman and Robert Kargon (eds.), *Victorian Science: A Self-Portrait from the Presidential Addresses of the British Association for the Advancement of Science* (Garden City, New York, 1970). Charles Babbage, *Reflections on the Decline of Science in England* (London, 1830) is a classic manifesto that has lost none of its energy with the passage of the years. John Herschel's *A Preliminary Discourse on the Study of Natural Philosophy* (London, 1832), which was widely read in its day, is invaluable for early-Victorian ideas of science and the scientific habit of mind. J.S. Mill's *A System of Logic* (vols. 7 and 8 of Collected Works, Toronto, 1967), contains the great Victorian statement of the empiricist theory of science. The opposing idealist view is to be found in Robert E. Butts (ed.), *William Whewell's Theory of Scientific Method* (Pittsburgh, 1968).

The study of the history of higher education may best be begun in J.W. Adamson, *English Education, 1789-1902* (Cambridge, 1930), an old book but one still valuable for understanding the universities in their larger educational context. Michael Sanderson (ed.), *The Universities in the Nineteenth Century* (London, 1975) is an interesting collection of contemporary items on the universities, with a good introduction that emphasizes the provincial universities. The early-nineteenth century history of Cambridge is surveyed in D.A. Winstanley, *Early Victorian Cambridge* (Cambridge, 1940); and Martha M. Garland, *Cambridge before Darwin* (Cambridge, 1981). W.R. Ward's *Victorian Oxford* (London, 1965) is a highly detailed account focusing mainly on university politics. W.H.G. Armytage, *Civic Universities: Aspects of A British Tradition* (London, 1955) is a concise survey of university history from the middle ages through the 1950s.

The early Victorian concepts of university education have been exceptionally well analyzed. Robert G. McPherson, *Theory of Higher Education in Nineteenth Century England* (Athens, Georgia, 1959) is a clear, short exposition of the ideas of leading theorists, notably those of Copleston, Whewell and Pattison. Sheldon Rothblatt's *Tradition and Change in English Liberal Education: An Essay in History and Culture* (London, 1976) is a gracefully written essay on changes in the idea of liberal education from the eighteenth century to the end of the nineteenth. Rothblatt's 'The Student Sub-culture and the Examination System in Early Nineteenth Century Oxbridge', in Lawrence Stone (ed.), *The University in Society* (vol. I, Princeton, 1974) offers a fascinating description of student life as it changed under the new class-ranking system. Mortimer R. Proctor, *The English University*

*Novel* (Berkeley, 1957) gives a clear, thoughtful survey of novels about university life.

Published primary sources on the universities and higher education are unusually rich. S.T. Coleridge's *On the Constitution of Church and State,* in Professor Shedd (ed), *Complete Works of S.T. Coleridge* (vol. VI, New York, 1853) is the place to begin. Sir William Hamilton's criticisms of Oxbridge can be found in his *Discussions on Philosophy and Literature* (New York, 1855). The best statement of the traditional response to Hamilton is Edward Coplestone, *A Reply to the Calumnies of the Edinburgh Review* (Oxford, 1810). Perhaps the best fictional portrait of university life in unreformed Oxbridge is Thomas Hughes, *Tom Brown at Oxford* (2 vols., Boston, 1876). The two mid-century Royal Commission reports are invaluable: *Royal Commission on Oxford University* (1852) [Parliamentary Papers, *c.* 1482, vol. XXII]; and *Royal Commission – Cambridge University* (1852-3) [Parliamentary Papers, *c.* 1559, vol. XLIV]. Of the many memoirs, two stand out: C.A. Bristed, *Five Years in An English University* (New York, 1873), which is a fascinating account of Cambridge in the 1840s by an American; and W. Tuckwell, *Reminiscences of Oxford*, 2nd edn (New York, 1908), a charming collection of vignettes from unreformed Oxford.

**Chapter 4: 'The Impact of Science on Victorian Intellectual Life'**
For the impact of science on intellectual life, many of the works cited in the previous section are useful, especially those by Cannon, Cardwell, Thackray, Chadwick, Adamson and Armytage. J.G. Crowther, *Statesmen of Science* (London, 1965) offers useful if simplistic studies of various advocates of science in Victorian England. Wemyss Reid's *Memoirs and Correspondence of Lyon Playfair* (New York, 1899) is the indispensable source for Playfair's career. Huxley has received much attention. The fullest biography is the uncritical 'Victorian' work by Leonard Huxley: *Life and Letters of Thomas Henry Huxley* (2 vols., New York, 1901). Cyril Bibby, *T.H. Huxley: Scientist, Humanist and Educator* (New York, 1960) is a recent, readable biography by another Huxley enthusiast. William Irvine's *Apes, Angels, and Victorians* (Cleveland, Ohio, 1959) is an entertaining dual biography of Darwin and Huxley, and a brilliant study of the reception of their ideas. Gertrude Himmelfarb has been criticized on technical points in her *Darwin and the Darwinian Revolution* (Garden City, New York, 1962), but the book is still a good introduction to the subject. Alvar Ellegård has analyzed the public reactions to Darwin in *Darwin and the General Reader* (Götesborg, 1958). The conflict between science and religion is

carefully dissected in Josef L. Altholz, 'The Warfare of Conscience with Theology', in Josef L. Altholz (ed.), *The Mind and Art of Victorian England* (Minneapolis, 1967, pp. 58-77). The conflict is placed in its context of cultural history in Robert Young, 'The Historiographic and Ideological Contexts of the Nineteenth Century Debate on Man's Place in Nature', in Mikulas Teich and Robert Young (eds.), *Changing Perspectives in the History of Science* (London, 1973).

The late-Victorian concern about the erosion of religious belief by science is sensitively analyzed by Owen Chadwick in *The Victorian Church*, Part II; and by Basil Willey in *More Nineteenth Century Studies*. A.W. Brown, *The Metaphysical Society: Victorian Minds in Crisis, 1869-1880* (New York, 1947) interestingly describes the club in which eminent late-Victorians debated the claims of science and religion. Frank M. Turner provides clear biographical chapters on the theme of reactions to science in *Between Science and Religion: The Reaction to Scientific Naturalism in Late-Victorian England* (New Haven, 1974).

The institutional aspects of the rise of science can be examined in a number of perceptive studies. Roy McLeod, 'Resources of Science in Victorian England: The Endowment of Science Movement, 1868-1900', in Peter Mathias (ed.), *Science and Society, 1600-1900* (Cambridge, 1972, pp. 111-66) surveys the various institutional claims by scientists. A.J. Meadows, *Science and Controversy: A Biography of Sir Norman Lockyer* (London, 1972) is a well-written biography that offers much information on *Nature* and the Devonshire Commission. Robert Kargon's *Science in Victorian Manchester: Enterprise and Expertise* (Baltimore, 1977) is a thorough study of the evolution of provincial scientific organizations. Two excellent studies of university-based science are: Gerald L. Gieson, *Michael Foster and the Cambridge School of Physiology* (Princeton, 1978), a good illustration of the tendency to found 'schools' of science; and Michael Sanderson, *The Universities and British Industry, 1850-1970* (London, 1972), a big book emphasizing the connections between provincial universities and industry.

Primary sources on the rise of science include: Francis Galton, *English Men of Science: Their Nature and Nurture* (New York, 1895), a classic analysis of the scientific community of the 1870s, emphasizing nature over nurture; and Charles Darwin and T.H. Huxley, *Autobiographies*, ed. by Gavin de Beer (London, 1974). Huxley's autobiography is brief and clear; Darwin's is simultaneously naive and candid. The articles by T.H. Huxley are essential — and still good reading. Some of the best are: 'Agnosticism' (*Collected Essays*, vol. 5);

'On the Educational Value of the Natural History Sciences' (*Collected Essays,* vol. 3); 'On the Advisableness of Improving Natural Knowledge' (*Collected Essays,* vol. 1); 'A Liberal Education and Where to Find It' (*Collected Essays,* vol. 3); and 'Universities Actual and Ideal' (*Collected Essays,* vol. 3). Cyril Bibby (ed.), *The Essence of T.H. Huxley* (London, 1967) offers a good selection from Huxley's writings, topically arranged. The Devonshire Commission reports are also invaluable: *Royal Commission on Scientific Instruction and the Advancement of Science* (1st and 2nd Reports, 1872), [Parliamentary Papers, *c.* 536, vol. XXV].

## Chapter 5: 'The Impact of Science: The Case of History'

The starting point for the study of Victorian historiography should be G.P. Gooch, *History and Historians in the Nineteenth Century* (Boston, 1959), which is a massive compendium of information, not oriented towards the sociology of knowledge, but useful for summaries of the various interpretations of the past offered by nineteenth-century historians. Herbert Butterfield's *Man on His Past: The Study of the History of Historical Scholarship* (Cambridge, 1955) is less encyclopaedic and more interpretive, with good chapters on German scholarship, Acton and Ranke. Felix Gilbert, 'The Professionalization of History in the Nineteenth Century', in John Higham, with Leonard Krieger and Felix Gilbert (eds.), *History* (Englewood Cliffs, New Jersey, 1965, pp. 320-39) is a brilliant comparative essay.

For British historiography, one should consult P.B.M. Blaas, *Continuity and Anachronism: Parliamentary and Constitutional Development in Whig Historiography and in the Anti-Whig Reaction between 1890 and 1930* (The Hague, 1978), which is weak on professionalization but strong on the Oxford School. The best single study of Victorian history in its general literary and intellectual context is an unpublished PhD thesis by Rosemary Jann, 'The Art of History in Nineteenth Century England: Studies in Victorian Historiography' (Northwestern University, 1975). Herman Ausubel, J.B. Brebner and E.M. Hunt (eds.), *Some Modern Historians of Britain* (New York, 1951) has good essays on J.A. Froude, Goldwin Smith and S.R. Gardiner. Richard A.E. Brooks, 'The Development of the Historical Mind', in Joseph E. Baker (ed.), *The Reinterpretation of Victorian Literature* (New York, 1962) is a thoughtful introduction to an important aspect of Victorian thinking. Olive Anderson's 'The Political Uses of History in Mid-Nineteenth Century England', *Past & Present* (April 1967, pp. 87-105) is an excellent study of a crucial framework of Victorian political ideas. Duncan Forbes, *The Liberal Anglican Idea of History* (Cambridge, 1952) offers a full exposition of the ideas of early-Victorian broad churchmen like Thomas Arnold.

Fortunately, there are excellent biographies of many nineteenth-century English historians. G.O. Trevelyan, *The Life and Letters of Lord Macaulay* (2 vols., New York, 1875), remains a classic. John Clive's *Macaulay: The Shaping of the Historian* (New York, 1973), is a graceful and thoughtful reinterpretation of the first part of Macaulay's life. Joseph Hamburger presents a tightly-argued interpretation of Macaulay as a 'trimmer' in *Macaulay and the Whig Tradition* (Chicago, 1976). J.M. Robertson, *Buckle and His Critics: A Study in Sociology* (London, 1895) is highly partisan but indispensable. For the Oxford School, there are useful older biographies: Leslie Stephen (ed.), *Letters of John Richard Green* (New York, 1901); W.R.W. Stephens, *The Life and Letters of E.A. Freeman* (2 vols., London, 1895); W.H. Hutton (ed.), *Letters of William Stubbs* (London, 1904); Louise Creighton, *Life and Letters of Mandell Creighton* (2 vols., London, 1905). Gertrude Himmelfarb's *Lord Acton: A Study in Conscience and Politics* (Chicago, 1950) is a brilliant intellectual biography. C.H.S. Fifoot, *Frederic William Maitland: A Life* (Cambridge, Massachusetts, 1971) is a recent straightforward study, which can be supplemented with H.E. Bell's concise, critical exposition of Maitland's work, *Maitland: A Critical Examination and Assessment* (London, 1965). Doris S. Goldstein, 'J.B. Bury's Philosophy of History', *American Historical Review* (October 1877, pp. 896-919) gives a technical but clear discussion of Bury's concept of history.

The history of disciplines other than history has only just begun to be written. J.W. Burrow, *Evolution and Society* (Cambridge, 1970) is a well-written account of evolutionary social science in Victorian England which illuminates the differences between positivism and German historical scholarship. Philip Abrams, *The Origins of British Sociology, 1834-1914* (Chicago, 1968) shows how sociology reflected changing values and social problems. In *Ethics and Society in England: The Revolution in the Social Sciences* (Berkeley, 1978), Reba N. Soffer makes a bold but confused effort to explain the foundation of a number of professional social science disciplines. Melvin Richter's *Politics of Conscience: T.H. Green and His Age* (London, 1964) contains some interesting suggestions about the origins of professional philosophy in England.

Of course, the best sources for the history of Victorian historical writing are the works of the Victorian historians. Useful editions of some of the best are: *Thomas Carlyle, The French Revolution: A History* (New York, 1934); T.B. Macaulay, *The History of England from the Accession of James II* (Everyman's Library, 4 vols., London, 1972); E.A. Freeman, *The History of the Norman Conquest of England,* edited by J.W. Burrow (Chicago, 1974); William Stubbs, *William Stubbs on the English Constitution,* edited by Norman Cantor (New York, 1966). Essays and lectures on the concept of history, its standards and techniques, are also invaluable: Thomas Arnold *Introductory Lectures on Modern History,* 4th edn (London, 1849); T.B. Macaulay, 'History', in *Critical and Miscellaneous Essays* (vol. 1, revised edition, New York, 1861, pp. 145-87); and Macaulay, 'Machiavelli', 'Hallam', and 'Von Ranke', in *Critical and Historical Essays* (London, 1883, pp. 28-51, 51-98, and 541-63); J.A. Froude, *Short Studies on Great Subjects* (2 vols., London, 1867-1871); E.A. Freeman, *The Methods of Historical Study* (London, 1886); William Stubbs, *Seventeen Lectures on the Study of Medieval and Modern History* (Oxford, 1887); and Lord Acton, *Lectures on Modern History,* edited by J.N. Figgis and R.V. Laurence (London, 1960).

### Chapter 6: 'The Reform of the University System'

On this topic, one should consult a number of authorities cited for Chapter 3, including Adamson, Sanderson, Ward, Armytage, Rothblatt and Proctor. One older account of university reform that remains useful is Lewis Campbell, *On the Nationalisation of the Old English Universities* (London, 1901), which is particularly good on the abolition of religious restrictions. C.C. Gillispie's 'English Ideas of the University in the Nineteenth Century', in Margaret Clapp (ed.), *The Modern University* (Ithaca, New York, 1950) provides a clear, brief survey of conservative and reformist ideas. J.P.C. Roach, 'Victorian Universities and the National Intelligentsia', *Victorian Studies* (December 1959, pp. 131-50), though not well focused, introduces some good questions on the role of Oxbridge in Victorian society and culture. D.A. Winstanley, *Later Victorian Cambridge* (Cambridge, 1947) is the standard survey. By a long way the most important work on the mid-century reforms at Cambridge is Sheldon Rothblatt, *The Revolution of the Dons: Cambridge and Society in Victorian England* (London, 1968). This is an original, path-breaking study of the aims of the reforming dons, particularly their professional orientation. In 'Emerging Concepts of the Academic Profession at Oxford', in Lawrence Stone (ed.), *The University in Society* (vol. I, Princeton,

1974, pp. 305-52), Arthur Engel offers an excellent analysis of reform impulses at Oxford. George Haines IV, *Essays on German Influence upon English Education and Science, 1850-1919* (Hamden, Connecticut, 1969) is a thin but suggestive introduction to an important subject. Christopher Kent, *Brains and Numbers: Elitism, Comtism, and Democracy in Mid-Victorian Britain* (Toronto, 1978) reveals the elitist tendency among university radicals.

For biographies of some of the leading university reformers, one should consult: E.G.W. Bill, *University Reform in Nineteenth Century Oxford: A Study of Henry Halford Vaughan* (Oxford, 1973), which gives a thorough depiction of a 'professorial' advocate; Evelyn Abbott and Lewis Campbell, *Life and Letters of Benjamin Jowett* (2 vols., London, 1897), which is an excellent example of Victorian biography; John Sparrow, *Mark Pattison and the Idea of A University* (Cambridge, 1967), which is a graceful, perceptive interpretation of the ideas and personality of Pattison; and A. Dwight Culler, *The Imperial Intellect: A Study of Newman's Educational Ideal* (New Haven, 1955) which is less a biography of Newman than a careful exposition of his idea of a university.

The published primary sources on university reform are exceptionally rich. John Henry Newman, *On the Scope and Nature of University Education* (Everyman's edn, London, 1965) offers a classic advocacy of a broadened version of a liberal education. Mark Pattison's *Memoirs* (London, 1885) are essential for an insider's view of both the mid and late-Victorian university reform movement. Pattison's *Suggestions on Academical Organisation* (Edinburgh, 1868) is one of the two crucial manifestos for the endowment of research. The other is C.E. Appleton, *et al., Essays on the Endowment of Research* (London, 1876). The Reports of the Oxford (1852) and Cambridge (1852-3) Royal Commissions of mid-century are essential for the aims of the reformers. The Third Report (1873) of the *Royal Commission on Scientific Instruction and the Advancement of Science* [Parliamentary Papers, *c.* 868, vol. XXVIII] is an exhaustive survey of the state of research in many fields at Oxford and Cambridge in the early 1870s.

### Chapter 7: 'The Tradition of Cultural Criticism and Alienation in Literary Life'

A good starting point for this topic is Raymond Williams, *Culture and Society* and Jerome Buckley, *The Victorian Temper,* listed under Chapter 1. Leslie Johnson, *The Cultural Critics* (London, 1979) offers brief analyses of critics of British culture from Matthew Arnold to the present. John Lester, *Journey through Despair, 1880-1914: Transformations in British Literary Culture* (Princeton, 1968) gives an agonistic interpretation of British literature, mainly poetry, at the beginning of the modern period. David Perkins, *A History of Modern Poetry* (Cambridge, Massachusetts, 1976) includes a thoughtful as well as comprehensive survey of British poetry and poetics at the end of the late-Victorian period. But by far the most important work on the ideas of late-Victorian literary figures is Graham Hough, *The Last Romantics* (New York, 1947), a brilliant combination of intellectual history and literary criticism of various figures from Ruskin through the decadents.

Aspects of the institutional context of literary life can be explored in a number of works cited under Chapter 2, especially Dudek and Griest. Simon Nowell-Smith (ed.), *Letters to Macmillan* (New York, 1967) offers a fascinating collection of letters especially illustrative of the authors' growing impatience with Mrs Grundyism. There are two good studies of *The Academy:* Diderick Roll-Hansen, *The Academy, 1869-1879: Victorian Intellectuals in Revolt* (Copenhagen, 1957), which is aggressive and provocative, and is especially good on connections of the journal to the university reform movement; and John Curtis Johnson, 'The *Academy,* 1869-1896: Center of Informed Critical Opinion', unpublished PhD thesis, Northwestern University, 1958, a useful survey of the subjects and opinions presented in the *Academy.*

Many of the intellectual trends of the late-Victorian years have to be traced in biographies. For Ruskin, Quentin Bell's *Ruskin* (London, 1963) is an excellent, brief, critical biography, while Joan Evans' *John Ruskin* (London, 1954) is a longer, thoughtful book, surprisingly critical of the great art theorist and social critic. Lionel Trilling, *Matthew Arnold* (Cleveland, 1968) remains the best intellectual portrait of Arnold. Of the many biographies of William Morris, the most comprehensive and provocative is E.P. Thompson, *William Morris: Romantic to Revolutionary* (New York, 1977). Gerald Monsman, *Walter Pater* (Boston, 1977) is a good, concise, critical study. Malcolm Browne, *George Moore: A Reconsideration* (Seattle, 1955) is the best book on this unusual Irishman. Carl Weber's *Hardy of Wessex: His Life and Literary Career* (New York, 1940) is the standard treatment. Leon Edel's magisterial biography of Henry James is very useful for late-Victorian aestheticism, especially *The Middle Years, 1882-1895* (New York, 1978).

The primary sources for the history of literary life in the late-Victorian period are almost numberless. The novels of Meredith, Hardy, Gissing and Samuel Butler are essential. So also is Mrs Humphy Ward's novel of religious faith and doubt, *Robert Elsmere* (3 vols., London, 1888). For the ideas of Ruskin, one may consult Kenneth Clark (ed.), *Ruskin Today* (London, 1964) which gives an excellent selection from Ruskin's works, topically arranged. Of the many works by Matthew Arnold, the essential ones for this chapter are: *Culture and Anarchy,* edited by J.D. Wilson (Cambridge, 1969); 'The Literary Influence of Academies', in *Complete Prose Works of Matthew Arnold,* edited by R.H. Super, vol. III (Ann Arbor, 1962, pp. 232-57); and *Schools and Universities on the Continent,* in *Complete Prose Works,* vol. IV (Ann Arbor, 1964). William Butler Yeats, *Autobiographies* (London, 1961) is a brilliant, provocative essential source.

**Chapter 8: 'Conclusion, The World of the Intellectuals, 1870-1900'**
To understand Gissing and his view of literary life, one should consult Jacob Korg, *George Gissing: A Critical Biography* (Seattle, 1963), a solid biography emphasizing the tension between Gissing's radicalism and aestheticism; and Adrian Poole, *Gissing in Context* (London, 1975), a tough-minded analysis of Gissing's work in the late-Victorian social and publishing context. But the most vivid portrait of late Victorian literary life and attitudes is Gissing's *New Grub Street* (2 vols., Leipzig, 1891).

To consider the English intellectuals in comparative context, one might begin with Edward Shils, 'The Intellectuals: I. Great Britain', *Encounter* (vol. IV, no. 4, pp. 5-16), an interesting essay on the contemporary English situation, stressing the 'London-Oxford-Cambridge Axis'. It was part of a series of articles in *Encounter* on intellectuals in various nations. Shils also has provided food for comparison in his *The Intellectual between Tradition and Modernity: The Indian Situation* (The Hague, 1961). Lewis Coser's *Men of Ideas* (cited under Chapter 1) offers case studies of intellectuals drawn mainly from modern English, French and American history. Fritz Ringer's 'Higher Education in Germany in the Nineteenth Century', *Journal of Contemporary History* (July 1967, pp. 123-38); and *The Decline of the German Mandarins: The German Academic Community, 1890-1933* (Cambridge, Massachusetts, 1969) brilliantly analyze one cultural aspect of the history of German intellectuals. Richard Pipes (ed.), *The Russian Intelligentsia* (New York, 1961) is a good introduction to a subject on which there has been considerable work. Christopher Lasch, *The New Radicalism in America, 1889-1963: The Intellectual As a Social Type* (New York, 1965) is a thoughtful and provocative essay on certain radical intellectuals in America. Burton Bledstein, *The Culture of Professionalism* (New York, 1976), is an exhaustive and energetic exploration of the rise of professional academic life in nineteenth-century America, with much to say about the middle class and their universities. Thomas Haskell, *The Emergence of Professional Social Science* (Urbana, Illinois, 1977), is a thorough study of professionalization of American sociology in the context of a 'crisis of authority'.

# INDEX